Emlyn Williams

Emlyn Williams

A LIFE

James Harding

Welsh Academic Press
Cardiff

Published in Wales by Welsh Academic Press, an imprint of

Ashley Drake Publishing Ltd
PO Box 733
Cardiff
CF14 2YX
www.ashleydrake.com

First published in hardback by George Weidenfeld & Nicolson Ltd in 1993

First paperback edition published by Welsh Academic Press 2002

ISBN 1 86057 0208

British Library Cataloguing-in-Publication Data.
A CIP catalogue for this book is available from the British Library.

Printed in Wales by Dinefwr Press, Llandybïe, Carmarthenshire
Jacket Design by www.darkangeldesign.com

For
SOPHIE WILLIAMS
who never knew her grandfather

CONTENTS

Contents

ACKNOWLEDGEMENTS

This book could not have been written without the generous and sympathetic co-operation of Emlyn Williams's family who gave me unrestricted access to all his correspondence, papers and documents. My thanks go to Mr Alan Williams, Mrs Alan Williams (Maggie Noach), and Mr Brook Williams. All quotations from published and unpublished material are made by permission of the Literary Executors and Trustees of the Emlyn Williams Estate. The opinions expressed are, of course, those of the author alone.

For many kindnesses and much hospitality I am indebted to Mrs Ann Plugge, friend and companion of the Williams family since the nineteen-thirties.

Sir John Gielgud, whose personal and professional association with Emlyn Williams goes back to 1934, kindly imparted his exquisitely phrased recollections. The impresario Mr Stephen Mitchell, another friend of many years, also gave me the benefit of his reminiscences, as did Mr John de Lannoy, who provided valuable documentary material. Miss Margaretta Scott delightfully recreated the atmosphere of 1930 and of *A Murder Has Been Arranged*.

I must also express my gratitude to Mr Robert Bolt; Mr Jeremy Brett; Mr Richard Briers; Mr Gary Broad; Miss Dora Bryan; Miss Wendy Craig; Mr Colin Firth; Sir Alec Guinness; Mr Richard Huggett; Mr Peter Lavender; Mr Tony Mendelson; Mr John Mortimer; Mr N.F. Simpson; Mr Victor Spinetti; Mr John Tydeman (Literary Executor); Mr Geoffrey Warren; Miss Joy Westendorp; and Mr Richard Whittington. I am grateful also to several informants who wished to remain anonymous.

As always, I am deeply indebted to Mrs Pauline Skinner for her patient secretarial skills and for her magical ability to decipher that which the writer himself is often incapable of untangling.

J.H.

ILLUSTRATIONS

Between pages 112 and 113

The photographs have been selected from the Emlyn Williams archives helds by his family. The author and the publishers will be happy to acknowledge individual copyright in any future edition.

"He was frank and generous and a very faithful friend . . . very sharp-tongued and, I imagine, a pretty lethal enemy, but he was also very funny and witty and incredibly industrious . . ."

Sir John Gielgud

"A strange and interesting man."

John Mortimer

BEFORE THE CURTAIN

Dr George Emlyn Williams CBE, MA (Oxon), Hon LL D (Bangor), FRSL, was both scholar and creative writer. He could have been, as his mother once hoped, an eloquent preacher, or, as his teacher expected, a schoolmaster specialising in French, German and Italian. Instead, he embarked on what his friend Noël Coward described as "the Cinderella story of all time" to become a famous playwright and actor. Yet he never lost his scholarly tastes. At first nights early in his career he would steady his nerve by reading Schiller and brushing up his German irregular verbs. In later life, on the island of Corfu where he owned a holiday home, he studied modern Greek so diligently that he was able to make speeches in the language and to act as compère at local functions.

The boy Williams spoke Welsh as his first language and only picked up English in later childhood. Coached by his inspired teacher Miss Sarah Grace Cooke, whom he was to immortalise in *The Corn Is Green*, he made his way via hard-won grants and scholarships to Oxford University. It was another world. From the narrow, poverty-stricken, chapel-haunted atmosphere of his native village he was delivered into a place of freedom and intellectual excitement. Here he discovered the theatre. He never went to a drama school and no one taught him how to act. Neither did anyone tell him how to write plays. That, in any case, would have been impossible. As he was to remark: "The elements of playwriting are the most elusive of all elements to capture, including the elements of fire and air." He acquired his craft partly through instinct and partly through alert observation. Like Molière's gentleman, he knew everything without ever having learned anything.

A strange duality pervaded his life. Known to his family and childhood friends by his first name of George, in his twenties he dropped it in favour of his second name Emlyn. Neatly and methodically, he obliterated "George" from his signature in books and on documents and replaced it with "Emlyn". It would, he thought, look better on theatre posters. But there were reasons for this other than professional. "George" stood for his stifling childhood, his quest for the love he did not receive from his gallant but cold and Spartan mother who struggled to keep the household together and to control his drunken father. "Emlyn", ambitious and tough-minded, fought doggedly to realise the dreams of a lonely boy fascinated by the world of literature and art which Miss Cooke opened up for him. "George" remained the inspiration of those plays in which he depicted Welsh characters with affectionate humour – although the Wales he portrayed belonged to an earlier, more idealised period than that of his youth.

He acknowledged the existence of this double personality by entitling his two volumes of autobiography *George* and *Emlyn*. They are among the finest and most engaging of all English theatrical autobiographies. The second volume ends, however, with the author in his thirtieth year and on the threshold of his first great success, *Night Must Fall*. There were still another fifty years to go. Although he contemplated a sequel that brought the tale of his life up to date, he only wrote a few scattered drafts. The rest of the story deserves to be told. Moreover, the survival of much of his correspondence with Miss Cooke and his family, starting in 1917, brings fresh light to bear on incidents which, though recounted with absolute truth, are subject to artistic arrangement.

His personality represents an inextricable tangle of George and Emlyn. Often one cannot tell where George begins and Emlyn finishes. George was a dutiful son and a thoughtful husband. Emlyn was a bravura actor who depicted with chilling intensity murderers and psychopaths, capitalising on his lack of conventional good looks and short stature to convey in a silvered voice untold depths of menace and horror. George was a loving father who adored his family. Emlyn was enthralled by evil and obsessed with the exploits of child murderers which he tabulated in absorbed detail. George invented stage characters of endearing Welsh homeliness and Dickensian humour. Emlyn created heroes driven by twisted minds and perverted psychology. When Epstein made a bust of him the sculptor commented that, while every male sitter had one profile masculine and the other feminine, he had never seen the phenomenon so marked as in Emlyn's case. This was shrewd. For Emlyn, Janus-faced, was always vulnerable to the charms of both men and women.

George/Emlyn was a leading theatrical figure of his time. His plays brought a *nouveau frisson* to the stage. The best of them can still hold an audience. When inspiration deserted him in his fifties he struck out in a bold new direction by reincarnating Charles Dickens, Dylan Thomas and Saki. Although his work languishes now in the purgatory that often follows immediately on the death of an artist, he left enough to convince posterity that, like his contemporaries Coward and Rattigan, he is not to be dismissed simply as a manufacturer of "well-made" plays. The theatre which has been named in his honour will not be the only reason why he is remembered in the annals of British drama.

And was it George or Emlyn who gave him the reputation of a sharp-tongued wit? There is a famous story about the sable-hued Queen Salote of Tonga who attended the Coronation of Queen Elizabeth in a coach escorted by a top-hatted dignitary. "Who is that?" enquired someone indicating the escort. "Her lunch," replied Emlyn. With some annoyance he was to see this quip attributed to Noël Coward.

Other sallies originated by Emlyn have also been passed off as Coward's. *On ne prête qu'aux riches*. At least Emlyn has had proper credit for his summing up of Paul Robeson as Othello: "Look black in anger." Or for his comment when Ivor Novello was convicted of an offence against the wartime petrol regulations: "Keep the home tyres turning." Coral Browne, another dangerous wit, was once invited to exchange civilities with Emlyn. "Oh," she answered cautiously, "I wouldn't want to find myself in the same room as *him*!" Her reaction was conveyed to Emlyn. "I wouldn't," he said, "want to find myself in the same room as *her*!"

CHAPTER ONE

(i)
Welsh Peasant

In the beginning there were generations of Welsh miners and peasants, millers and domestics, and, once, a tea-seller who owned a donkey and a cart. Some of the women occasionally distinguished themselves by rising to become ladies' maids. Hardly ever did these forerunners travel beyond the boundaries of Flintshire, their home county, although mention is made of an uncle on the maternal side who was a civil engineer reputed to have built a bridge in France. English was regarded as a foreign language and the city of Liverpool, not so far away, as "abroad".

Mary Williams, born in 1869, learned the elements of English at school, as did her brother Jabez and her sister Sarah, but could never write or spell it properly since outside the classroom everyone around her spoke Welsh. She lived in Treuddyn, a small village up on the hills overlooking the town of Mold, and was the daughter of Job, a miner, and Eleanor, a midwife, neither of whom could read or write. They were ardent chapel-goers, and their dark four-roomed cottage displayed on a shelf only one book, the Bible, presumably for its symbolic value. Despite his chapel upbringing Job was given to drink, especially on Saturday nights, when, emerging from a maudlin haze, he would dandle little Mary on his knee and splutter beery fumes over her curly hair. One evening his son Jabez, then nineteen and a miner, came home to see him attacking Eleanor the midwife in a drunken frenzy. Jabez beat him up and walked out of the family home. The young man, swearing never to drink strong liquor himself, emigrated to Liverpool, found work at a tea blender's, and became an energetic deacon of the Wesleyan Chapel in Bootle.

A year later Mary, at the age of fourteen, emulated her sister Sarah and went into domestic service. Brother Jabez met her in Liverpool and took her to the home of her new employer. As a housemaid she gave every satisfaction: the silver gleamed impeccably, the front-door steps shone whitely, the ironing was crisp and immaculate, and no dust ever settled for long on the furniture. She spoke little and bobbed deferentially to an approving mistress. Her sense of household economy was strong and inspired her to preserve, in a drawer kept for the purpose, odd bits of string as well as used paper bags folded away. On Sundays she was reunited with Jabez. It was a day of Sunday school, of chapel service, of tea and cold ham, of high-principled conversation. In the summer of 1889 an interesting newcomer joined the congregation. Thick-set, black-haired, he swaggered down the aisle with a sailor's walk. Following the custom of worshippers who were at liberty to come forward and testify after the sermon was finished, the crew-cut youth stood before the pulpit and begged the Lord to give him a voice. The Lord obliged, and tones that were sonorous and lyrical resounded through the chapel. The Welsh he spoke, Biblical, stately, throbbed with feeling. He had, Mary noted, a neat moustache and would be about her age. Later she remarked the deep blue of his eyes.

Jabez was impressed by his delivery, and after the service introductions followed in the porch as umbrellas were seized and black hats rescued. Mary could not help feeling a little startled by the chuckles and high spirits that now succeeded their friend's solemn demeanour at the pulpit. He made her laugh, too, although she could have wished for a little less mirth on a Sunday of all days. Richard Williams presented himself, a stoker on the ocean-going *Lucania*. Not only did he come from Ffynnongroew, some fifteen miles from Treuddyn, but he also had the same name as she did. Born in 1870, one year her junior, he had begun his working life down the mine. When he was five his family moved to Lancashire. There, at the age of twelve, some sort of argument arose, he stumped out in the middle of the night, tramped thirty miles to Liverpool, and signed up on a ship. Tripoli knew him, as did Panama and Trincomalee. He had, he told Mary with a grin, a wife in each of them.

Over the next five years he called on her each time the *Lucania* docked at Liverpool. They went for strolls and gaped at tempting shop windows. He brought her presents from exotic ports of call and charmed her mistress with his attractive manner and fine speaking voice. That lady thought his hands were particularly fine. Would Mary be going to marry him? she asked. Mary blushed and said no. She was not all that taken by him. Patiently, tenaciously, he continued his siege. They went to the local music-hall and heard "Oh, Mr Porter", "Daddy wouldn't buy me a bow-wow", and "Tara-ra-boom-de-ay." Once they sat up in a theatre gallery and saw a performance of *Romeo and Juliet.* The young lady's Wesleyan morals remained unsullied. "I did not understand much of what they said," Mary observed later, "because they talked so old-fashioned."

In 1894, when she was twenty-five years old and he twenty-four, they were married on the 3rd December at the Trinity Road chapel. Jabez gave her away, still not quite satisfied about her husband's financial prospects, and her employer, mourning the loss of a perfect maid, presented her with a clock, a tea-set and an affectionate hug. The couple went into residence at 39, Elwy Street, Toxteth Park. Here stood the possessions that were to accompany her through life: a grandfather clock, two horsehair chairs, a sofa with its antimacassar, a pair of brass candlesticks, glass ornaments that looked as if they were made out of spun sugar, a large wedding picture copied from a daguerreotype of a haughty groom and a meek bride, a hymn book and a dropsical Welsh Bible, a gift from the minister. In a corner cupboard lurked a handsome tea-set, too fine to be used, together with a cracked mug owned by her husband since the age of seven and bearing the mystic device, "On the Coming of Age of Llewelyn Mostin Esquire". Lace curtains, stiff and dazzling white, veiled a window that looked out into a murky street clamorous with the noise of trams and, on chilly nights, of Atlantic foghorns.

After a hasty three-day honeymoon Richard went off to sea for another voyage. Meanwhile his wife burnished the kitchen until it glittered like a jewel and ironed his shirts so that they crackled with crispness. On the day of his return she prepared a high tea of lobscouse in time for his arrival at six o'clock that evening. The chimes struck the hour. He did not appear. Seven o'clock pealed out from the grandfather clock, and then the strokes of eight. Had his ship gone down? Was he a corpse at the bottom of the Atlantic? Suddenly there were steps outside. Richard tumbled in, a beatific smile on his lips, and tripped while he sought unsteadily to give her a kiss. As he did so she caught a whiff of the smell that used to engulf her when her drunken father took her on his knee. It was of beer with a tincture of whisky.

"Shame on thee!" she hissed, and much else besides. He stared, hatred in his blue eyes. When she slammed his dried-up lobscouse on the table he gave her a last look and went out into the dark. That night she slept alone. In the morning he was back, though they did not speak until the end of the day. There were to be many other scenes like this between the prudent, economical, house-proud Mary and the careless, improvident and charming Richard. But divorce was unthinkable and, moreover, a strange, indissoluble attachment bound them together.

Drink was a problem, and so was money. He never told her what he earned, and doled out, each week, a given number of coins to her. The rest he spent in taverns. She became pregnant, and the consequence he recorded in the big Welsh Bible: "Jabez, born September 8, 1899." The next line read: "Died April 22, 1900, aged 7 months."

It was time, he thought, to give up the sea, strike fresh roots in Wales and settle down in his native district. She was delighted. They went back to Flintshire and took a little house in the village of Glasdir where Richard found a job as stoker at the mine he had worked in before. On fine evenings they went out for strolls through the hills and a glimpse of the sea beyond. A new inscription was entered in the family Bible: "Sarah Blodwen, born March 22, 1902." And then: "Died May 6 aged 7 weeks."

Richard tired of stoking and decided to take up greengrocery. They moved to another cottage and he turned the front room into a shop filled with blushing carrots and bulky marrows and fresh potatoes. "R. Wms, Greengr'c'y", announced a copperplate card in the window. He bought a horse and a small cart to go out on his rounds. The novelty soon faded. The greengrocer, bored again, sold his horse and cart, and, to Mary's horror, took over a public house not far away called The White Lion. Her dismay was softened by another pregnancy, and, before they moved to the White Lion, a boy was born amid the odour of staling vegetables. An hour after its birth the infant started to choke, but Mary's sister Sarah, who was staying with them, shook it vigorously and the breath came back. Richard described himself on the birth certificate as "general labourer". In the Bible he wrote: "George Emlyn b. Nov. 26, 1905." Underneath it, when their next child was born, he left, with pessimistic forethought, a blank line.

The White Lion, its roof grey-slated, its square walls white, stood on a hillock above Glanrafon, a hamlet of fourteen stone cottages that housed miners and estate workers. They spoke Welsh and only very rarely was English heard. The happy-go-lucky host gave them generous credit, charming them with a hearty welcome and matching them drink for drink. For nine years Mary lived reluctantly in a beery atmosphere that mocked all the righteous, chapel-going principles on which she had been bred. No licensing hours restricted the times of opening, and every weekday she toiled incessantly at keeping house and washing glasses, cooking meals and running down to the cellar to fill beer jugs, ironing family clothes and cleaning the bar. Only on Sunday could she rest, and even then the local people would call discreetly for refreshment at the back door. In 1908 a son called Job was born, and in 1912 another who was christened Thomas. They survived. So did George, whose earliest memories were of himself, quivering in his nightshirt as he sat on the draughty stairs of an evening and listened to the noisy laughter from below and the chink of mugs and the occasional raucous ditty.

In his frayed pinafore and red petticoat he would go down the hill to play with other village children. They floated biscuit-tin lids in the gutter, leap-frogged over each other in the fields and watched, thoughtfully, the sheep being sheared. Sometimes the thirteen-year-old drudge employed by his mother would take him and a friend out for a picnic. They sat on the beach of the Dee Estuary while he made the agonising choice, a precious halfpenny clutched in his hand, between cornet and wafer.

When he was four he began walking a mile each day to a convent school staffed by nuns. Cautioned by his Wesleyan mother against graven images, he was more disturbed at the tongue the wimpled sisters chattered. He looked furtively away from the plaster image of the Virgin and tried to understand what he heard. Although he knew only a few phrases of English he realised that it was some other language they were talking. A boy explained: they were French. So he began to pick up French even before he had properly grasped English. He played happily with his companions, but always, somehow, remained apart from them. Gentle, quiet, he led an inner life he could not share with them. One Sunday he read in the family Bible his father's inscription: "Jabez died April 22, 1900." This was the elder brother he might have had, a companion ready to help and comfort him when needed. Where, though, could he find him?

He peopled his loneliness with figures cut out of a stores catalogue, ladies and gentlemen wearing the latest fashions whom he set up in a mansion constructed from empty Woodbine cigarette packets and play bricks. They were given names, and around them he wove quaint fictions. A dim idea came into his mind of a book where each page represented a day in *George, His Story*. The worst of those days was Sunday, so longed for by his mother, so dreaded by him for its boredom. His Sunday-best clothes chafed, the street was empty and dull, no cheerful voice or joke was heard. After Sunday school came evening chapel and the monumental test of an endless sermon during which he austerely disciplined himself to watch the clock only at five-minute intervals. From the bare walls of the chapel his glance drifted to a bee climbing up a window pane, and from the bee it roved to the hat of the woman in front of him. Further and further he retreated into himself, desperate to find an escape but not knowing how.

A glimmer came his way from *Tales For Little People* and *What Katy Did*. There was also an enigmatic volume entitled *Pears Eng. Dic.* which offered page upon page of strange words. One morning his father, after a two-day carouse in Rhyl ostensibly to renew his licence, brought back an abridged edition of *The Water Babies* complete with pictures. Then the boy read *The Children's Gulliver* and imagined tiny people crawling up his legs. *David Copperfield*, after a few pages, turned out to be incomprehensible. The book that really caught his imagination was *A Welsh Singer*, a novel by the then popular author who wrote under the name of "Allen Raine". It gripped him completely. The life he knew shaded into unreality. His father's pub, the village around him, became insubstantial shadows. He lived only for the hero and the heroine whose adventures possessed him entirely. Even difficult words failed to put him off: *Pears Eng. Dic.* came to the rescue and helped him over "suspicious", "cynical" and "agitate". As he looked them up he mouthed to himself: "suspickuss", "kinnical" and "aggie-tate".

He had met romance, and soon he was to know death. A playmate friend died of "pew-monia", and, gazing into the open coffin, he touched an icy forehead. The funeral inspired an episode in *George, His Story*, and before the ceremony was over he had begun to imagine his own death. His eyes filled with tears. The bereaved father, moved at what he took to be mourning for the dead girl, patted his shoulder. Even more stirring was the occasion when Issmael Jones hanged himself in the slaughter-house nearby. (One catches, from time to time, an echo of *Cold Comfort Farm*.) There was Mister Jones, a farmer he'd often seen before, alive, healthy, breathing, now only a corpse that swung lazily on a hook. The boy's face turned white, his knees froze with a strangely pleasurable horror. That night in bed he saw the candle being lit, the noose tightening and the shadow rocking back and forth on the wall.

One Sabbath evening in January, 1914, he glanced through *The Sunday Companion*. It contained the first instalment of *'Neath Nero's Rule*. What, he asked his mother, did "Neath Nero" mean? "Neath," she said on reflection, "is in South Wales, your father went there when he was at sea, but I never heard him talk of Nero." He began reading and, between mouthfuls of bread-and-dripping, was swept away into the grandeur of ancient Rome. Each Sunday he waited breathlessly for the next instalment and cut it out to go with the others he had carefully preserved and stuck together. Amid the clutter of useful tips to housewives and notes on holy worship, he had caught another glimpse of romance. When the serial ended he was haunted by visions of bloodstained arenas and of golden-haired heroes mighty in stature.

That summer he left the nuns and frequented, reluctantly, a new council school at nearby Picton. Although he was eight years old he still lacked fluency in English and suffered the gibes of a bullying schoolmaster. While he polished a knife for woodwork the master observed: "Don't we need a little more elbow-grease?" "Yes, Sir," replied his victim, half-rising and then, confused, sensing the trap. "Weren't you going to fetch some elbow-grease?" "Yes, sir." "And where does one buy such a thing?" The boy realised that "elbow-grease" must be an idiom. "Please, sir," he riposted, "you buy it from the blacksmith, for the rheumatics, only you got to remember not to rub with the same arm that got the rheumatics, because if you do you cannot reach round to rub the elbow." A roar of laughter from the class showed he had won that round. Later, though, the master triumphed. The boy pronounced "reap and sow" to rhyme with "bough". His tormenter pounced. "Come, there must be a lot of pigs where you come from." In the playground afterwards boys chorused at him, "The sow of Pen-y-Maes!" At home he languished, dreading the return of each schoolday much as he dreaded the Sabbath and chapel. He confided the reason for his low spirits to Mam – but warned her not to tell his father. A little later, while at play during break, he saw, astonished, Mr Williams slip into the school office. Remembering his explosive nature he trembled at the thought of an awkward scene. Five minutes later, beaming and tranquil, his father emerged and went on his way, discreetly pretending to ignore him. The baiting ended.

Exotic serials in *The Sunday Companion* were followed by smudged photographs and maps and puzzling news of a distant war. It all came to life when he suddenly imagined the Huns occupying Chester and advancing along the Dee, his Uncle Jabez being hustled into chapel and shot, refugees swarming along the streets, and nuns from his convent school herded on to the lawn and raped. At the sound of jackboots on the stair he flung himself into a chest and closed the lid. A sabre clanged as it slashed into the bed. He woke up screaming.

Days at the White Lion grew still more sombre. Richard Williams now drank so much that he was even barred from the local public houses. Mary buried her face in her hands and wept, "Richard, Richard . . ." Yet for all his drinking, for all his terrible rages, she loved him. Their son George wanted to comfort her. His two brothers Job and Thomas were not old enough to understand. Neither did George entirely comprehend, but he at least felt he had something to offer which might have brought a response, a flow of emotion in return. It never came, and the reserve between mother and son crusted over with impregnable ice. In the absence of an elder brother he looked for companionship to the little maid who drudged for them, but she left after some obscure episode involving Richard and he felt lonelier than ever.

The lease of the White Lion was sold in July, 1915, for much less than its worth and the family moved to stay, all five crammed into a single room, at the house of distant and unwelcoming relatives. Eventually Richard found a cottage to let and papered the walls. Mam washed the floor with water from the rain-butt outside and soon their new home sparkled with cleanliness. George went to Trelogan Council School at the top of a hill which the headmaster, moustached and knickerbockered, ascended each day on a stately bicycle. In the hall was a glass case containing four New Testaments, brightly bound, in French, Italian, Spanish and Portuguese. George coveted them. As the boys marched one afternoon from the allotments they cultivated as part of their war effort, they passed his father, unshaven, bleary, glass in hand, at the door of the public house. He mouthed a benevolent if slurred greeting. Red with embarrassment his son strode mechanically on. Next day, as if to make up for the incident, a kindly headmaster took the New Testaments from their case and handed them over to the boy, who, overjoyed, fingered them with respectful affection and stared fascinated at accents and cedillas. "It's not as different from English as Welsh is," remarked the sympathetic pedagogue.

The money from the sale of the White Lion quickly vanished in drink, and Mary Williams, desperate, saw the workhouse looming. Christmas that year was bleak. The spring of 1916 promised better, for then Richard found a job as a munitions worker. It meant his living in lodgings during the week and coming home on Sundays. George's mother was left in peace to run the house and await the dominical visit of a sober husband who brought treats for the children and a share, a modest share, of his pay packet. George himself became enthralled by a new serial called "The Exploits of Elaine" in the *News of the World* and was inspired with an adventurous scenario about Chinatown for which he cast the various parts from among his brothers, parents and classmates. The telephone, a strange and unearthly instrument, played an important role and was to carry dramatic talk of blood, opium and motor cars.

It was a pity that his first experience of the theatre, or, rather, of a staged play, should have been so disappointing. His mother took him to a performance by an amateur group in a town hall. There were no curtains, no scenery, no lighting. Moreover, the play was given in Welsh, for him a language ineluctably associated with hours of chapel boredom while the preacher's eloquence battered his unappreciative ears. His introduction to films proved happier. While staying with his father one weekend the family visited a cinema. A lady at an upright piano hammered out ragtime and other lively measures, quite unlike the severe marches to which his class manoeuvred at school. A glowing curtain ascended to the heavens, another lady, quite beautiful this time, played a violin solo on stage, and then the flickering announcement "Pathé's Animated Gazette" was followed by views of London streets and of people jerkily moving through what seemed like snow showers and even of King George V emerging from the blinding dazzle of jumping white spots to greet a loyal subject. The main feature, called *The Juggernaut*, excited the watching boy unbearably and left him drained at the climax, a spectacular scene where a panting train roared on to a bridge and crashed into the river below. He passed a sleepless night in a phantom railway carriage, the only passenger who knew of the danger ahead and who tried, again and again, to warn the guard but was frustrated at every attempt. Morning found him exhausted.

Deep in *Westward Ho!* one evening he overheard his mother shouting at his father, hours late home from the pub, his dinner congealing on the table. She rushed after him into the street calling "Richard, Richard!" A crowd gathered and watched, fascinated, as he grudgingly threw down the money she begged of him to keep the household going. The boy would have gone out and helped her back into the house, had he not recalled the admonition she once gave him: "Whatever you do, keep out of it." That evening she muttered, "If he can drink, so can I." She poured a glass of stout and drank it as if it were medicine. The remainder stayed in the bottle until it was thrown away, undrunk. A little later Richard Williams had an accident at work and was taken to hospital. White-faced, she hurried off to Chester Infirmary. In the weeks that followed as his broken leg healed so, until their next clash, did their marriage.

In the summer of 1916 George Williams wrote a little essay at school. It was, said the English teacher, outstanding, with perfect punctuation and a good idea of English. His headmaster decided to enter him for a scholarship at Holywell County, the Welsh equivalent of a grammar school, and for three weeks he toiled over extra homework with special attention to decimals. Arithmetic was not a strong point, but suddenly, in a moment of ecstatic revelation, he grasped the mystery of decimals and the neat beauty of manipulating the decimal point. On the day of the examination he had bacon for breakfast, a luxury normally reserved to his father alone.

The market town of Holywell contained an ancient spring said to have been created by the severed head of the martyr St Winifred when it came to a halt after rolling down the hill. A less fragrant co-religionist, the notorious "Baron Corvo", had dwelt there in discontent some years previously. For ten-year-old George Williams the place was like a city bustling with more people than he had ever seen in one spot before. In Holywell County School the examinees bent over their desks and pens scraped laboriously. A sudden voice fractured the silence from outside. "Look here . . . !" it thundered. A woman appeared, white-bloused, high-booted.

There was a mistake, she explained to the invigilator. The scholarship candidates had been given the wrong papers. "Fair play," she boomed, "give me the book of rules." The correct papers were distributed. George set himself to write what he could about the Kingmaker, the Inquisition, the Rump Parliament. He battled with arithmetic and, thanks to decimals, produced a reasonable series of answers. He was glad that the white-bloused apparition had withdrawn. She was disturbing, larger than life.

Yet he could not forget her. She spoke English with explosive impact, each consonant, each vowel energetically mouthed. A pince-nez dangled from her lapel to be perched athwart her blue eyes and then impetuously dashed aside. Her gestures were impatient and commanding. The hair was brown and the face interestingly pale. The lips were full, the snub nose broad at the nostrils to give a negroid touch. George felt terror in her presence.

A week later he heard that he had passed thirteenth out of twenty-one candidates and won a scholarship of £4 a year. His father bought him a new Sexton Blake story as a reward and his mother worried about food and clothes. Each day was to mean a ten-mile journey on foot, five miles to get there and five miles to come back.

(ii)
Who Am I?

Miss Sarah Grace Cooke hailed from Leeds in Yorkshire. She was thirty-three years old in 1916, had been a pupil teacher at the age of thirteen and thereafter taught herself the craft of teaching. Following Ripon Training College and a period at a school in France she obtained an external honours degree in English and French from Liverpool University and went on to an MA. After teaching in Cumberland she came to rest at Holywell County School in 1912, though "rest" is hardly a word to be associated with this buoyant, emphatic character, or "English freak" as George at first classified her.

On a September Monday morning, at the rise of the sun, he started his five-mile journey with a satchel at his back containing one shilling and eightpence for his five daily dinners and six half-crowns to pay for books. On his first day at Holywell County he made the acquaintance of Latin, and, as he walked the five miles back home that afternoon, thought he glimpsed Roman legions gathering on the wooded hills beneath the setting sun. Gradually he came to know the teachers. The headmaster was a benevolent man of peasant origins who spoke English as if it were a foreign tongue. Often he would consult with the authoritative Miss Cooke to check a point of grammar. "She tells the masters what to do," George reported to his father who loved hearing gossip about the looming woman he'd nicknamed "the Suffragette".

Through the rains of autumn and the snows of winter George ploughed back and forth between school and home. Geometry and algebra left him unmoved, but Latin was different. If *puella* meant "girl", it was obvious that *puellae* meant "of the girl", because Welsh had the same constructions. Over forty years afterwards, looking back on his adventures into Latin, he wrote: ". . . *puellae pedes nautarum lavant*, the girls wash the feet of the sailors. I saw the yellow Mediterranean sands, the purple-sailed galley rocking in the bay, the bronzed boys in their togas, sandals in hand, the white-robed girls kneeling with bowls of sea water. *Ave Caesar* . . . and nominally intricated with the pictures, was the grammar: the nominative girls verbly wash the accusative feet of the possessive sailors." At Christmas his school report, weak on arithmetic and geometry, bloomed into "good" for Latin and English, and "vocabulary excellent".

In the spring of 1917 he was told that he could transfer to French classes with Miss Cooke. He felt like a commoner summoned to Buckingham Palace. *Pont*, he realised, meant "bridge" in Welsh, just as "ffenestri", or *fenêtre*, meant window. "Ceffyl", the Welsh for horse, was *cheval*. Within a few weeks he easily caught up on the other pupils who had started before him. Miss Cooke began to take notice. After his five-mile slog of a morning, she pronounced, he could do with a cup of good hot cocoa. He called at her lodgings and gazed wonderingly around him at piles of exercise books, a copy of the *Observer* sprawled over the arm-chair, books, books, and yet more books in Latin, French and even Spanish. She was never there when he called, but each time her landlady came forward with the steaming cocoa which he sipped as he looked inquisitively about him.

One sleety morning Miss Cooke stopped him in the school hall. Her family, she explained, were to do with leather. Would he draw his foot on the sheet of brown paper she thrust at him? He did so and handed the tracing back. A week later he found, next to his daily cup of cocoa, two boots made of stout Yorkshire leather. They were strong and comfortable, superbly designed for conquering mud and slush. "Dear Miss Cooke," his father wrote, "we are very thank-full to you for taking interest in our son's well-fare, and let us hope he will be a credit to us all we remain Yrs. Obediently R. & M. Wms."

There came a day when members of the French class were deputed to recite chosen dialogues from their textbooks. George's was a passage with another boy about eating frogs and he prepared it carefully in advance. The school hall was packed, and, although he felt extremely nervous, he was aware of a strange inner calm. He spoke clearly and heard his voice ring out over the audience. Then, at the end, he delivered the master-stroke he had rehearsed and perfected in the silence of country lanes as he walked to school. The dialogue, a flat series of interchanges about English people eating potatoes and French people eating frogs, ended with the English boy learning from his French interlocutor that he had unknowingly eaten frogs: *"Des grenouilles? j'ai mangé des grenouilles? Non . . ."* When he delivered this line as the English boy, George added a piece of business that raised a howl of laughter. *"J'ai mangé des grenouilles?"* he said incredulously, eyes a-stare. A nauseated expression passed over his face, he put both hands to his suffering stomach, and, muttering *"Oh non, non, non,"* he ran from the platform amid renewed laughter. He could not have contrived the effect in everyday life. Yet for a moment, concealed behind the screen of a foreign

language and another personality, he had been, triumphantly, someone else.

His Easter report announced that he was top in Latin and high in
English. As for French, Miss Cooke wrote: "Excellent, phenomenal
progress. S.G.C." His mother pointed with her bread-knife at the
word "phenomenal" and asked what it meant. "Good," said George.
That Sunday his father came home as usual and saw the report. "Top!"
said Richard Williams, "What's pheno-meenal, George?" "Better
than anybody else," rejoined his mother. They gave him a bicycle, and
now he could get up at least an hour later than usual before skimming
the five miles to Holywell County.

In July 1917 Richard Williams found a permanent job as fireman at a
steelworks and the family moved to Connah's Quay. Happily George
could stay on at Holywell County and the school offered to pay the
four pounds each year that his train fare would cost. The new home
stood in a slum near a railway embankment where noisy engines
coughed smuts over Mrs Williams's neat line of washing. At night the
Irish Mail roared through, shaking the walls and throwing kaleido-
scopic lights into the bedroom. The Williamses were aliens here, for
the town stood on the threshold of England. Soon George's brothers
Thomas and Job became Tom and Joe. Before the year was up his
mother and father were speaking English at home. In time the
neighbours' children gave up taunting the brothers with chants of
"Taffy was a Welshman, Taffy was a thief," which they delivered in
broad Staffordshire accents.

The new home was below sea-level. Throughout the winter damp
seeped in, crumbling mortar and staining wallpaper that peeled away
in melancholy strips. For warmth the boys and their parents crowded
into a kitchen already full of the red oak dresser, the ancient horsehair
sofa, a table with an old newspaper for cloth, and Richard Williams's
favourite hard-backed chair. Upstairs George slept in a tiny bedroom
beneath faded pictures entitled "God is Love" and "Jesus wept".
Outside, in the yard, stood the crazy shed that served as lavatory. In
the yard, too, was the tap where kettles and bowls had to be filled,
whatever the weather.

Richard Williams was soon promoted to foreman. Regular work
and steady wages brought more stability to the household, but still
there were occasions when his dinner crisped to a cinder and he did not
stumble in at the door until late, irritated by the way each member of
his family looked uneasily away from him and regretful for the scene of
jollity he had left behind at the New Inn. Once, deep into the night,

George heard an altercation down below and rushed to take his mother's part. His father grabbed him by the ear, hustled him upstairs and threw him back on his bed. There were, however, not so many scenes like this now, though the ritual allotment of housekeeping money remained grudging and hesitant. The days between recurrent Fridays still brought, for George's mother, nightmares of financial insecurity.

George escaped from the slum into books and during the holidays read greedily the volumes Miss Cooke lent him. They were rivalled by a new attraction which absorbed him quite as fully and which cast a spell no less potent. For twopence ha'penny he could see Charlie Chaplin at the local cinema and, for another penny, enjoy fish and chips in newspaper sodden with grease. There were serials featuring Pearl White, Pathé Gazettes hot with actuality, "side-splitting" one-reelers and women, beautiful women whom he crudely sketched in notebooks. Connah's Quay melted away and left the foreground to Blanche Sweet and Dorothy Gish, William Farnum and Norma Talmadge. There was magic in everything to do with the cinema: the swish of the window curtains to blot out the sunshine before the Saturday matinée began, the lady at the piano rustling the pages of her music as she prepared her accompaniment, the elegant subtitles that flowered and dissolved, even the censor's certificate which declared that the film had been passed for public exhibition. Sometimes, between films, variety turns grimaced and postured against a painted backdrop. George watched and, later at home, mimicked the "Bing Babies" who pirouetted and sang in high-pitched tones which he reproduced in his yet unbroken voice. "Poll," laughed his father, using the nickname he gave his wife in mellow moments, "we've got a houseful o'clever little ladies!"

On evenings when he did not go to the cinema he loitered outside and watched the audience entering that place of excitement whence the chatter of an agitated piano could be heard. One way of sating his hunger was to stare at the posters dotted throughout the town, garish drawings of episodes from the next serial instalment, bloodcurdling pictures of the heroine in the clutch of a monster octopus or suspended, bound and gagged, from a towering pagoda. He wandered along the railway line between sooty thorn bushes and strolled among slag-heaps under the dull evening light and smoke from the steel-works, all the time seeing himself as the hero of the latest comic film. Even the subtitles materialised, ready-made and unhidden, within his feverish brain.

Books reasserted themselves. Dickens came back and the noisy tumbrils in *A Tale of Two Cities* drowned out *The Perils of Pauline*, the charm of *Lavengro* exorcised the sweet profile of Louise Lovely. His homework improved, and Miss Cooke showed him how to make systematic notes on his reading. And then he went to his first pantomime at the Royalty Theatre in Chester. Amid the reek of gas-jets and newly peeled oranges he heard the orchestra play an overture which sounded far richer, more full-bodied than anything rapped out on a cinema piano. The stage filled with colour and the glitter of tinsel. Yet, because he could not identify with pantomime, films kept their hold on him. All the same, he became confusedly aware of another sort of magic, and he knew that only in the theatre would he be able to find it.

By spring of the following year he had learned how babies were made. The information, passed on by a schoolmate in vivid terms, made him incredulous. Would Lorna Doone or Jane Eyre, he wondered in Chesterfieldian disgust, have submitted themselves to such crude grapplings? The summer holidays were passed in long lonely walks beside the railway line and around the rubbish dumps. One day a boy he knew was drowned in the turbid water of the Dee. Boatmen rescued the corpse with hooks and took it to the mortuary. Strict warnings forbade swimming in those treacherous deeps, but George, secretly, would creep down to the sands, undress, and plunge into the frigid current with a shock of agonised delight. In the mortuary lay a body, in the water lurked death, and each time his naked body hit the bitter chill of the waves he experienced a distinct sexual thrill.

The Armistice celebrations in 1918 were overshadowed for him by the novel he had just begun to write. At the age of thirteen he embarked on *Hearts of Youth*, a seventeenth-century romance in which the hero rescued his lady-love from a Turkish harem. Having completed sixty-eight pages and written "The End" on the final sheet, he proudly handed the manuscript to Miss Cooke. She returned it to him with the tactful comment: "You have certainly given your imagination full play."[1]

A viewing of *Intolerance* at the cinema dazzled him with sights of

---

[1] Twenty-nine years later the manuscript turned up in an autograph dealer's catalogue. It was priced at £25. "The Author's plays are well-known," wrote the cataloguer, "and in years to come the above manuscript will, to the fortunate owner, become increasingly precious as an example of the earliest work of the Author of *A Murder Has Been Arranged*, *Night Must Fall* and *The Corn Is Green*."

ancient Paris and the massacre of St Bartholomew, of Babylon and its decadent grandeur. He fell in love with the epicene Mountain Girl who was auctioned as a slave in the Babylonian episode. She, this sexless being, metamorphosed into the companion he wanted so much. He looked in the glass at home and ruffled his hair so that the reflection threw back at him a vision of a wild-eyed exotic creature. When everyone had safely gone to bed he brushed soot over his lips and contemplated his profile in a shaving mirror. George Williams would be a film star. Or would he become a dramatist? Never having so much as read a play before, he cast a piece of homework in the form of a drama forty pages long and called it *The Blue Band*, an epic with twenty half-minute scenes based on the massacre of St Bartholomew. Then he turned novelist again and confected *The Tomb of Terror*, a Theban adventure story nourished by Dickens, Lord Lytton and subtitles from *Intolerance*.

In July, 1919, he sat for and passed with distinction the junior examination of the Central Welsh Board. He had prepared it with the rigour of a general laying out his dispositions for battle. Geo. Wms. was a good examination candidate who knew the value of a well-thought-out timetable and a detailed revision schedule. His English teacher, the amiable Miss Morris, not so trenchant a body as Miss Cooke but quite as percipient, gave him *The Lure of The Pen*, a treatise by a Fleet Street journalist on the art of writing. With this manual at his side he looked again over *The Tomb of Terror* and blushed at the hysterical exaggeration of what he had written. He had, in any case, plunged his hero into a situation where a magic snake was about to turn him into stone, and he had no idea of how to rescue him. The manuscript was left unfinished.

Each year on St David's Day the school held an Eisteddfod. George was to give a recitation and chose, after much indecision, one of Mrs Nickleby's monologues from *Nicholas Nickleby*. He fattened it up with extracts from her other speeches, and lay in bed at night mouthing until he knew every word by heart. Then he practised, on journeys to school, the mincing tones of a dotty Mrs Nickleby. For a moment, as he stood on the platform to announce his piece, he wondered if he would lose his nerve and give a simple recitation. He did not. Hands clasped, face beatifically wooden, he launched into a soaring whoop, "Kate my dear, a warm day always puts me in mind of roast pig . . ." The audience quivered and a giggle swept through them. The loveliest sound on earth, the noise of laughter and applause, filled his ears, and he won first prize.

Acting and reading and writing were still not enough. He idled on solitary walks beside the river and looked, unwittingly, for casual encounters. One, a leering old man, was too drunk. Another, a soldier home from the wars, lit up a Woodbine and, encouraged by the crafty fourteen-year-old, spoke about Germans who raped women. "What's rape?" enquired George, all innocent and wide-eyed. They crouched down on the man's old khaki overcoat. Afterwards he walked home, "at peace but guilty," he remembered, "guilty but at peace."

By the winter term of 1920 he had passed his "senior" exam and shed the subjects that bored him in order to concentrate on French, English and History. He now belonged to a choice group of seven who made up the Honours Form destined to take the "Higher" exam in a couple of years' time. Miss Cooke dominated as never before, acting out the revolutionary drama of Victor Hugo's *Hernani*, slipping into urbane seventeenth-century mode with La Bruyère, and reverting to epic tones in Vigny's *Moïse*. It was her idea that pupils should correspond with members of a French school. George was told, a little airily, to expect a letter from a teacher at that establishment who would set him essays and correct them. Within a few days an envelope bearing stamps of the French Republic arrived on his tea table at 314A, High Street, Connah's Quay, near Chester, Angleterre. "Cher George Williams . . .", he read. It was the first letter he had ever received.

On a massive typewriter intended for pupils learning shorthand and book-keeping he hammered out essays which speedily came back to him neatly annotated and corrected. In between composing dissertations on "*la différence entre Thomas Hardy et Arnold Bennett*", he started another novel. His blood was not yet clear of the virus of *Intolerance*, and on his fifteenth birthday he trudged four miles to Flint library where he made careful notes about life in ancient Babylon. These, which ranged from average temperatures to building techniques, were distilled into *The Mists of Babylon*. "Between the hill and Merkes Babylon looked like a heart across which is a purple robe sown with jewels," he wrote, "huge flaming orbs and tiny points of white fire – and across the purple robe a velvety shimmering band is laid – Euphrates." He displayed a Simenon-like absorption in the weather and dwelt on atmospheric detail: "A yellow ball hung in a void of mist; it was the sun at its rising. The vapours shuddered and parted like rent veils . . ." The noblemen at the court of Merodach were ". . . young and beautiful; they wore gold fillets in their hair, that fell gleaming and black like ebony on their necks; they wore cylinders of agate on their wrists; they wore mantles embroidered with gems on their shoulders;

they wore hide sandals on their long, lithe feet; they wore sweet smiles and sweet words . . ." In January, 1921, he reached the end of Chapter VII ("Shamed") but could write no more because all thought of Babylon was suddenly driven from his mind by an abrupt intervention from Miss Cooke. "Look here," she said, dropping her pince-nez and staring at him, "would you like to go to France?"

It could have been an invitation to the moon. What about the cost? She would look after that, she replied, it was an investment worth making. His mother, startled beyond measure, was undecided. His father, amused and excited, took the news in his cheerful stride. That Miss Cooke was at her tricks again: "Trust her to keep us on the hop with her marching orders, she'll be in the House o'Commons next." Lugging with him a shabby trunk that contained, among other things, a sophisticated pair of pyjamas instead of his usual night-shirt, he set off from the station for Haute-Savoie where he was to stay with his correspondent Mademoiselle Jeanne Tardy. "Goodbye, Miss Cooke, thank you very much . . ." "Thank me when you get back, I'm taking a small gamble on this, and it's up to you to see I bring it off, goodbye, my regards to Mademoiselle Tardy . . ." On this occasion, the first time he had ever left home, he thought his mother might have kissed him goodbye. She did not. Their relationship excluded such gestures.

At Euston he was met and escorted to his hotel by a representative of Thomas Cook ("a relation of Miss Cooke, Mam, that would take me across London"). Along Shaftesbury Avenue the talismans flashed: Evelyn Laye, Marie Lohr, Owen Nares, Charles Hawtrey, Beatrice Lillie. After posting his "safe arrival" cards home he stole an evening at a music-hall, unable to believe that he, Geo. Wms., was sitting in a London theatre. Next morning, nannied again by Thomas Cook's man, he embarked for Calais and then Paris and glimpses of posters bearing the incantatory names of Sacha Guitry, Raimu, Yvonne Printemps, Maurice Chevalier. On the night-train he thought he would never get to sleep and then dozed off immediately to wake up, alone in a compartment chill with the ice-blue dawn. At Bellegarde Mademoiselle Tardy awaited him, brown-eyed, short, with delicate hands and feet. "*Enchanté de faire votre connaissance, Mademoiselle,*" he stammered. They caught a local train to her home in Vincentiers-en-Genevois. How was Miss Cooke? she asked. Ah, she added, "*Miss Cooke est une brave personne.*" The remark fell oddly on his ears.

At the age of eighteen she had met Miss Cooke when they were pupils at Rumilly College. Later she studied English in Bournemouth and went to visit the Cooke family in Leeds where "Mees Cooke's" father aroused her devotion. She had kept in touch ever since with her old college friend. During the three months George stayed in what she described as *"mon* humble home" he acquired a beret, worked hard to perfect an uvular r that was truly Parisian, and even took piano lessons. The Welsh peasant began to assume a Gallic sheen. Miss Cooke also arranged for him to have private tuition in Italian. He wrote her long and regular letters in French that was gradually becoming more fluent. How should he end? "Affec. à vous", he ventured hardily. She replied "Yours affectionately," with the admonition: "By the way, don't ever abbreviate letter-endings, i.e. 'affec.' for affectionately." He complied. Even at a distance of many miles she remained forbidding.

He went with Mademoiselle Tardy and several other women teachers at the school to see Geneva. As they travelled through Ferney they spoke of Voltaire, and at Lausanne he mentioned (it was unavoidable) Gibbon. When they visited the Château de Chillon they were impelled (also unavoidably) to discuss Byron's poem. At the lycée of Vincentiers, where classes began at eight in the morning, he found delightedly that he came top in French dictation, a result of having learned the language in the old-fashioned way, by reading and writing, unlike the native speakers who had picked it up by ear. He looked at his fellow pupils with curiosity. One of them, in particular, caught his eye, a slim, black-haired, fresh-faced boy who wore a tight-fitting white jersey. He noted a perfect profile and generous lips. His name was Lambard and his unapproachable beauty a source of frustration. A gift of chocolate served as an introduction to friendship. One day Lambard invited him to stay at his home in a nearby village. Ecstatic, George told Mademoiselle Tardy. At first she replied icily that such an arrangement was not *convenable*, despite the approval of Lambard *père*, but he got his way and set off with a fluttering heart. The two boys tramped throughout the day and Lambard chattered inexhaustibly. As evening fell George ran out of subjects to talk about. A haze of, was it boredom?, descended. They reached Lambard's home, a dreary farmstead, and ate a family meal so drenched in garlic that George's stomach rebelled. Lambard's volubility ceased only when they undressed to spend the night in a double bed. He was still as handsome, still as attractive, but the spell was broken and the charm vanished. They fell into bed and almost immediately were asleep.

In August he spent a last sight-seeing day around Annecy with Mademoiselle Tardy whom he now called "Tante Jeanne". The prim thirty-four-year-old spinster and her boy companion sailed over the lake in a steamer and carefully avoided talking of their imminent separation. She saw him off on the night train to Paris, and as the carriage moved away she looked nervously around and clasped her hands in an effort at self-control. *"J'écrirai, j'écrirai, Tante Jeanne!"* he called despairingly, his eyes blurred.

Miss Cooke herself stormed up to meet him in Paris and he winced at her stentorian tones after the delicate nuances of Tante Jeanne. They booked seats at the Comédie Française and saw *Les Femmes Savantes*, Miss Cooke chuckling heartily at Molière's tilts against bluestockings. On her instructions he took notes of their tour through the Louvre and a ritual inspection of the Mona Lisa, and at Napoleon's tomb he fell, momentarily, into a dazed sleep. Calais, Euston and Connah's Quay were soon reached, and people glanced curiously at the beret he wore. *"Qui suis-je?"* he muttered pathetically to himself, "Who am I?", as he unpacked his trunk.

Mademoiselle Tardy rendered her account to his mentor with school-mistressy precision. Miss Cooke's allowance of two thousand one hundred francs had been overspent by two hundred and eighty-six. There were the Italian lessons, the train fare to Geneva, a dictionary, and a beret to be considered. The cost of an outing to Chamonix was not included, she explained, as that had been taken on her own initiative. Miss Cooke paid up and wrote in her firm hand on the letter "Final settlement". Yes, Mademoiselle Tardy concluded, she would be glad to continue their pen-friend arrangement. George browsed over a map of Haute-Savoie and traced with his finger the routes he had taken, the places he had not yet visited. He wrote long letters to Tante Jeanne and pined incessantly for French voices and French people. That month the National Eisteddfod awarded him top prize of three guineas for an essay he wrote on the League of Nations. It was the first money he had earned. It failed to cure his longing for Chocolat Meunier and *œufs sur le plat* and the smell of Gauloises.

The new term began and Miss Cooke amazed him by criticising as affected the Parisian r which he rolled so proudly. She decreed that he should sit London Matriculation in January and thrust him into a crash-course of Latin, Italian and Greek. Extra tuition came from a London correspondence course for which she herself paid. He passed. More interestingly, he played Shylock in a school production of the trial scene from *The Merchant of Venice*, having based himself on old photographs of Tree and Irving and rehearsed the effect of his beard in a mirror. An ingenious piece of business he had evolved, the flick of a knife suddenly brandished, was peremptorily censored by Miss

Cooke. "Don't do that," she hissed, "it'll frighten the younger children." He was incensed and did not forgive her for weeks.

At Girl Guide functions and Church teas and social evenings he started to give recitations for half a crown apiece. He meditated an historical drama about Owen Glendower for the Eisteddfod. There was a moment when he nurtured the impossible dream of producing *She Stoops to Conquer* in a church hall. His nerves were strained. At home his mother annoyed him by her apparent lack of interest in his school work. He taxed her bitterly. If, he told her, it hadn't been for Dad he wouldn't have even been at school. "If it wasn't for your father, indeed . . . If it wasn't for me, your father wouldn't be here, nor you nor any of us." She did not, as he feared she might, break down in tears, but turned away, cold-eyed, impenetrable as ever.

His last year at school began with Miss Cooke in more dictatorial mood than usual. She sent him on demeaning little errands and hailed him, abruptly, as "Williams", her pince-nez quivering. He felt easier if she were at a distance, as when, during the school holidays, she posted him books to read and he thanked her with long letters in his small neat handwriting. One Easter he was absorbed in the French classical drama and preparing an essay on the character of Pauline in Corneille's *Polyeucte*. He did not find her as attractive as the heroine of Hugo's *Hernani*. "Frankly I think she's tiresome. Doña Sol mayn't be much, but she's far more real than Pauline, whom I can't even imagine eating! Surely it is very factitious to show people as if they did nothing from morning till night but dissect their souls." At the end he formed an opinion which, in a seventeen-year-old boy, shows rare critical instinct. "But the raptures of Polyeucte, and the language altogether, are wonderful! I think it is the language there, just as in *Hernani*, that makes up for the defects in characterization. At least not that exactly, for the language of *Polyeucte* has more thought, more strength behind it than Hugo's, which is all glitter and nothing underneath." One can see why Miss Cooke preserved so religiously the letters her protégé wrote to her.

He sat through the performance of a Welsh play and thought it ". . . marvellously true to life, quite to compare with Hardy's Wessex peasants . . . Perhaps some day a time will come when a Welsh novelist will combine this faithfulness in depicting ordinary life with the Celtic mysticism and passion; then we shall have our Hardy, one which will perhaps outrival the Saxon one." He read Alphonse Daudet's sequel to the popular *Tartarin de Tarascon* and decided that ". . . the humour is so child-like and effervescent. Still these books, written for an aviduous [sic] public asking for more, are never as good as the first, are they?" More modern literature engaged him in the shape of *If Winter Comes*. Perhaps sections of it were "too patently clever" and the style was "painful, almost hectic at times", but these "blemishes" were redeemed by the novel's "intense vigour". Why were the critics so prejudiced against it? Because it was amazingly popular and because they thought that ". . . to be of any value a book must be read of the few."

His adventures in French literature continued with Maeterlinck, about whom he could not make up his mind. "Sometimes I think it is very simple and beautiful indeed, at other times it is both childish and incoherent, but it is every bit very thrilling." Loti's *Pêcheur d'Islande* occupied him for several hot weeks in summer as he struggled to translate it into Welsh for an Eisteddfod prize contest. He concluded with despair that it was particularly hard to render "even into English".

Gradually the theatre began to intrude. "I saw a little of the poetry in *The Playboy of the Western World* but I am afraid that was all I ever saw in it." Fifty years later, however, he was to find Synge useful at least to the extent of suggesting a title for his "Saki" performances. And he wrote to Miss Cooke with a chance but decidedly eerie foresight: "So Genevieve Ward is dead at last! I suppose Ellen Terry will not survive her by many years. Isn't it curious to think that as soon as actors and actresses are dead, their work becomes immediately a tradition, since they have no definite heritage to hand down to posterity, as authors have? If I were an actor, and seriously ambitious, I should begin to feel very handicapped and discouraged."[2]

In the spring of 1923 he declared a truce with Miss Cooke. We do not always find it easy to forgive those who do us good turns, and kindness is one of the most difficult human virtues to acknowledge with an open heart. He had begun to resent her constant gifts of money, of books, of newspapers, however much she tried to disguise her charity with a gruff dismissiveness. It embarrassed him when he remembered the boots she had given him during his early days at Holywell and the discreet financing of his three months in France. Gratitude was checked by an urge to rebellion. After months of haughty insolence he came to realise that she, too, was a human being,

---

[2] John Gielgud has described Genevieve Ward (1838–1922) as "a terrible old battle-axe", and recalls her dressing-room tiff with Ellen Terry which ended in the latter's remark, "You always were a cat, Ginny." She was, however, he adds, "a fine tragedienne".

that she felt unease as well, and that her domineering attitude was a clumsy attempt to spare both their feelings. They shook hands and made up.

A day later she called him back and suggested he enter for an Open Scholarship in French to Christ Church, Oxford, worth eighty pounds a year. It was a long shot, and he would be competing with the brainiest pupils from all over England, but it was worthwhile, she remarked, "for the fun of it". Once again he drew up a detailed timetable of study for Latin, Greek, English and Italian, to run concurrently with his preparations for the Welsh Higher. Was Oxford by the sea? his mother enquired, and who would pay his fare to sit the exam there? Oh, Oxford would, he assured her, although of course it was Miss Cooke who provided the money. He arrived in Oxford, a little disappointed that the railway station had no dreaming spires and looked more like Connah's Quay station, though bigger. For two days he translated Heredia into English, construed Greek and Latin, and sought, in his English essay, to define the word "Romance". At his interview an elderly don enquired kindly, over sherry, about his sex-life. "Aren't Welsh women supposed to be very passionate?" he persisted, gimlet-eyed. The candidate departed, bemused with sherry and formulating the witty ripostes that might have lightened the bizarre ordeal but did not occur to him at the time. Before catching his train home he lingered at the notice board beside Tom Gate. A handwritten note was pinned to it: "July 6, 1923, The following election has been made: To an Open Scholarship in French, Mr G. E. Williams, signed H. J. White (Dean)."

At Connah's Quay his mother prepared a celebration tea that included the luxury of a boiled egg. His father smoked a jubilant pipe and greeted him in Welsh as "man of Oxford". There were still many things to be done, not least the passing of the Welsh Higher, but exhilaration persisted. George wrote to Miss Cooke that his mother was ". . . everlastingly talking about clothes and handkerchiefs and towels, it reminds me of when I went to France. She is trying to get those marked initial-slips, if they are not too dear, and she has also been making enquiries already after most of the other things. As for a trunk we have discovered my father has a very good one already, made of strong tin, almost new, with several locks, and we think it will do nicely. Do you think so? It is really very strong and looks quite presentable." It was, in fact, not of tin but of solid oak, thickly riveted and of daunting tonnage.

The Welsh Higher was confidently attacked and despatched with success. Then hubris intervened. He went to the National Eisteddfod buoyed up on the unbroken current of triumph and expecting to hear that his drama about Owen Glendower had won the hundred-guinea prize. He had already spent the money in imagination. The result was announced. Or rather, there was no result, since the judges decided not to award the prize because the standard of the entries was so low. In particular, it was thought, the entry by "Gwnfab" (G. E. Williams) leaned towards old-fashioned melodrama. Old-fashioned!

He made up for this setback by winning a County Exhibition of £60 a year to add to his Christ Church Scholarship. A private benefactor, appealed to by his headmaster, contributed another £40 for three years. At a farewell school party his teachers gave him a set of hairbrushes, three pound notes and some books. His father helped with pride to carry the heavy trunk, and his mother presented him with a bacon sandwich. She waved once as the train pulled out, and then again, and he left Connah's Quay behind him.

"G. E. Williams" said the freshly painted notice outside his rooms in Tom Quad. The cheapest available, they comprised an oak-beamed attic and a friendly bedroom where he distributed his books and modest belongings. Lewis Carroll once lived on the same floor. Had anyone ever heard of *him* at the time?

His tutor spoke vaguely of an essay each week on, for example, the philosophy of Diderot or the Tristan legend. Perhaps the new undergraduate would care to attend lectures at the Taylorian when he saw fit? There was no hectoring, no jollying along such as he had come to expect from Miss Cooke. At meals in Hall he distinguished gingerly between fork and fish-knife. When his scout served breakfast it included cornflakes, a dish he had never seen before. "Dear Miss Cooke," he wrote, "life is new and strange . . ." And to Vincentiers: *"Ma Chère Tante Jeanne, la vie est nouvelle, étrange . . ."*

A few days later, alone in his room, he tried to work. It was impossible. The urge had gone, the power to concentrate evaded him. In this atmosphere of total freedom he was confused, disorientated. He resembled a prisoner who did not know what to do with himself once the long period of incarceration had ended. At Connah's Quay he had longed for escape, and study had provided the means of liberation. Now he was free and it meant nothing to him. What *did* he want? Gradually a thought crystallised in his mind and he began to feel better. "I want to be in the Theatre," he said aloud.

(iii)
Theatre

"Dear Miss Cooke, I have decided it is a part of my Oxford education to study plays, so have bought, at Acott's, a book of Playhouse tickets . . ." The converted "Playhouse" was in fact a museum replete with stuffed animals in the Woodstock Road. It had been taken over by James Bernard Fagan, an Irishman of voluble charm who learned his trade under Benson and Beerbohm Tree after having studied for the bar and dallied with the Indian Civil Service. Fortified by much enthusiasm though little money he produced, or directed as we would say nowadays, plays of an avant-garde or classical interest. Apart from an unfortunate habit of casting his second wife in his productions (for she was not a good actress), he showed inventiveness and imagination. These qualities triumphed over the material poverty of his Oxford theatre, where the seating consisted of wooden chairs balanced on planks, there was no curtain, and the cast, presenting a new play each week, never knew where to find the prompter of whom they often had a desperate need.

Fagan's Oxford repertory season taught George about Ibsen, Strindberg, Wilde, Yeats, Shaw and most of the playwrights an aspiring dramatist needed to know. It was the only training in acting and writing plays he ever received. Among the young men of the company was an immensely tall character named Tyrone Guthrie. An elfin Richard Goolden flitted across the stage from time to time, and the women included a pallid Flora Robson. At a performance of *Love for Love* George heard a woman say of the leading man, "Poor boy, how *does* he pronounce it, John *Jeel*-good?" The *Isis* had trouble with the name, too, and praised "a very interesting performance by Mr Gielgerd."

The French Club invited him to play a small part as Maitre d'Hôtel in the Labiche comedy *La Poudre aux yeux*. He read the script, decided that the role had possibilities, and made his first appearance on the stage with a performance both assured and effective. Afterwards, as he slyly told Miss Cooke in his regular weekly letter to her, ". . . you would not believe how good it has been for my French." From this he ascended to the OUDS and to *Hamlet* directed by J. B. Fagan himself. At the last minute the prompter had to withdraw, and George, ordered to take over, sat enthralled beside the red plush curtain amid the warmth of footlights and the smell of size and the mysterious draughts that suddenly rippled the painted flats. Night after night for a whole week he studied the performance at close quarters, observing how pauses were calculated, how effects were timed and climaxes prepared. He became, himself, a part of the illusion so cunningly nurtured.

In the spring of 1924 he gained two more scholarships, worth £75 and £70, one of them to be spent on travel in France. With a fellow-scholarship-winner he travelled to Paris where their French studies were encouraged by *En Pleine Folie!*, the latest attraction at the Folies-Bergère. Afterwards, anxious to rid themselves of their virginity, they bargained with two *filles de joie* who, when negotiations broke down, pocketed the money already offered and drove them away screaming abuse. "Dear Miss Cooke, Paris is rewarding, much to see and tie up with study . . ."

By summer he was rehearsing for an OUDS production of *Love's Labour's Lost* and struggling to lose his Welsh accent. Aiming at Biron the hero, he was cast as Dull the constable and had his reward in a mention by Ivor Brown writing for the *Manchester Guardian*: "Mr Williams made a small part large by a rich suggestion of the well-intentioned lackwit hopelessly at odds with a world of scholars." He still had money left over from the travelling scholarship, and during the vacation he set off with his Raleigh bicycle, a birthday present from Miss Cooke, on a tour of the French provinces. In the birthplace of Corneille during a session *à trois* with a burly sailor and an obliging Rouennaise, amiable and expert, he at last disposed of the virginity which so embarrassed him.

Winter dribbled away in attempts at playwriting: *Sinner in the Sun*, which never got beyond two pages, and *Cinderella*, which went off to an agent and as promptly came back. Miss Cooke described the latter as "too much a mish-mash of realism and poetry", and gave him a typewriter for his birthday. On a trip to London he saw the young American actor Tom Douglas who in 1925 dazzled both women and men with his boyish look and handsome features. George forgot *la belle Rouennaise* in a hungry obsession with this beautiful young man whose presence made *Fata Morgana*, an adaptation from the Hungarian, into the hit of the season. Twenty-one years old, slim and vulnerable, Douglas was already a veteran of D. W. Griffith films and adored by a large following. George reverently studied his name in the telephone book, dreamed of speaking to him, imagined creating plays for him. He nerved himself to write – "This is not a fan letter though I am a sincere admirer of your work" – and had, overjoyed, a benignly vague reply addressed to "G. Emlyn Williams Esq." He never met his idol and the image remained untarnished.

At the OUDS he played several roles in *Peer Gynt*, an old man in the Gilbert Murray translation of the *Medea*, and a head waiter and a notary in Rostand's *The Two Pierrots* and *The Fantasticks*. He acted Pirandello in the original Italian (*Lumie di Sicilia*), and, at the Presbyterian Church Hall, Connah's Quay, performed in his native tongue for a single presentation of *Y Bobl Fach Ddu*. In *Buy Degrees*, an "informal smoker", he did a drag act parodying a music-hall cocotte, lyric by G. E. Williams. Made up as Yvette, purple-dressed, cloche-hatted, he later had a photograph taken and sent it to Miss Cooke. "Mm . . .", she drily commented, "striking, but I prefer Dull."

Oxford meant the theatre, acting, playwriting, making-up. It fluttered with circumambient shades bearing names like Betjeman and Driberg and Acton and Howard and Ketton-Cremer. It meant playing in Chekhov's *The Bear*, ("Lukka", said the programme, "Evelyn Williams"), and doubling as Silence and Morton in *Henry IV, Part 2*, and rushing early next day for the *Sunday Times* to check on James Agate: "I think I spy an actor in Mr G. E. Williams, who gave the small part of Morton very well." Oxford meant a fortnight's charity tour of local villages with a revue called *Twenty-One*. Oxford, too, meant ploughing the end-of-year "Divvers" and a fainthearted excuse to Miss Cooke that he had been over-working. "Your letter makes very sorry reading," she bombinated by return. "I've no use for slackers who can't stick it."

A three-month holiday in Italy during the vacation took him to Rome, where, in the shadowed coolness of his room, he made a noble attempt to acquire the command of Greek essential for his next assault on "Divvers". In Assisi he studied Spanish, and in Sorrento found with delight that his landlady was named Signora Gobbo. Wherever he was, though, he could not resist turning to the theatre list in *The Times* and running his eye over a litany more firmly anchored in his mind than any Greek gospel: the Ambassadors, the Adelphi, the Apollo, Drury Lane, the Duchess . . . and Noël Coward in *On With The Dance*, Sybil Thorndike in *The Lie*, Tallulah Bankhead in *The Creaking Chair* . . .

He was already the author of *Vigil*, a one-act piece of Grand Guignol presented by OUDS under John Fernald's direction. It took place in a lonely manor house on the Welsh border and had three characters: the farmer's boy Issaiah, a stranger, and a permanent guest, both English. The benighted stranger arrives in the small hours and learns from Issaiah about the master of the house who never appears but who exercises hypnotic power over the people who come there. The permanent guest has been immured four years and cannot break out: "I had a brilliant future before me, and I have lost my soul. I tell you, my soul! He has taken it away from me, as a grown-up man takes away a toy from a naughty child." The two men plot to murder their captor and escape. They are forestalled, however, by his illiterate servant Issaiah who himself has been detained there for ten years. An off-stage bell clangs furiously and then stops as suddenly as it began. "He has called me," says Issaiah dreamily. For a month Issaiah has awaited the tolling of the bell at night. He has been systematically poisoning his master, he explains as the bell rings again, sharp and insistent. Three single strokes are heard, each weaker than the last, then a muddled clatter and finally silence. "It is finish," Issaiah continues placidly. "He breathe strong not now. It is finish." The others escape and leave him alone with his terror. He picks up the candlestick and shuffles fearfully towards the room of his dead master, a snatch of weird song on his lips.

Vigil was written very quickly in a sudden spurt of inspiration. It shows what later were to be characteristics: the ability to conjure up an atmosphere swiftly and convincingly, a relish for strange terrors, and an absorption in characters of sinister ambiguity. After the OUDS production, when the cast included Robert Speaight as one of the two Englishmen, the script was printed in an Oxford magazine. A copy went, inevitably, to Miss Cooke and another to Connah's Quay. George's father replied: "Your play is well mixed together, more power to you."

In the spring of 1926 a General Strike gave the young playwright a welcome excuse for deserting his books and helping, with other students who also enjoyed the lark, to unload ships at London docks. It also, for a time, distracted him from a new infatuation. But only for a time. Back in Oxford he was haunted by the profile of an undergraduate who had been assistant stage manager for *Vigil*. Warm, kindly, the friend was yet unattainable. George knew it, and the fact of his idol being beyond reach, like a Proustian *être fuyant*, only made him the more to be desired. He could bear the strain no longer. He wanted to die, he told a sympathetic doctor who gave him sedatives and patted his arm comfortingly. Then he went back to his rooms, fell into a bottomless sleep, and awoke, puzzled, to see his father come to take him home.

The telegram received at Connah's Quay had spoken of a nervous breakdown. Again he fell asleep, and when his eyes opened and he saw his brothers Job and Tom in their neighbouring bed he realised that after all he had only exchanged one prison for another. Miss Cooke bustled up, striving to conceal her astonishment at this wholly unexpected turn. "You'd feel better, you know, if you got your hair cut," she vociferated while his father grinned appreciatively. It was the first time his parents had met her. "She's got the bark, George," said Richard Williams afterwards, "but God bless her, no bite."

Having a "brain-fever" he was excused chapel. He felt marooned in a family he loved but with whom he could not communicate. Miss Cooke escorted him to a doctor in Liverpool who testified that he was unfit to take examinations and should defer them for a year. "Wms. from working-class home," reported the medical man, " – diff. between home and Christ Church a strain on adaptability." He was wrong. The chameleon George had had no trouble at all in adapting to Oxford the moment he realised that his fellow undergraduates were not all the heirs of dukes and millionaires and that quite a few of them were the sons of solicitors and building contractors from the Home Counties. His problem was the handsome, the unavailable assistant stage manager.

At first he could do little more than sit in his room and melt from time to time into bouts of weeping. Occasionally he wandered beside the Dee and lay face down on the scrubby grass, aching for his lost love – or was it really "lost", since he had never consummated it? Miss Cooke lent him novels which he read slowly and unenthusiastically. From a drawer he took out a bundle of poems he had written, thin typed sheets bearing translations of Welsh and French poetry and meditations inspired by Versailles. They included a long epic on Byron and original pieces with titles like *"Moment Pathétique"* and "Departure of a Lady". The verses meant nothing to him now.

As his strength gradually returned he diverted himself with the novelty of a cat's whisker wireless set, a bundle of straggling wires and ear-phones. A friendly school inspector put him in touch with the Lloyd George family and he gave French and Italian lessons to the children, among them a twenty-four-year-old Megan, "the most attractive girl I had ever seen." For nine shillings an evening he ran French classes at the suggestion of a bank manager in Criccieth. At the public library, where he called every day to read the theatre page in *The Times*, he saw that J. B. Fagan's new play about Pepys called *And So To Bed* had just opened successfully. It was September, 1926, and he recalled writing a play entitled *Full Moon* over the past confused recuperative months and sending it to, among others, Fagan. Everyone, except Fagan, had acknowledged it, kindly but non-committally.

Full Moon was set in the Italian Alps and drew on the old Welsh legend, Breton as well, about a city drowned under the waves of the sea whence may be heard by lovers, at the time of the full moon, the clamour of distant bells. With this was interwoven the conflict that opposes an expatriate Englishman and a half-Italian girl, the cause of their disagreement being his young son. As love flowers at the end of the first act bells are heard from the drowned steeples and "a tremor of moonlight" flickers over the stage. By the curtain of Act Two the full moon has begun to rise and all the characters are deeply embroiled in their problems. In the final act the son speaks resentfully to his possessive father: "I have been your son, if you like . . . but yesterday . . . last night when the bells rang . . . I was myself! And I was there, with her – it was the loveliest thing I had ever dreamed of – and now the bells are dumb – that loveliest thing – *you* have killed it! Dead!" Anger subsides, and bittersweet reconciliation is achieved, and the curtain falls with another "tremor of moonlight".

In September, 1926, a letter arrived at last from Fagan agreeing to do *Full Moon* at the Oxford Playhouse. What impressed him must have been the deft stagecraft and the assurance with which the plot was managed. The strong emotion generated by the scenes between father and son owed something as well to George's relationship with his own parent. He read and re-read with feelings of disbelief the blessed letter written on paper headed "Savoy Theatre, London". It was difficult to credit that the fantasy he created on paper would soon be bodied forth by flesh-and-blood people on a stage. Within the family circle he deliberately played down the wonderful news. Miss Cooke abetted him: "Hmmm . . . As I told you, it's an interesting play, and as to respect for the Unities, Racine would have approved. But don't build castles on sand, find yourself a goodly piece of rock in the shape of an MA Oxon, that'll outwear a week at any old Playhouse . . ."

Castles on sand! Why should he not be entitled to build a few of them when the name "Emlyn Williams" appeared on Fagan's programme among those of Shaw, Chekhov, Barrie and Strindberg? ("Fancy," said his mother, "you taking up the Emlyn and dropping the George, is that for good?") On February 28, 1927, *Full Moon* had its première at the Oxford Playhouse. Fagan's telegram to Connah's Quay announced: "Your charming piece played beautifully do come see it." *The Times* discerned ". . . something of Tchekov and

Strindberg . . . mystical, with touches of whimsical humour . . ." He
rushed to Oxford and for two enchanted, dreamlike hours had the
bizarre experience of listening to other voices speaking the words he
had set down in his lonely room. The leading male roles were played
by Alan Napier and Glen Byan Shaw, names later to be distinguished
in the theatre, and they were just as he had visualised them. So were the
rest of the cast. He only awoke from the dream at the end, when he
hurried out to avoid hearing any comments by the departing audience.
"I don't often advise this," said Fagan, "but have you thought of going
on the stage? When you've done your Schools, of course. Come to me
if you need help." At the stage-door an envelope was handed over. In it
were five one-pound notes, the first royalties he ever earned.

At Fagan's invitation, and expense, he passed a few days in London
on theatre visits. When he returned to Connah's Quay he felt
unsettled, as if his personality lay about like the random pieces of a
jigsaw puzzle. In that uneasy atmosphere he quarrelled with his
brother Job, a squall predicting the storm that soon afterwards broke
as a result of some trivial disagreement. His mother snapped, his father
thundered. Without a word he left the room and counted out the four
pounds twelve shillings which remained of his royalties on *Full Moon*.
Early next morning, speaking to no-one, he slipped quietly out of the
house and booked a railway ticket to Euston. In London he
confidently expected to assemble all the pieces of the jigsaw puzzle. He
remembered Fagan's promise and called on him at the Savoy Theatre
where *And So To Bed* was installed. Fagan did not let him down.
Unusually direct and for once free of his Irish vagueness, he offered
him £3 a week in the walk-on part of Pelling's 'Prentice. There was one
condition. "As an old Trinity man," he added, "I insist that you take
your Schools and get a respectable Second, a degree never did anybody
in the theatre harm." The part had six lines – six lines! – and Emlyn/
George scribbled them down on the back of an envelope at the stage-
manager's dictation: "Is Mistress Pepys within . . . ?" He walked,
ecstatically, to Bloomsbury where in Mecklenburgh Street he had
taken a little room. Beside his shabby bed he hung up a theatre-list cut
out of a newspaper. From a chemist he bought the traditional make-up
sticks of "five and nine". Then he studied his part over and over again.
The envelope on which he had written it contained a letter from Miss
Cooke: "Hmmm, I was afraid of this. But I have faith, and three cheers
for Mr Fagan of Trinity."

And So To Bed, a comedy of charm and quick humour, was destined
for a long run both in London and New York. It featured as Charles II

an actor called Allan Jeayes, resonant-voiced and solidly built, who in plays and later films built up a repertory of judges, police inspectors and men of authority. Mr Pepys himself was the Welsh actor Edmund Gwenn, an admirable piece of casting, for he had an air of quizzical roguery and a mischievous grin accompanied by diction that was velvety and insinuating. He graced the West End for over forty years, after which he emigrated to Hollywood and began another long career specialising in tetchy but kind-hearted old gentlemen and, more interestingly, venerable ancients with a strong hint of villainy underneath their bland exterior. His wife, Mrs Pepys, took on the appearance of Yvonne Arnaud, a much loved actress now commemorated by her own theatre in Guildford. She was unmistakably Parisian and at the age of thirteen won first prize for her piano playing at the Conservatoire, afterwards touring the world as a child prodigy. Almost by chance, and certainly without any training whatsoever, she made her stage debut at the Adelphi when aged nineteen as Princesse Mathilde in *The Quaker Girl*. Her immediate success led to roles such as "Mam'selle Trălala", "Georgette St Pol" and "Chiquette" in numerous musical comedies, and once she even ventured into an Aldwych farce. By then she was an established favourite, long settled in England, where her apparently effortless acting style concealed a sense of timing as deft as Marie Tempest's. As the years went on her French accent grew more and more jagged, for although off-stage she had fluent English, she knew, like Maurice Chevalier who enjoyed a similar popularity here, that Anglo-Saxons dearly love an entertainer who murders their language with Gallic brio.

The curtain went up on the matinée of April 4, 1927. Pelling's 'Prentice stood in the wings having duly made up with "five and nine" and hoping that no one had remarked his inexperienced fumbling with the Leichner sticks. He thought of his lines and ran over the directions he had scrawled for himself on the envelope. Despite the heat of the footlights he was cold and his hands trembled. The prompt nodded and he sauntered forward. What if he fell down? Yet although his nerves played up he was aware of watching himself, of taking a curiously objective view as if he had been someone else. It was the feeling he had experienced at school when he performed in the Anglo-French dialogue or impersonated Mrs Nickleby. He crossed the stage and delivered his lines. "Iss Misstress . . . Peeps . . . within?" They splashed out in a torrent of Welsh vowels and hissing sibilants. Afterwards, he recalled, "I was as tired as if I had just played King Lear."

In a dressing-room that reeked of powder and sweat he creamed off make-up and changed his clothes. As he went out of the theatre the murmur of voices from the stage was drowned in the clatter of traffic. The immensity of London daunted him: "You take a bus up to Hampstead Heath," he wrote to Miss Cooke, "and for two moments a green tree and a pond with a duck on it give you the illusion of the countryside. And then you climb on [an] eminence, and London is still all around you, as far as you can see! The suburbs are wonderful – rows and rows of drab dining-rooms, grocers' shops, with tramlines in between, shimmering in the heat, miles and miles, every shop an exact and grubby copy of every other."

While he paced the London streets killing time until the evening and his one-minute appearance, he had a sudden queer vision of home at Connah's Quay. He saw the neat kitchen and his brothers sitting at the table covered with a newspaper to save the cloth, eighteen-year-old Job, now a worker at the steel plant, and Tom, four years younger but already helping the family income as a paper boy. While his mother, reserved, white-haired, cut bread and butter, his father sat nearby genially immersed in the betting pages of the *Liverpool Echo*. It would, he thought, be a long time before they met again, although he still kept discreetly in touch through Tom. As he explained to Miss Cooke, who had been startled by his abrupt departure: "I quarrelled with my family on the Sunday, and left Monday morning first train. Father has never forgiven me for my previous 'nervous breakdown'. Others might fail their exams and remain quite amusing, but I was a solid rock of respectable learning, and he lost confidence completely when that happened. And of course this business of the stage disgusts the whole family. And I don't get on with Mother, she doesn't really like me as much as my middle brother, and things got so strained, father burst out and said I was good for nothing and was in the way . . . So I ran away with no money and no prospects." He had never forgotten the occasion when he told his mother: "I want to stand before crowds of people and make them laugh and cry." "Oh, you want to be a preacher!" she replied delightedly. "No, I want to be an actor." His mother had been appalled.

From Bloomsbury he moved after a few weeks to Chelsea, for he had quickly made acquaintances of a sort he would never have encountered in Connah's Quay. "I am living with a French Corsican friend whom I met in Paris," he wrote with tactful mendacity to Miss Cooke, "in a lovely studio in Chelsea, with rafters and orange curtains, for which I pay fifteen shillings a week – he cooks beautifully and we are going to keep house. The studio's at the top of girls' school where he teaches French and Spanish in the intervals of writing a novel, exactly as I did at Criccieth."

The "French Corsican friend" was the "comte" Pierre de Rilly, born in Pittsburgh as Peter O'Reilly, a pasty-faced queen thirty years old, my dear, if a day, and ornamented with a monocle. Manresa Road, Chelsea, represented Bohemia for the romantic young Welshman, and he learned with pleasing alacrity the argot of the new world that beckoned him in. "Chicken" "cottage," "TBH," "a little plain knitting," "rent" . . . the phrases tripped fluently off the tongue. "Bugger's such an *ugly* word, don't you agree?" twittered Pierre in his American-cum-British-cum-music-hall-French accent. "Sodomite has so much more panache!" After two days the amusing chatter palled and Emlyn moved house again, this time to the solitude of a grim but thankfully silent room at King's Cross. Yet desire remained, ever present, ever demanding fulfilment, and he became a familiar shadow in such notorious meeting places as that fake Tudor temple of daintiness the Tea Kettle, the more boisterous Long Bar at the Trocadero, and the ambiguous Chalice Bar in Coventry Street. Since, however, his taste did not lie with the girlish clientele that frequented those purlieus, he drew more satisfaction from brief encounters outside. In Hyde Park or around Hampstead Heath, on hot sunny afternoons while mechanically perusing a book, he would sometimes find a virile neighbour beside him. Casual glances and non-committal chat led to stealthy manoeuvres beneath a negligently spread newspaper, the pleasure considerably heightened by the agreeable but dangerous possibility of a watchful policeman lurking not far away.

And So To Bed dragged on through the critical warm months of summer. He discussed French literature with Yvonne Arnaud who had graduated from the Sorbonne before plunging into musical comedy and who confessed that Racine was her favourite poet and that she disliked Corneille. Someone asked her if she studied at the Berlitz School to preserve her French accent. "Of course," she said gaily, "it eez my bread and my bitter!" These frivolous tutorials with Mademoiselle Arnaud were the lighter side of study for "Schools" which was now becoming desperate. He knew, he told Miss Cooke, that he would not get a First and he was ready to settle for a degree of any sort. His head buzzing with French Morphology, with the development of the tonic enclosed E, with the syntactical nuances of the *langue d'oïl* and the *langue d'oc*, he went to Oxford on June 2, 1927, for his final examination and, a few days later, the dreaded Viva.

Miss Cooke cheerfully paid the five-pound fee, a loan which increased the debt he already owed her to forty pounds. Schools were "terrifying", the Viva even more so. Did Mr Williams *really* think that the fifteenth century was one of unexampled prosperity in France? Had he *never* heard of the Battle of Agincourt? Was Mr Williams *quite* correct in speaking of Rutebeuf's "delightful descriptions"? The victim twisted fearfully as the inquisitors, his hastily scrawled paper before them, impaled him on one after another slyly wielded skewer.

While awaiting the result he played in a brief season Fagan arranged at the Oxford Playhouse. In London, before the Oxford programme opened, he had walked on in Strindberg's *The Spook Sonata*. "It is a quite incomprehensible play," Miss Cooke was informed, and, last word in opprobrium, " 'highbrow' if anything is, and yet by the end of the week the theatre was packed to overflowing . . . The ways of the theatrical public – the pit especially – are incalculable." At Oxford he had one line in *Uncle Vanya*, small roles as a Burglar in *Heartbreak House* and as a Footman in *The Circle*, and a splendid opportunity as Sir Andrew Aguecheek. He felt uneasy in *Twelfth Night*, could not get to grips with the lines, and was told by a kindly friend that the knight may have been a fool but was not the village idiot. He cheered up when he read the Oxford Class lists in *The Times* and saw that G. E. Williams had achieved a Second with "distinction in colloquial French". Henceforward, a man of solid achievement, he would be allowed to style himself, after the necessary formalities, "MA Oxon."

In September the *And So To Bed* company went on a brief provincial tour which enabled him to spend a short time with Miss Cooke in her home-town of Leeds where she was holidaying with her sister. She had not changed. The voice rang out as stridently as ever, the eyes flickered with challenge. "Well," she announced, "I reckon a Second isn't to be sneezed at considering, dash it all you were working under a handicap, well you seem in pretty good shape, I expected you to look theatrical." He left her feeling refreshed, invigorated, and went back to London where the company prepared for a season in New York. By now he was reconciled with the family, at least to the extent of correspondence, and his father wrote: "Dear Goerge" – he had never quite mastered the spelling of his eldest son's name – "Dear Goerge, I see by the Liv. Post that you lot are signed on the dotted line to have a whack at the Great White Way . . ."

Emlyn's signature on the dotted line guaranteed him a first-class passage by sea and a weekly salary of twelve pounds. "As life is twice as expensive there it works out at six pounds," he told Miss Cooke, "which is very good, don't you think?" Promoted to a slightly larger rôle as Pepys's Boy and given responsibility as Assistant Stage Manager, he spent more time during the voyage trying out a play he had just written than he did in the contemplation of his new duties. The group of players, voluble, flamboyant, attracted the attention of other passengers, among them a large detachment of the American Legion, ex-soldiers who had made their yearly pilgrimage to the Western Front. "Goddam British pansies, *all* of them!" the veterans chorused, expressing a general opinion. "Pansies?" enquired Yvonne Arnaud. "And what piece do they think we will play in their countree, 'And So To Flowerbed'?"

The lights of New York, thought Emlyn, made Piccadilly Circus look like a country fair. Millions of electric bulbs flashed and dazzled along Broadway spelling out incandescent exhortations on behalf of cigarettes, chewing-gum, plays, films. After a first night spent in a hotel he paled when he saw the bill, nearly half of his weekly wage, and promptly moved out to a modest but economic room at 246, East 23rd Street. At dress rehearsal in the Shubert Theater he was constantly on his feet from nine o'clock one morning until three the next. Another blow fell when he was obliged to join American Equity at a fee of seven pounds. Quickly, though, the frugality he inherited from his mother asserted itself, and by limiting his budget to three and a half dollars rent a week and twenty-five cents for meals at the Soda Luncheonette he was able to bank savings which soon would help clear his debt to Miss Cooke. A diligent scholar still, each evening in the prompt corner he brushed up his German irregular verbs and studied Schiller.

And So To Bed continued to draw good houses throughout the winter, although, as he reported to Miss Cooke, "Things are getting worse and worse in our happy little family party." Between Mary Grey, Fagan's wife, and Yvonne Arnaud, all but a state of open war had been declared. Despite the exchange in public of many a "Darling!" and many a "Chérie!", behind the scenes enmity flourished. "*La dame à côté*" was Yvonne's cold denomination of Miss Grey, whose jealousy and lack of professionalism she deplored. More discord arose when "la Grey's" brother was introduced into the cast as King Charles. He had for some years been kept by the actress Nazimova whom he left when money ran short, and he was an even worse player than his sister. Known to Yvonne as "*cet homme-là*", he destroyed, she claimed, her performance in the second act. Worst of all, the company discovered that "Fagan is not the mild-eyed kind benevolent man we thought he was, but a mere crooked weakminded creature who has vaguely good instincts but is the absolute tool of an extraordinary wife." Working for him had become a matter of "Queen Mary Grey holding court over a little group of obsequious – or rebellious, as the case may be – sycophants to whom she had done the great favour of admitting to her court. It becomes intolerable." Yvonne Arnaud longed to cancel her contract, and only the thought of the compensation she would have to pay deterred her from walking out – although she was earning a large salary of two hundred pounds a week, the parsimonious instinct which urged her to wear her oldest clothes and to live with strict bourgeois economy recoiled at the expenditure of any sum that was not vitally necessary.

Her sense of financial prudence was shared by the junior actor who played Pepys's Boy. By February, 1928, he had enough in his bank deposit, garnered through months of careful living, to pay off his debt to Miss Cooke. "Enclosed a cheque from the richest man in America," he jubilated. The company was now preparing to mount *The Cherry Orchard*. When he first saw it at Oxford he had been bored with it, ". . . but on closer acquaintance I find it exquisite. The very things I found irritating before are now the beauties of the play. The thing it is difficult to realise at first is that it is a picture of real life in the most literal sense, when people say and do things that have no obvious artistic bearing on the situation, exactly as they would off the stage. It is such a relief to see a play which has no climax at the end of the second act and a dénouement in the third." This is a revealing observation from a future dramatist who was obsessively fascinated by technique and who was to write plays demonstrating smooth mastery of every device associated with a conventional stagecraft far removed from Chekhov's approach.

He did not, after all, appear in *The Cherry Orchard*. When he asked for a rise in salary, given the extra matinées, Fagan refused and dropped him from the cast. In any case the Chekhov play met with complete and ignominious failure and soon had to be withdrawn. *And So To Bed* was not doing well either. Casting difficulties led to the brief engagement of Claude Rains, the silky-voiced English actor lately recruited to Hollywood, but he did not fit in and left before his contract expired. "La Grey" continued to throw fits of temperament, to keep the curtain waiting and to storm at Fagan, while Fagan in turn stormed at the stage manager. "It is not all strawberries and cream for these spoilt children," sighed Miss Cooke's pupil.

Homesickness could not be kept at bay, and when Miss Cooke sent him a little box of Flintshire earth and Flintshire moss and Flintshire snowdrops he kept it for days on the table in his little room. Other desires were more easily assuaged. A visit to a well-known Turkish Bath plunged him into a labyrinth of dim corridors that wound between dark windowless cubicles. From time to time a cigarette-end sparked in the gloom as shadows draped with greyish bath-robes padded quietly along. One of them would hesitate, push at the door of a cubicle and, if it gave, slip inside, to remain or, a few seconds later, to emerge and pursue the hunt elsewhere. A bedspring creaked, an occasional whisper susurrated, a door shut stealthily, a moan refused to be stifled. A phantom drifted by, nonchalant, replete. Another, rejected after urgent parleys, scuttled noiselessly to a cubicle further down the way. A cathedral-like hush presided over the casual meeting of bodies in manoeuvres as formal, as decorous, as those of a quadrille. Only occasionally was the silence fragmented by a sudden wincing cry or an "ouch!" that could not be suppressed.

The last and two hundred and fifth performance of *And So To Bed* was given at Easter, 1928. Emlyn went to the bank and drew out savings of nine hundred and fifty dollars, some two hundred pounds, which he had accumulated with loving prudence. "It's a year since I left home," he told Miss Cooke, "and I'm not sorry for three reasons (1) I'm going to write lots of plays (sounds like a threat) and I've already got a much better grip on the very material conditions, stage management and such things, a knowledge of which is essential to the production of an actable play. (2) I've met jealousy and gossip etc etc, and it has been very interesting, and, ultimately, amusing, and of course I must know how to deal with that side of it if I'm going to have a hand in producing plays, (3) the most important. I'm keener on acting than I ever was ... I want more experience. Sounds like a prospectus, I know." After which he resumed for the moment his study of Schiller's *Wilhelm Tell* – "an episodic historical play in rather pedestrian blank verse" – and Goethe's *Hermann und Dorothea*, "a charming elegiac idyll with much delicacy and humour." More suited to his immediate ambitions was Eugene O'Neill's *Strange Interlude*, "undoubtedly America's most important contribution to world drama – a profound psychological study ... The result is something very original and very powerful." Miss Cooke, once the teacher, was now becoming the taught.

CHAPTER TWO

(i)
Glamour

On his return to England in May, 1928, he found London dark and rainy but "full of nice old smells . . . beautifully old", and it was good to hear English spoken again. He made a final decision to drop the first name of George which his father had given him as a respectful nod to the monarch. Henceforward, he resolved, he would be known as Emlyn, or "Emma-line" or "Emil" as New Yorkers had sometimes confusedly addressed him. The name was professionally striking, memorable, and blazoned moreover his proud Welshness.

For a time he stayed in north London with rich friends he had made at Oxford. They persuaded him to buy his first new suit in three years, contributing, thanks to a lucky coup of theirs on the Stock Exchange, seven of the fifteen guineas it cost. At the Embassy night-club, where they took him as their guest, he saw Prince George talking to the then Duke and Duchess of York. Nearby, at another table, sat "an incredibly small and incredibly thin lady in black with a grey boyish haircut and an irregular face so very bright and intelligent as to give the impression of very great beauty." It was the Countess of Oxford and Asquith accompanied by Prince Bibesco. Across the dance floor swayed the elegant film actor Adolphe Menjou. "Don't you wish you were seeing *life*?" Emlyn exulted to Miss Cooke. "It was great fun after 8 months of *Democracy*."

But "life", apart from this glimpse of high society, was more concerned with his daily trudge through London streets in search of a room at an economic rent of fifteen shillings a week. At last he found one in a house at 34, Vincent Square, Westminster, just off the Vauxhall Bridge Road, a building of dilapidated respectability. Miss Cooke suggested he deposit his New York savings in her bank and arrange to cash cheques at a branch nearby. He did so, and, having had a telephone installed, ordered writing paper printed with his address and the essential number in a handsome type-face. He sat back and waited for calls from managers to whom he had written and from casting directors he had importuned. The telephone remained, except for occasional wrong numbers, pathetically mute. "You ask for news," he lamented to Miss Cooke, " – I'm afraid I have none to speak of, beyond the fact that eggs have gone up a farthing in the Vauxhall Bridge Road . . ."

At mass-auditions for walk-on parts, humiliating affairs where actors shuffled forward in a queue to be briefly looked up and down by cold-eyed directors like prison warders, he found that the OUDS, *And So To Bed*, New York, meant nothing. He saw a young actor called Laurence Olivier in the current hit, *Bird in Hand* at the Royalty, and was impressed by his "darkly romantic looks and an interesting stillness". The play was shortly to go on tour and he auditioned for the part, having loitered self-consciously in the run-down waiting-room of a theatrical agent with other candidates whose bright nonchalance failed to conceal taut nerves. He did not get it. At Vincent Square the telephone never rang.

In his little room, by the light of an Aladdin oil-lamp he had bought to replace the feeble flicker of gas, he began work on a play. In between rounds of agents and auditions he completed it after four weeks of concentrated attention. Then he cut and timed it with all the benefit of professional experience gained under Fagan. When it came back from the typing agency, immaculately presented, stage directions laid out in red, speeches neatly arranged, he sent it out to various managements. He was satisfied with it: "Much less 'highbrow' (horrid word) than *Full Moon* . . . I think it is a sound hopeful money proposition and hope managers will think so too. It has considerable 'heart interest' as the girls' weeklies say and that is always attractive." He had little else to tell Miss Cooke apart from his trip to a party in a Chelsea studio with Yvonne Arnaud: "A roomful of manly women and womanly men all in stages of drunkenness and all talking utter nonsense all at once. Yvonne, who is the essence of respectability, fled at once . . . The only interesting person there was Edmond Dulac the painter."

At first he called his play *Happiness* and then, using a new word just come into vogue, rebaptised it *Glamour*. The piece was deliberately built around the star part of an actress who is the leading lady. Gladys Cooper? And Edna Best for the ingénue role, Ronald Squire as the man-about-town, Ellis Jeffreys as the malicious friend? Miss Cooke was told of the need for ". . . a woman who is beautiful, can act, but is thirty-seven and a trifle *passée*. Three well-known London actresses have turned the part down, for reasons which you can guess." Yet eventually there emerged an impresario who had faith in the play, a minor producer called Williams with the initials C.B., like those of the great Cochran himself, which augured good luck. He was an agreeable man who wore pince-nez, looked like "an unworldly Welsh deacon", and specialised in provincial tours of obscure musical plays. *Glamour*, Miss Cooke learned, was to be "tried out for a week at Woking on November 12 and opens at the Embassy Theatre in Hampstead on the 19th or 25th. If it is a success it will be moved further into the West End. My contract is for five per cent royalties on gross receipts at every performance." In addition to his royalties, Emlyn was to receive, unexpectedly, five pounds a week for playing the young Welshman Jack. Instead of Gladys Cooper and Ronald Squire the other parts were filled by supporting players unknown to fame. For reasons of economy there were no understudies. If it was a success, he thought, he would invite Miss Cooke up for the weekend. If not, he sternly told himself, he would not break his heart and throw himself into the river, as it was a piece of good fortune to have the play put on at all. A telegram bearing the joyful news to Connah's Quay brought a characteristic response from his mother: "Received your telegram. I hope this will have no effect on your health. I enclose a muffler as the winter is coming on."

On the strength of his promised five per cent royalties, and feeling very patriarchal, he sent a pound note to brother Tom for his sixteenth birthday. The first night took place, in the event, at Aldershot Theatre Royal on a rainy December night. At rehearsals the minimum of direction had been offered and there were no discussions of the script. The scenery, plucked from here and there by a thrifty management, was shabby and unsuitable. Moments occurred when a laugh struggled through, when a speech made its point, when the dim mass of faces in the audience appeared to register contact with the actors on the stage. Applause, at curtain-call, was fair. It came from a house largely "papered" with the free list. On the second night the audience was even smaller, for by then the free list was exhausted.

The setting of *Glamour* is the London flat of Eve Lone, a famous leading lady, who, like Emlyn's compatriot Ivor Novello, lives over a theatre. She is about to reach the dreadful age of thirty-two. (In fact, she is thirty-three, but keeps her terrible secret dark.) She suddenly realises how empty her life is, how sterile is the "glamour" created by sensational first nights and the luxurious existence of a star. Eve is Welsh by birth, and the irruption into her life of two cousins, Jack and Jill from the home country, awakens a nostalgic longing for her simple origins. Jill is soon transformed into a Mayfair beauty and starts a

41

successful acting career. Jack, a budding artist, falls in love with Eve and they plan to marry. Eve decides to relinquish her lead in a new musical comedy to Jill. Alas, Jack is told by a specialist that he is about to go blind. How can Eve live with a sightless husband? She changes her mind, takes back the lead, and contemplates marriage to her lover, a wealthy sponsor of plays. Jill now realises that it is Jack whom she really loves and plans a life back in Wales devotedly tending him. *Glamour* is a fairy-tale in which even the unpleasant people, the snobs and the careerists, turn out in the end to have hearts of gold.

The structure of *Glamour* is conventional in its preparation for the entry of main characters. "Yes," says the maid answering a telephone call at the rise of the curtain, "this is the flat of Miss Eve Lone, the famous actress." Other background details are provided by exchanges between minor characters. The plot becomes melodramatic with the introduction of Jack's blindness which gives the dialogue a stilted quality hard to bear: "My darling," says Jack to Eve, "do not look so sad! Honestly it does not matter, honestly it does not! The only thing that can make me unhappy now is to see you like that. Eve, don't! . . ." The most egregious improbability of all is Eve's decision to make way for Jill: breathes there the leading lady with soul so mad that she will throw up the chance of a lifetime in favour of a younger, more beautiful rival? As Emlyn was to observe years later: "When I had told myself I knew what I was writing about – Welsh people and the West End theatre – the first could be true, the second was not."

The play, "this schoolboy play" as the *Daily Sketch* contemptuously dismissed it, transferred, unbelievably, to the Embassy in London and then to the Royal Court, where it opened on one of the worst possible dates in the theatrical calendar: New Year's Eve. In between Emlyn took the train to Connah's Quay for the first time since his embittered departure nearly two years before. He found Mam washing up, and she greeted him with a smile but no kiss, no hug. His father beamed and flourished the bundle of much-thumbed press cuttings he had garnered about his clever son. Brother Tom came in, upright and elegant in his new Salvation Army uniform. "God be with you," he said as he went off with his cornet to rescue the perishing. Presents from London were distributed. For old times' sake, Emlyn scraped soot from the kitchen chimney and cleaned his teeth with it at the backyard tap.

By the Thursday of *Glamour*'s first week his five per cent royalty amounted to just over two pounds. Audiences dwindled in spite of feverish papering, and that night in the gallery, which could not be papered, there were three lonely spectators. *Glamour* evaporated, leaving him with the lesson that he had confused what he wanted to say with what the audience wanted to hear.

Full Moon emerged briefly for a Sunday night performance at the Arts Theatre. Other modest engagements followed, chiefly in single performances of avant-garde plays mounted by the indomitable J. T. Grein, a critic of Dutch descent who, with the genial assistance of his wife, herself the author under a pen name of many plays, bravely attempted the conversion of London to Ibsen and the European drama. (How, one wonders, did he acquit himself when professional duties obliged him to review one of Mrs Grein's dozen or so plays?) At a guinea a performance Emlyn acted in a French-speaking adaptation of Zola's *Thérèse Raquin*, in Sarment's *Le Pêcheur d'ombres* and in other French and German productions. One day there came to his rooms a gaunt figure, its pate cinct with blanched hair, its figure bent, its lungs convulsed by the ascent of narrow winding stairs. The apparition folded up coughing into an armchair. He was William Poel, instructor to the Shakespeare Reading Society, founder of the Elizabethan Stage Society, author of *What Is Wrong with the Stage?*, and quondam "discoverer" of Edith Evans. The "doubtful" plays attributed to Shakespeare were his meat, and the obscurer pieces of Webster and Beaumont his drink. His latest obsession was *The Conspiracy and Tragedy of Charles, Duke of Byron*, an Elizabethan drama of which no one else had ever heard, and on the strength of Emlyn's reply to his advertisement in *The Stage* he had come to interview the postulant. The visit became a disquisition, uttered in the style of Moses handing down the tablets, on the Poel Method of Voice Production. Emlyn heard him out politely, flattered that the venerable gentleman had taken such trouble and daunted by the famous Method which, in some arcane way, depended on an elaborate system of breathing. If, he reflected, Edith Evans had survived it, so could he, and gladly he accepted the customary guinea for uttering six lines of incomprehensible verse.

He had the chance of acting in a play that lasted more than a night when he was engaged by Ernest Milton to join a brief repertory season at the Queen's Theatre in February, 1929. The programme consisted of *The Mock Emperor*, a version of Pirandello's *Enrico IV*, and *Mafro, Darling!*, a new play by Milton's wife the novelist Naomi Royde-Smith. Milton, then not yet forty, was already a distinguished Shakespearean actor, and with husbandly courage had ventured to put on Mrs Milton's not very good play. On a draughty stage lit by a single naked flame the cast assembled for a run-through, peering at their scripts, flicking cigarette ash into dirty tins beside their chairs, and reading the lines with matter-of-fact emphasis. Next day moves were blocked out, the company began to "act", and speeches started lying in the memory. Ominously, as rehearsals went on, much rewriting became necessary. As early as the first-night interval the little play gave off an aura of doom, and within a few days it was replaced with *The Mock Emperor*. Listless, worn out by the strain of his uxorious gesture, Milton yet bestirred himself to give a performance as the Emperor of overwhelming pathos. It was no good: within a week the notices went up. Yet the failure of this nobly-intentioned venture had, like *Glamour*, taught Emlyn a double lesson, in this case the art of holding an audience as demonstrated by Milton and an example of professionalism in the face of adversity. He learned more from it, he was to say later, than from ten years at a drama school.

Miss Cooke paid a lightning call on him in London, descending at Vincent Square with a bulging hat-box so full of books that it threatened disintegration. They went to see Maugham's new play, *The Sacred Flame*, and talked of old times and old pupils. Tactfully, she did not mention his future, and after he had seen her off he realised they had not spoken of the theatre. It was August, and when he examined his Holywell bank statement he saw that of the £190 he had bought back from New York only fifteen remained. An unexpected letter arrived from Connah's Quay. "Dear Goerge," wrote his mother, "i am enclosin this 10/– note so you can gett some nourishment . . ." Instinct had told her "there was something wrong . . ." His eyes blurred. Then a thick, hearty screed from Miss Cooke fell heavily on the carpet at the front door. "I see your acct. here is v. low," she told him. She was therefore putting £100 into it, and if that started to sink she would arrange monthly credits of ten or fifteen.

In October he found work at last understudying four small parts and walking-on as required in a new Charles B. Cochran production. Cochran always paid well, and even such a minor job was rewarded by what was then the handsome wage of £12 a week. A major event loomed, for the play was Sean O'Casey's *The Silver Tassie* which had been rejected by the Abbey Theatre because of its anti-war theme and the elaborate stage effects required. From Augustus John himself Cochran had wheedled a middle-act setting which the impresario considered to be "a masterpiece of theatrical design". Moreover, Cochran gave the leading role to Charles Laughton, at that time a rising young actor whose technique had lately startled London with its unusual realism and power. Laughton worked hard at his Irish accent: "Will oi ever get it roight, damn and blast?" he wailed. Though he was deep in the intricacies of his part he by no means ignored other people in the cast, even the humblest. One day Emlyn mentioned the name of a friend to him. "He told me you're a good actor," rejoined Laughton abruptly.

Cochran's flair, which told him the time was ripe for a play on the subject of war, had for once deceived him. *The Silver Tassie* opened to empty seats and a very short run that made it another of his honourable failures. Emlyn was again out of work. In his depression he suddenly grew sick of his room at Vincent Square. A fellow actor joined him to look for a flat they could share, and they found what they wanted in 12A, Wellington Mansions, at the Monmouth Street end of Upper St Martin's Lane. It was gloomy, the kitchen windowless, the stair that led up to it of stone, but for thirty shillings a week, to which Emlyn contributed ten because he only had the small room at the back, they could boast a flat in the West End at the heart of the theatre district.

Two months later he was engaged for another war play called *Tunnel Trench* and inspired by the classic success of *Journey's End*. It starred Brian Aherne, a youthful matinée idol who within a few years was to establish himself in Hollywood and to become, for a while, the first of Joan Fontaine's quartet of husbands. Emlyn's rôle, as younger brother to the hero, was a splendid cameo part. As he rehearsed it on his own the drabness of Wellington Mansions vanished into a haze of sparkling promise. At the preliminary read-through the director beamed approval. Rehearsals began and Emlyn happily built on his conception of the part, adding a gesture here, a new inflection there. The director called him aside. He regretted, he said in the voice of one reporting a bereavement, that he was not really suited to the part, he was too emotional, too Welsh. Back in the solitude of Wellington Mansions he burst into tears. Next morning's rehearsal saw him doubling walk-on parts and agreeing, with a fixed smile, to understudy the rôle from which he had been sacked. A mediocre actor was better than none at all if the principal could not appear.

A curious incident distracted him from his humiliation. The cast, all except for one, were called on stage and Brian Aherne addressed them gravely. The absent player, he stated, had "made an indecent suggestion" to a colleague, and the rest of them must be on their guard. A sudden spurt of anger shook Emlyn at this prim announcement. They were adults, not schoolboys. "You mean he raped him?" Not quite, a flustered Aherne replied. And he went on, in response to a further sarcastic question from Emlyn, that it was, he imagined, something to do with a wandering hand. "Anyway," said Emlyn, "aren't we all men and able to defend ourselves?" Aherne, embarrassed at his unwanted role as head prefect, agreed, and everyone laughed. The public school ethos of Sir Gerald du Maurier was not yet wholly extinct, ("Are you a bugger?" he once demanded of Charles Laughton), and several years were to elapse before Binkie Beaumont reigned over the Uranian solidarity of the West End theatre.

Tunnel Trench faded very quickly within a week of its first night, a victim of the same deluded instinct which had misled even so experienced a showman as Cochran. Emlyn was not displeased, although on examining his accounts he found that, over the past nine months, he had made some eighty pounds, a rate of just over two pounds a week. His brother Tom, an apprentice greengrocer, could not be earning much less. Moreover, his flat mate had decided to marry and so would be leaving Wellington Mansions, and although he had not been the most congenial of companions his departure meant that another pound a week was needed to pay the full rent. The telephone remained obstinately silent. Miss Cooke's loan showed signs of exhaustion. If he did not find something by Christmas Eve, Emlyn decided, he would sign up with Gabbitas-Thring to become an embittered schoolmaster. And then, on December 15, the telephone rang.

He was offered the small part of a French interpreter in a two-month season of the comedy *French Leave*. Charles Laughton, his ally from *The Silver Tassie*, was the star and greeted him jovially: "You'll be pleased to hear, my dear chap, that I've been promoted from Private to General." Madeleine Carroll was the heroine, and the part of the Gallic landlady fell to May Agate, sister of James. She had fluent French and in her youth had been an intimate of Sarah Bernhardt about whom she wrote a little book which is the best on its subject in either English or French. An "altercation in French" being indicated by the script, she and Emlyn worked up an impromptu shouting match that won delighted grins from Laughton and the others. "Emma-lyn," said Laughton with the stutter of embarrassed sincerity, "you're very g-good you know." There was a scene in which Emlyn had to say to him: "*Mon général*, I have my suspicions." The French for "suspicion" being *soupçon*, Emlyn tried out the line as: "*Mon général*, I have my soupspicions." Laughton was enchanted and cried out: "But that's perfect – exactly the way a Frenchman would say it!" In this warm atmosphere Emlyn's confidence blossomed anew.

The play opened in January, 1930, and brought him £12.10s. a week. It closed when Laughton departed for *On The Spot*, a new crime melodrama by Edgar Wallace. Emlyn kept afloat with occasional Sunday performances and linguistic excursions on behalf of J. T. Grein and his European avant-garde dramas. He took out his accounts book and calculated his earnings: during the financial year to April, 1930, his average weekly wage now amounted to £4 a week. The telephone rang again. Someone was being replaced for a small part in *On the Spot* and Mr Laughton had suggested him. Within minutes he raced down Upper St Martin's Lane and through Newport Court to Wyndham's Theatre in the Charing Cross Road.

There, under the working light, Laughton was moulding himself into the part of the gangster Tony Perelli, muttering phrases, experimenting with styles of walking and trying out business. Emlyn's role was that of his henchman Angelo. The lines were few but telling, and the part itself a gift since Angelo was on stage for most of the action. Uncertain of American idiom, Emlyn slyly suggested speaking his lines with an Italian accent. "I like that," said Laughton. "Fine," agreed Edgar Wallace, who had by now absorbed the racing news in an early edition of the *Evening Standard* and was ready for action. "You're E.W. are you – well wi' those initials your future's in the bag," Edgar chaffed, Cockney, genial. His business manager proposed, unasked, a weekly wage of £20. "It's what I had in mind," replied Emlyn brazen-faced. But as the days passed there was no sign of a contract. Unpleasant memories of *Tunnel Trench* surfaced. A schoolmaster's future threatened again as he realised that Edgar, unaccountably, seemed to be paying more attention to others in the cast. He lay awake at night fearing the sack. At the last minute his contract materialised. Of course, he had been imagining things! Years later he heard that Edgar had indeed changed his mind. It was Laughton who saved him by remarking: "Edgar, I promise you he'll be all right. Let him stay."

Edgar Wallace had already conquered a vast readership with dozens of crime and mystery novels which he wrote, or rather dictated, at astonishing speed. One of them he produced, for a bet, in the course of a weekend. During the late nineteen-twenties he turned to the stage and displayed a gift for melodrama in a series of plays that thrilled audiences with sensational effect. If one of them failed, as they sometimes did, he quickly wrote another, and his successes were as dazzling as his flops were spectacular. On a recent trip to America he had been taken by a police official on a tour of Chicago's underworld.

There he inspected the scene of the St Valentine's Day massacre, the shop where a notorious racketeer had been put "on the spot", and the places where rival gangsters fought out their battles with machine guns. He was charmed. Here was a criminal milieu infinitely more villainous and brutal than the cosy underworld of London which up to then he had depicted in his novels. Crime held a boundless fascination for him and he revelled in the extravagance of gangsters who dripped jewellery and lived like millionaires while running their private kingdom with utter ruthlessness. Al Capone intrigued him above all. In that sinister figure he discovered inspiration for the character he had always dreamed of creating: the master criminal, supreme, magnetic, terrifying.

Having, as he estimated, given nearly a hundred newspaper interviews in his New York hotel and shaken the hands of one thousand two hundred and fifty American fans, he set sail for London. On the five-day voyage he worked out the plot and the characters in the play he meditated. Once home he started his task, in front, as usual, of a roaring fire, windows closed, a glass screen round the desk to keep away draughts. After a day of writing lubricated by incessant cups of sweet tea and chain-smoking through his long cigarette holder, he was ready to dictate the remainder of his play. There was no mystery in it, the identity of the evildoer was known from the start, but Edgar, as his audience did later, found himself swept along by the excitement of what he was imagining: the malevolent Perelli lavishing upon his women diamonds and on his enemies coffins, and, in moments of eerie tranquillity, playing the organ. Within four days *On the Spot* was complete and Edgar collapsed exhausted into bed.

He was a good director of his own plays, and he handled *On the Spot* with a confidence born of the opinion that it was his best. As the first night approached the cast grew jumpy and monosyllabic. In the dressing-rooms they moved with a calm precision belying the tension that straitened their nerves. Buttons were checked as a last-minute precaution, final glances taken in mirrors, costumes smoothed down, properties stroked, as if in a hypnotic trance. The curtain rose, and instantly every cough, every rustle of the audience, every slight change in the atmosphere, engraved itself indelibly on the mind. Laughton emerged, dark-skinned, thinly moustached, plump body encased in a black and white suit, eyes glittering beneath false lashes. Applause came, then laughter, and Edgar, sitting in his box, detected enthusiasm quite soon. Emlyn, too, sensed triumph, and he knew that he had scored a big laugh with one of his few but effective lines. Afterwards

Edgar threw a typically lavish party, and the early editions of the newspaper confirmed that *On the Spot* was a success.

The Times was characteristic of the warm notices the play received. Author and star were praised for having made of Perelli "a living man, not an adventurous poet." Emlyn, too, had a generous mention: "Angelo, Perelli's chief assistant, while providing the humour of the evening, is never content with humour alone: he too is for ever entangling the plot, wheeling in divans to receive corpses, deceiving women, baffling the police and generally, with Mr Emlyn Williams's most ingenious mixture of innocence and guile, thrusting forward the adventure." It was necessary, though, to wait until the weekend and the *Sunday Times* to know what the most formidable of the critics thought. "A success . . .", wrote James Agate. "Mr Williams reminds us, as Angelo, that likeableness and a naive, almost cherubic degeneracy may be combined . . ." From Connah's Quay a jubilant note arrived: "My dear Son Goerge . . . The Rev D. M. Griffith told your Mother that he knew years ago in Chapel that you would enter the Theatrical Profession, hows that for second sight, I must get him on to the Horses." The eldest son, who refused to become a preacher or a schoolmaster, had redeemed himself.

It seemed, too, that at last he had discovered the friend, the companion, the elder brother whom he had been seeking throughout his lonely childhood and unsatisfied youth.

(ii)
Bill

There is a type of actor who never achieves major billing but who can always be relied upon to give a solid supporting performance. His name is not always familiar to the audience, though his face usually is, and he is often recognised at his first entrance as something of an old friend. He is rarely out of work, and within the profession he is valued for his dependability. William Cronin Wilson, known as "Bill", was one of this sort. He began his career in 1906 as a member of the company run by Lewis Waller, the glamorous actor whose virile good looks so excited his women fans that they organised a group baptised the KOWB, or "Keen on Waller Brigade". Bill Cronin Wilson made his début in a swashbuckling production of *Robin Hood*. After five years learning his job in the romantic costume melodramas which formed Waller's speciality, he went into modern plays and earned a name among theatre managers and producers for his neat impersonations of majors, baronets, detectives, judges, police inspectors, doctors, and any sort of rôle where quiet authority was required. He had just such a part in *On the Spot* as Detective Commissioner Kelly, who, according to *The Times*, "very shrewdly played by Mr Cronin Wilson, makes his visits with so much swiftness and determination that each sentence seems to advance the tale."

In 1914, at the age of twenty-seven, he went to war in France. Up to then he had been an ordinary, handsome young actor, popular with the girls and wanted at every party. What he saw of the ghastly life in the trenches, the dead bodies, the mud and desolation, changed him ineluctably. He never spoke of those days and he did not choose to mention his war service in any book of reference. Neither did he give his date of birth nor any detail of his parentage, education or address. All he wished his colleagues to know about his background was a bare list of the fifty or so parts he had played, the brief tours of America and South Africa, and the three plays he wrote, two in collaboration with the American dramatist Eugene Walter. Although a sociable drinking companion and agreeable acquaintance, he remained a man of mystery. No one ever heard from him the secret of his illegitimate birth, a result of the passing union between a chorus girl and a nobleman closely related to the royal family. There was something in his manner, not of condescension, but of kindly superiority, as of a prince mingling with his troops. The indefinable air made him all the more popular since Bill was the most clubbable of men.

He lived in a room at Wellington Mansions where the main item of furniture, apart from the cracked mirror, was a huge well-worn trunk that contained all the essential belongings of a man who had no real home. His laundry was attended to by the obliging wardrobe-mistress of *On the Spot*. Emlyn sometimes encountered him on the stair returning from a late-night carouse. His step was unsure, his gait none too certain. *On the Spot* brought the older man and the young actor closer together, and they went out for drinks at the Cavour, then a well-frequented meeting place for theatre people. Sometimes they would eat a snack in a pub or take a quick meal at a cheap cafeteria. Bill was a more approachable man than Charles Laughton. Emlyn dined one evening with Laughton and found him ill at ease. The actor who as Perelli looked at him full in the eye and collaborated perfectly on stage was, in private, awkward, shifty, unable to keep his gaze on him for very long. Laughton's uneasiness raised a barrier between them which Emlyn regretted, since he admired him as an actor and was grateful for the very real help he had received from him. Could it be, he asked himself, that Laughton, an actor incarnate, did not come to life unless facing an audience, and that without it he relapsed into an insecure child? Now, Bill, he felt, was just as complex a personality, and yet there was an instant sympathy with him.

After the evening performance of *On the Spot* Emlyn would take off his make-up, change into street clothes and walk back home up St Martin's Lane. There, before going to bed, he pottered a while as the tension of the evening's work loosened and the adrenalin ceased to flow. One night he sat in his room sipping a chaste cup of Ovaltine and reading *Madame Bovary*. Someone knocked at the door. He put down his volume of Flaubert and went to open up. It was Bill, a confused grin on his face, and, Emlyn judged, in the mellow, good-natured stage of drunkenness. " 'Lo ole boy, still up?" He ambled into the room, burly, genial, his clothes well worn but obviously cut by the best tailors. His hair, above a strong forehead, was trim, the mouth full, and the teeth had been well looked after. Only the eyes had a wounded look, with the crinkled bags underneath and the mesh of fine lines at the corners. Below, the chin lapsed into jowl. As he lifted a cigarette to his mouth the hand trembled.

He accepted a glass of whisky from a half-bottle which his economical host kept in reserve. Coughing, he sank into an armchair while Emlyn sat primly on a stool. With a bemused smile he leaned over and put his hand on Emlyn's knee. "One day at rehearsal," he said, " – er – I thought, that kid's an actor an' what's more – er – he's attractive. An' what's more – er – the little devil knows it . . ."

They looked steadily at each other. Strangely, Emlyn felt much more at ease with him than he had done with Charles Laughton over their dinner recently. Had Laughton been wanting to say what Bill said, and had he been unable to find the resolve?

"Do you agree," said Bill, "this calls for another." He rose, swaying, to his feet. Cigarette smoke writhed around him. The aroma of whisky that mingled with it reminded Emlyn of the smell he caught when, as a small boy, he had been taken up in an alcoholic embrace by his father. It was, in turn, the same smell his mother sensed when as a little girl she had been hugged by *her* father.

Two lonely people sat and talked in Wellington Mansions. Bill stayed the night.

After that they were often together. They went on trips to the country in the Green Line bus: Epping Forest, Box Hill, Whipsnade. "Haven't done this sort of thing since I was younger than you," said Bill, "in Lewis Waller's company and taking the girls out." They spent hours in drinking-clubs and raffish bars where Bill, having drawn big advances on his weekly pay, stood treat to old acquaintances and reminisced about adventures on tours long-forgotten except by the old actors who had taken part in them. Yes, there had been women in his life, the latest four or five years ago. But women tended to be difficult when they turned possessive.

Few among his bar cronies knew of Bill's secret life. When he was seventeen, he explained to Emlyn, Oscar Wilde had been dead four years. No one of Emlyn's generation could appreciate the effect that any mention of Wilde had on the theatrical profession. "Normal young actors, members of the Green Room, were terrified of being misunderstood at some point, and then branded." He lit, with the ever-shaky, nicotine-stained hand, another cigarette.

He was alone, he said, he had nobody. That was the reason for everything. "My dearest boy . . ." "Bill, it's not true that you haven't got anybody," rejoined Emlyn. "You've got me." His shoulders hunched together. "Bill, there's no future in this for you. Why don't we take a flat together?"

They found a place at 60, Marchmont Street in Bloomsbury over a butcher's shop. This was a cause for celebration and for what Bill called "a snifter". They sat down, tumblers brimming, and Emlyn recited the story of his life while discreetly avoiding any enquiry about Bill's. He spoke of his reading, and Bill mentioned the writer Saki, a name Emlyn did not know. Saki's *Collected Stories* was the only book Bill owned, and, putting on his glasses, he read aloud a favourite passage. Then he broke off to prepare the scrambled eggs for their meal. When he came back he engulfed yet another large whisky. Emlyn's head was reeling. "Bill, don't you agree we've had enough?" "Wozzat, ole man? Speak for yourself." He lurched into the kitchen. Emlyn hid the bottle.

"Where's bo'le?" asked Bill on his return. "I've put it away." ". . . You've *what*? You've *hidden* it?" He glowered hatred, his face twisted with anger. A flow of invective spewed out larded with obscenities. "You drunken bastard," shouted Emlyn, remembering, too late, that such he was in fact. Bill rooted around and found the bottle. "Sucks to you. What *you* know 'bout life, you post-war upstart, you lily-livered loon?" A shred from the Shakespearean drama he had played under Lewis Waller surfaced in his muddled brain.

"My liver isn't lily," retorted Emlyn, "and I can drink you under the table."

"Can you, by Jove?" Bill proffered the bottle and Emlyn swigged the burning liquid. It nearly choked him. "Now get out and make a pig of yourself." More expletives flew.

He fell on the bed and drifted into oblivion. Next morning, alone, he awoke to find the lights still blazing and the gas-fire still popping. He remembered, with a start, that Miss Cooke was due that evening on the bus from Chester to see *On The Spot* and to spend the night in a room he had booked for her at the Kenilworth Hotel in Great Russell Street. After vomiting and a long day's sleep, he disinfected his ashy mouth with Listerine and met her for tea. She chatted about her latest pupils' successes and the new political developments, while he, head throbbing, stomach queasy, listened with courteous attention. At the theatre he introduced her to Bill. Afterwards he saw her off on the train to Paris for the rest of her holiday. He had kissed her on the cheek, instinctively and for the first time.

Once Miss Cooke had gone he thought of Bill again. When they first met he had pitied him and thought he was doing Bill a kindness. But pity had soon become an affection that turned into love. He wanted him to the extent of needing to dominate him absolutely. It did not matter that Bill was old enough to be his father. The situation is a familiar one. Kept at a rigid distance by his mother, remote from his father, separated from both parents by virtue of intellect and emotion, Emlyn sought an older man for the love he could not find with either of the pair who had created him. "Nobody's ever wanted to do anything for me before," Bill had said mildly at their reunion after the drunken night. "Dearest boy . . ."

Emlyn went to see him once more. Bill coughed and smoothed his collar with a trembling hand. They embraced, bear-like, in an acrid wave of nicotine and whisky. "We've got used to each other," said Bill, "haven't we? I've never loved anybody before. And I love you as a friend, and as a son." He would, he promised at Emlyn's urging, cut down on tobacco and reduce his drinking. They set up house in Marchmont Street. He chewed gum heroically and restricted himself to one, just one, whisky and soda a night. "But it's unbelievable," people would say to Emlyn, "he looks ten years younger." The eyes were no longer bloodshot, the face regained its healthy colour, the walk became firm.

Their new routine was peaceful and reassuring. At night they slept in a double divan. Breakfast was made about ten o'clock by their charwoman, whereupon they sat around talking and reading. By noon they were drinking a beer at the Cavour before going to see a film. After tea they were ready for *On the Spot*. When they came home, having bought provisions on the way, Bill, calm and sober, prepared his speciality of scrambled eggs. Their conversations taught Emlyn a great deal, for Bill was a sensitive judge of acting. What, Emlyn asked him once, was the test of a good performance? Bill reflected. "It's a performance," he at last replied, "when every sentence sounds as if it's being said for the first time."

Rummaging in a drawer one day Emlyn came across two well-worn snaps. One was of a private soldier, no more than eighteen years old, fresh-faced and cherubic. "Who's he?" Bill glanced at it. "Lord, it's little Gareth, my batman, beautiful boy, Welsh. And damn good value, as I remember." The other photograph showed an officer, tall, slim, in his late twenties and very attractive. "Who's he?" Bill fumbled with his glasses. "Good God . . ." It was himself, fifteen years ago, the most handsome man Emlyn had ever seen. He felt a sudden stab of jealousy. He was jealous of the young officer with the sensuous mouth who stared at him provocatively out of the faded snapshot, and jealous of the years that had stolen him away. The snap was carefully fitted into his wallet, and from time to time he took it out when he was on his own and studied it hungrily.

One evening after supper he tried to find out as much as he could about Bill's past. The childhood, wrapped in luxury and privilege, was, he knew, forbidden territory. Bill's mother? He bored her. His youth? Normal, girls and all that, until the war. He joined up, and to begin with it was fun: no responsibilities, always on the move. Then came France and the real thing, weeks of shattering bombardment, friends blown to bits, and, in the carnage, a sharp awareness of living, healthy bodies. Drink helped, and the casual promiscuity and intimate friendships of trench and dug-out. Bill's batman Gareth, he told Emlyn, "talked like you when you get worked up, it's what I first noticed about you." Gareth was engaged to a girl from another Welsh village and always wore a ring on his left finger. On the night of a particularly heavy bombardment when shell and shrapnel were flying like hail, Bill and Gareth took a bath together. The inevitable happened. Then, a week later, Gareth was blown up. Bill's eyes veiled with grief. All that was left of the batman was the ring by which he identified him.

In August, 1930, Emlyn suddenly felt very ill. Acute tonsillitis was diagnosed and he took to his bed, fussed over by Bill who rushed off for medicine and warned the theatre. He promised to be back by "eleven-fifteen at the latest" after the play. Emlyn lay in throbbing pain. Watching the clock, he imagined the house lights dimming, the action of *On the Spot* proceeding, and the last fall of the curtain. A quarter past eleven came and went. The minutes became hours. His mind drifted back to a scene he had often known in youth: his mother awaiting, in angry frustration, the return of his drunken father late at night while dinner shrivelled in the oven. The pattern of events was grotesque.

A noise awoke him. He looked at his watch and saw that the time was half-past two. Bill stood in the doorway, a vague smile on his lips. "Hello, ole boy, berrer?" He had bumped into friends, they had gone to the Club . . . "You're in the other room," said Emlyn firmly. He knew he could never trust him again.

(iii)
Murder

It was 1929. Ever since the muted triumphs of *Full Moon* and *Glamour* he had been writing plays. At Marchmont Street he had written *Patrick's Mother*, a one-act comedy set in "the drawing-room of Lady Helen's home in Mayfair". Another play called *Tom* was closer to his roots, being a three-act comedy which took place in Flintshire. The hero won half a million pounds in the Welsh Miners' Sweepstake, but, ill at ease with the grand life money brought him, gave his winnings back to the miners and returned to the sweetheart he had left in his native village. No West End manager responded, and the neatly typed script grew worn and dog-eared on its travels through the post.

A more distinct possibility, he told Miss Cooke, was the play "I'm going to write now, a frankly commercial thriller called *A Murder Has Been Arranged*." It was completed while on a short holiday in Connah's Quay at a rate of ten hours' work a day. "Tomorrow I shall finish *A Murder Has Been Arranged* after exactly a week's work," he wrote to Miss Cooke. "Thirty-six thousand words on my little typewriter! one hundred and twenty pages of a printed book! I think it's rather a feat of endurance! It's a complete thriller and if I don't sell it I'll eat every one of the one hundred and twenty pages." After which, having learned from his experience with *Full Moon* and *Glamour*, from watching other writers' plays and from his own performance on the stage, he set about revision, scribbling at various points in the margin the sort of ironic remark Miss Cooke would have made about one of his more pretentious essays. Ruthlessly he cut and trimmed away everything that did not help to develop character and forward the plot.

He had by now evolved the technique he was to use for the rest of his career. The idea for a play might come from anywhere: from a paragraph in a newspaper, a remark overheard, a snatch of conversation, a book he happened to be reading at the time, even a face in the street. After the first thrill of inspiration had evaporated he would often find that someone else had already used the idea. If, however, the notion seemed original and capable of development, he would write a short synopsis of no more than five hundred words or so. This helped to fix the situation in his mind and to outline the problems that needed a solution. In the days and weeks that followed he jotted down in a notebook random thoughts which floated to the surface: isolated exchanges of dialogue, names of characters, suggestions for props, details of clothes. It was important, at the earliest stage, to fix the title of the play, because this gave substance to a creation as yet vague and shadowy while somehow strengthening his confidence in the project. At no point, even to his closest acquaintance, did he ever talk about the play until it was completed. The most he would say was "It's a thriller set in a theatre," or "It's a comedy with a Welsh setting." This resulted from his fear of running aground half-way through and from a superstition that if he revealed any detail of what he was writing the charm would vanish and inspiration desert him. This did, in fact, once happen when he incautiously spoke to a friend about scenes unwritten. He never did so again.

Although ideas normally flowed in the act of writing, he always kept to a scheme which had been planned with care and in advance. One of the tasks he did first was to arrange the climax and then work backwards. This was the method of those French masters of comedy Labiche and Feydeau, whose farces resembled beautifully constructed watches controlled by an intricate mechanism that ticked over with immaculate precision. Each development of the plot, however outrageous, led on through a chain of unforgiving logic to the next with which it was intricately bound. This perfect smoothness of narrative line was achieved by writing the *dénouement* first of all, and then by sketching out the play in reverse so that every strand in the plot could be seen to run inexorably toward the finale when all the strings were eventually untied. *A Murder Has Been Arranged* followed this classic line with a first act in which the situation is posed, a second where the plot burgeons into a sensational ending, and a third in which all the threads are neatly gathered up.

Described as "A ghost story in three acts" and dedicated "To S.G.C." (Sarah Grace Cooke), *A Murder Has Been Arranged* takes place in the theatre where it is being played. A frightened woman interrupts the overture when she emerges through the parting of the curtain and pleads for it to be lifted. The theatre is haunted, and that very night Sir Charles Jasper is holding a fancy dress party on stage, in a set left over from a recent play, to celebrate his fortieth birthday. By the terms of his late uncle's will, he is to inherit two million pounds if he is still alive by eleven o'clock in the evening. Should he die, the fortune goes to his sinister cousin Maurice Mullins. The which he does, suitably poisoned by the wicked Mullins dressed as Caesar Borgia. Everyone in the audience has known since his first appearance that Mullins would be the killer. The ingenuity of the plot depends on the way Jasper has been tricked into writing a suicide note, the mingling of the theatre's ghostly legend with the actuality on stage, and the device by which Mullins is persuaded to confess the murder before eleven o'clock, thus forfeiting his claim to the money. There is little attempt to draw character, although Jasper and especially Mullins offer good opportunities to the actors, and interest is sustained wholly by unexpected twists to the narrative.

Bill liked the title of *A Murder Has Been Arranged* and persuaded Emlyn to send it to the Repertory Players, a Sunday performance club. It caught the attention of Henry Kendall, a well-known actor and producer. Kendall began his career as a juvenile in Shakespeare at the Old Vic, afterwards emigrating to the West End as an ornament of drawing-room comedies to which he brought a debonair appeal and sprightly charm. During the war he had served in the Royal Air Force with Ivor Novello and won the AFC, although the medal, contrary to malicious gossip, was not intended as a reward for having survived his friend's catastrophic attempt at piloting an aeroplane. He invited Emlyn to lunch at the Ivy. Wearing his best dark suit, impressed by the atmosphere of a restaurant which then formed a setting for all the brightest and most fashionable in the London theatre, Emlyn heard Kendall propose a Sunday towards the end of 1930 as the date for a performance of his play. What was more, Kendall suggested, Emlyn could direct it himself because the stage directions he had incorporated were "so right". The young playwright/director went back to his script and started pencilling diagrams of the set and moves for the cast. A curious memory suddenly arose: he remembered himself as a child of six fashioning empty Woodbine cigarette packets into little people and moving them around.

The Duchess Theatre was booked for the one Sunday performance. The set used was that of *It's A Boy*, a Leslie Henson farce currently running there. As he contemplated it from an empty auditorium one bleak October morning, Emlyn realised that with careful lighting it would provide the ideal setting. Rehearsals went happily and the cast reacted to their young director with sympathy. On the evening of Sunday, November 9, he treated himself to a nervous drink and then wandered into the theatre just as the orchestra began the overture. Suddenly, to the startlement of the audience, a woman burst out through the curtain and silenced the music. "Stop! I'm frightened – I can't stand another minute alone on this stage! Mrs Wragg! Please – please lift up this curtain!" All was going as planned. He fled.

He walked the streets and sat in a pub dipping into a German dictionary he had brought with him to pass the time. When he returned to the theatre he heard, from the wings, noisy applause. The play had been a success and, next day, the notices were excellent. "Not for many years has any author made my flesh creep so goosily," wrote the *Daily Telegraph*. *The Times* observed: "Here is a dramatist who can throw over the theatre an icy and continuous spell." James Agate alone struck a jarring note. He agreed that a dramatist can only horripilate for a limited period of time, which is why Grand Guignol is so short. Emlyn only truly horripilated, he claimed, in the last ten minutes, and the previous two and four-fifths acts of preparation had brought in extraneous material and went on too long. This is fair criticism of a play which, towards the end, becomes Grand Guignol itself and, not content with one ghostly apparition, features two of them.

Such reserves did not inhibit the eleven managements who clamoured next morning for the rights to *A Murder Has Been Arranged*. These were finally given to the Daniel Mayer Company on the unusually handsome terms of a flat ten per cent of takings rather than beginning at the customary five per cent and then rising gradually. It was the sort of agreement only Bernard Shaw then enjoyed. From Connah's Quay a despatch reported celebrations everywhere, ". . . your only critics being the Sally Army, Tom says Commander Watson is sorry you gave your play such a Murderous title. I expect they would like it better if you called it 'A Salvation Has Been Arranged' but I think you would lose custom that way."

The play transferred on November 26 to the St James's, until its demolition one of the prettiest little theatres in London. It also had the advantage, from Emlyn's point of view, of a reputation for being haunted. The first-night reception was polite, appreciative, certainly quieter than the ecstatic cheers that greeted the Sunday performance. Had it been over-praised? Would it have gone better if it had been launched cold? One famous visitor was disappointed: "An evening of claptrap . . .", wrote Arnold Bennett in his journal. But Emlyn was now earning a hundred pounds in royalties a week, whereas a year ago he had been making no more than twelve.

Henry Kendall, naturally, was very much the leading man and played his villainous role with panache. The youngest member of the cast was Margaretta Scott, then eighteen years old and but recently graduated to the West End stage in *The First Mrs Fraser*. Her part as Lady Jasper in *A Murder Has Been Arranged* was her biggest and most rewarding to date. The management wanted to engage established names for the St James's production, Fay Compton, for example, but Emlyn, impressed by Miss Scott's glowing beauty, insisted on retaining her and, indeed, all the original cast who had worked so loyally for him. He was young, not all that well-known, and he was taking a risk. The fidelity of his players rewarded him. The backstage atmosphere during the run at the St James's was happy – during intervals, when the curtain was down, the cast remained on stage around the dinner table which featured in the set and chatted amicably together instead of making off to their dressing-rooms. That the play did not run very long was partly due to the situation of the theatre, which, rather tucked away from the centre, lacked the passing trade of Shaftesbury Avenue.

All this time he had been playing in *On the Spot* which ended its run in January, 1931. While Bill went on tour with the company Emlyn decided to take a holiday. He would go, he thought, to Berlin, "the wickedest city in Europe, ducks," as one of his queeny friends had giggled to him. On arrival he looked first at the theatre advertisements – *Auf den Fleck*, said one, or "On the Spot" – and chose instead to tour the "wicked" places. Very soon he tired of the sickly lads propped up in bars and the boys in drag. He would go, he resolved, to a centre of real wickedness. He would go to Hanover, scene of crimes committed by the butcher Fritz Haarman who murdered twenty-seven boys and then, using his craftsman's skill, chopped them up and disposed of the bones for soup.

In the station waiting-room where Haarman preyed on his victims a brief seven years before, Emlyn studied the cold, weary drifters who lazed there. It was easy to imagine the burly, commonplace, middle-aged man wandering among them, picking one up to offer the warmth and hospitality of his room, taking him back, and producing, after dalliance, the butcher's knife which he used so expertly. There was his front door to be looked at, Number 7, Rote Reih, and Police Headquarters to be visited. An obliging official laid out documents and photographs of piles of bones, childlike faces, and even Haarman's bedsitting room with its pious text on the wall, "God Bless Our Home". And there was Haarman himself, plump, stolid, indifferent. It was his ordinariness that chilled the blood.

Emlyn spent three days in Hanover, his nights haunted by sleeplessness and visions of mean streets dark with fog. In dreams he saw a nineteen-year-old student from Oxford, a scholarship boy, arriving in Hanover to improve his German. By chance he met a friendly older man who invited him back for tea or coffee or something. The man listened with kindly interest as the boy spoke of his travels in France, his Welsh homeland, his interest in the theatre. They moved closer together. The cosy room grew warm. At the moment of climax a knife flashed and blood spurted. Meat was deftly sliced from the bone.

How could so monstrous an evil reside in so nondescript a man? Was true wickedness more likely to be found in a shrinking bank clerk than in a flamboyant sinner? Might this be the case with Bill, so gentle that he would not step on an unoffending insect: were there depths within him that would terrify if they were glimpsed? Or in Emlyn? The problem of evil fascinated him, and the trip to Hanover encouraged an interest that was to provide him with several major themes. It was dusk when he returned to the lonely flat in Marchmont Street, for Bill had not yet come back from touring, and as he put his key into the lock his eye caught the window of the butcher's shop on the ground floor. He thought of slashed corpses under a vague electric light and ran upstairs.

Before appearing in Edgar Wallace's next play he acted in another French-language piece, *Devant la Porte*, and once again impressed an intellectual audience at the Arts Theatre. Then, in November, it was back to gangsters and kidnapped heiresses in Edgar's latest melodrama, *The Mouthpiece*. Bill was with him in yet another reliable piece of characterisation, and so was Mabel Terry-Lewis, one of John Gielgud's maternal aunts, the prettiest of three and also the sharpest-tongued. Although a talented actress (her Lady Bracknell was a model of gentility), she rather looked down on the theatre and did not take it seriously, to the extent, once, of asking Gerald du Maurier, her then employer, if she could absent herself from a matinée in order to attend the Derby. Perhaps amused by this aristocratic nonchalance, he let her go. Early in the century she retired from the stage to live with her husband in a Dorset manor-house where white doves cooed on the lawn. When she became a widow she returned to the theatre. "Her style and technique were quite unimpaired by her long absence ... Her carriage and diction were always faultless ..." records Sir John. Unfortunately neither she, as the plebeian "Mrs Smith", nor Bill, nor Emlyn as Commissioner Neufeld, managed to save *The Mouthpiece* which, at its first night, was greeted with cries from the gallery of "None of your rubbish!" when Edgar came out to make a speech. Within ten days it had to be taken off. Three weeks after that disastrous opening Edgar had written and staged, with his usual tearing speed, another drama to take its place.

For once Emlyn, who had become a member of Edgar's unofficial repertory company, did not act in the latest production. He preferred instead to accept the challenge of playing a sixteen-year-old French schoolboy in *Etienne*, one of those adroit boulevard comedies by that skilful dramatist Jacques Deval. It is a witty concoction about a precocious youth who turns the tables on his overbearing father and checkmates the latter's mistress, the whole lightly sprinkled with a hint, just the lightest hint, of the Oedipus complex. The play was done at the St James's where *A Murder Has Been Arranged* had but lately triumphed. The omen did not save it, for *Etienne*, having failed to travel well, vanished from the bills in less than a fortnight. James Agate, who had seen the play in its native Parisian setting, commented that Emlyn looked like "an out-of-work Welsh miner". On the other hand, Agate added, ". . . he looked gypsy enough to be at least un-English and so possibly French." Finally the critic pulled himself together and pinpointed what became Emlyn's most notable feature as an actor: "Mr Williams used so much artistry and intelligence that he overcame natural disadvantages and generously succeeded where the better-graced juvenile, who relies solely upon his graces, must have failed."

A Murder Has Been Arranged had gone out on tour under Donald Wolfit and was making money. No engagements at that moment beckoned. Emlyn frequented the shady Long Bar near Piccadilly Circus and killed time in brief encounters. Impelled by a mood that hungered for experiment within a more conventional type of sexuality, he set up a threesome with one of Bill's cronies and a fat whore of whale-like proportions. While the crony watched drunkenly, Emlyn did his best to cope with ballooning bosoms and thighs the width of oak trees. Post-coital melancholy made him feel very old and he thought longingly of Bill.

His doctor advised a cruise and he set sail for Egypt. At Marseille he experienced deadly boredom in a brothel. Was it his destiny to end up always in places like that? Port Said and its ethnic mish-mash gave an idea for a play, or rather a character, a native woman who has a child by a visiting Englishman. In Colombo he wandered into the public library and took out a volume of *Punch*. It contained a review of *On the Spot* with caricatures of "Mr Charles Laughton" and "Mr Cronin Wilson". Again he thought wretchedly of the letter he had hoped to find awaiting him at the hotel. It had not been there, for Bill was more at home with words spoken rather than written. Emlyn had to content himself with memories: the sound of a voice, the smoke of a cigarette, the wounded look in the eyes.

The sun, fierce and sulphurous, vanished behind clouds and a monsoon broke over Ceylon. As the rain clattered down with a spiteful hiss Emlyn found a name for his heroine and a title for his play. She would be Narouli Karth, half-caste woman of primitive beauty, and the play would be called *Port Said*. But he was restless, ruled by his obsession, and after a brief six days he began the return journey. By the time the ship reached Aden he had completed his first act. When they docked at Port Said he went ashore and noted local colour: an advertisement in the street, a muezzin's cry, a veiled face at a doorway. On arrival in Marseille he could wait no longer and booked a passage on an aeroplane, all struts and tinny fuselage, which, bearing two other passengers strapped in like him, bumbled gently over a mirror-like sea to Croydon Aerodrome. A bus delivered him and his fellow travellers in the Haymarket. "God, I've missed you," said Bill, squeezing his knee. It was what Emlyn had travelled six thousand miles and back to hear.

Soon they were together again on stage, for Edgar Wallace had conjured up yet another play, *The Case of the Frightened Lady*, in between editing a Sunday newspaper, writing a daily racing column, chairing a film company, electioneering for Lloyd George, and at the same time maintaining a torrent of novels and journalism. The frightened lady of the play is a young woman whom a domineering aristocratic mother is attempting to marry off with her son, the last and most degenerate of his line. The action includes two murders by strangulation and a classic final scene where the criminal is revealed as Lord Lebanon himself, a homicidal maniac whose insanity has up to then been a family secret. Among the cast was Gordon Harker as a morose and cynical detective sergeant who flavoured his lines with a dry Cockney wit, the sort of rôle he enacted many times, and to perfection, in plays and films of the nineteen-thirties and forties. Bill, also typecast, was the stolid Chief Detective Inspector, and to Emlyn fell the part of Lord Lebanon. He did not at first think much of it. In the early scenes the young lord is not much more than a silly ass. So cunning was Edgar's handling of the plot, however, with its false clues and deceptive hints, that only when Emlyn came to the last scene did he realise what a chance he was being given. This, a melodramatic confrontation between the Detective Inspector and Lebanon, builds up the tension until Lebanon, veering abruptly between icy logic and madness, shoots himself with a despairing flourish. At home Bill and Emlyn rehearsed the scene. By transposing some of the lines and adapting the business they believed that they had made it more effective. Would Edgar agree? They played it out before him on the Wyndham's stage. He waved his cigarette-holder expansively. "That's magnificent," he said, "never play it any differently."

They opened on August 18, 1931, and the bloodcurdling scene made its point. "Mr Wallace does it again!" said newspaper headlines – with, it might have been added, a little assistance from the twenty-six-year-old Mr Williams. Emlyn always maintained that his favourite part was that of Lord Lebanon thanks to the chance it gave of portraying the evil madness which he relished depicting as an actor. *The Case of The Frightened Lady* ran for more than a hundred and ninety performances at Wyndham's Theatre. Since he had already played more than three hundred and fifty performances of *On the Spot*, he was well and truly qualified to wear the house tie. This, known as "Wyndham's tie", was the perquisite of actors who had played over two hundred nights at the theatre. Striped with black, white and deep purple, it was based on the racing colours of Sir Charles Wyndham who had built the theatre, and the old Harrovian tie worn by Sir Gerald du Maurier, one of its most distinguished actor-managers. Emlyn wore it to greet his brother Tom who visited his dressing-room one day. Tom, gorgeous in his Salvation Army uniform, gaped at the mirror and the sticks of make-up. Emlyn offered him a seat for the show. Tom primly refused. The Salvation Army, he explained, forbade him to attend theatres or cinemas. But, Emlyn objected, he was in a theatre at that very moment. Yes, replied Tom, but he wasn't watching anything, was he? Having inspected the temple of impurity, he went out for a walk in the park. "After that," Emlyn complained to Bill, "serve the Army right if somebody tries to pick him up." Bill mused, unexpectedly: "I don't like to think of that, I've never seen any lad with such beautiful ignorance."

He had finished *Port Said* by now and was looking for a manager to present it. No-one rose to the bait. Then he remembered that Edgar Wallace's wife held the lease of Wyndham's Theatre and might be ready to gamble on a Sunday night performance. She was, and casting began. Marie Burke, then a famous name, was persuaded with little difficulty to play the beautiful Narouli Karth. May Agate joyfully agreed to impersonate an elderly French prostitute out of Toulouse-Lautrec, and a boyish Jack Hawkins took a juvenile rôle. Emlyn was to direct. The leading man's part, that of an embittered drifter, had been specially written for Bill. At preliminary readings he did well and caught exactly the note of desolation Emlyn wanted. Rehearsals found him, however, uncertain. Emlyn as director confused and embarrassed him. On the Thursday before the performance he lost his voice. There was no alternative: Emlyn must play the part himself. Bill took to his bed, relieved, and Emlyn learned his words in sixty hours or so. The Sunday night show, on November 1, attracted a large audience alerted by the presence of Marie Burke and the success of *A Murder Has Been Arranged*. He had certainly captured the local colour in his play, as a *Daily Sketch* review acknowledged with the heading: "Gutter symphony of colour. Love, violence and gaudy squalor of 'The Sink of the World' ". Was this drama of mixed blood, enquired a critic, the result of the author himself being Welsh/English? Others, more soberly, pointed to the inordinate length, three and three-quarter hours, of *Port Said*, and its restless, unnecessary complications. Too late, he remembered Miss Cooke's ingemination: cut and simplify, cut and simplify. Two years afterward he revised it savagely as *Vessels Departing* for the Embassy Theatre when Bill, restored, took the part originally intended for him and an embrowned Flora Robson played the heroine, while May Agate once more enjoyed herself as the ancient French whore. Despite ruthless surgery the play ran for only a week or two.

Equally short-lived was his next engagement, the part of a young Frenchman opposite Celia Johnson in *The Man I Killed*, an adaption of Maurice Rostand's play by Reginald Berkeley. Right up to the first night in March, 1932, he had been preoccupied with an unusual activity, or rather lack of activity: daily sittings of three hours each for his bust. It was Miss Cooke's idea. For some time she had wanted

Epstein to make a sculpture of her star pupil. Enquiries were launched, a fee of two hundred pounds was mentioned, and the best-known sculptor of his time, admired as much as he was execrated, began flicking and shaping a grey mass of clay. He worked in silence except for an occasional banal remark about the weather, and darted acute professional looks at his model perched on a shabby stool and appraised new angles in the light from the studio window. Every male sitter, he remarked, had one masculine profile and the other feminine. "I've rarely seen it so marked as in this one." At last the head was complete and draped for protection with an old dish-cloth. Epstein lit a cigarette, burly, diffident, looking like a caretaker. "I think that's all," he smiled, showing his irregular broken teeth. At his exhibition in May next year, the bust of Emlyn Williams Esquire stood next to that of Joseph Conrad and a lowering series of "Primeval Gods" which had absorbed the sculptor ever since 1910 and demanded over twenty years to complete.

Emlyn repaid Miss Cooke's gesture by helping her finance a deserving pupil's studies at a Spanish university. "I remember a schoolteacher of mine saying 'Never lend, *give*,' " he wrote back to her enclosing a cheque. He was doing well and beginning to earn rewards that are the lot of the successful playwright, his work resembling a capital investment that goes on paying all sorts of unexpected dividends in the shape of rights and royalties. The American amateur rights of *A Murder Has Been Arranged*, for example, had just netted three hundred and forty pounds. In the years to come there would be film rights, television rights, broadcasting rights, translation rights, serial rights and permissions, quite apart from performing royalties. Now he was at last able to execute an idea that he had been nurturing for some time. He went down to Connah's Quay. It was Monday, wash-day, and his mother, wearing an old cap of his father's, was scuttling about in a chilly wind carrying loads of damp linen. She was sixty-three years old, his father sixty-two. He went for a walk in the countryside beyond and saw newly-built bungalows for sale at five hundred pounds each. The builders showed him a plan, he signed a contract and paid a deposit.

While his mother darned socks and his father attacked dinner, Emlyn took out the plan and showed it to them. At first they did not realise what he was talking about. As his meaning dawned on them incredulity shaded their brow. They were too old, protested his mother, they were past shifting about. "We've lived here fifteen years," she said, "since you was eleven. How much is this goin' to cost?" He refused to tell her. With gentle determination he finally persuaded them. As soon as he returned to London he consulted a solicitor and had an agreement drawn up. This arranged for his parents to receive an annuity ". . . in consideration of the natural love and affection which the Grantor has for his Father and Mother (the Annuitants)." The document, granting a tax-free annual allowance, was duly signed by George Emlyn Williams and witnessed by W. Cronin Wilson. A first instalment of £19.8s.10d. arrived at Connah's Quay. An account of stewardship recorded that brothers Job and Thomas were each allotted five pounds, Mam five pounds, and Dad £4 8s.10d. ". . . I hope you are not Robbing yours self for us all," wrote his mother, "all we want is to know that the three of you boys are happy as we are alright now we are quite comfortable all through you . . ."

At the Albert Hall in May the Salvation Army held a giant ceremony where, among others, brother Tom was to be commissioned as an officer. Mr and Mrs Williams travelled up from Connah's Quay to be present and to see their eldest son in a new play called *Man Overboard* by Sutton Vane, author of the very successful *Outward Bound* which had in the past charmed numerous audiences with its mystico-sentimental maundering. His latest play won no such triumph and expired within a fortnight, although this did not rob Emlyn's parents of the awe they felt at beholding, outside the Garrick Theatre, the illuminated sign which spelt out "EMLYN WILLIAMS IN MAN OVERBOARD". The white-haired, apprehensive little woman and her bluff, confident husband took high tea at Lyons. They were introduced to Bill – "Mr Cronin I presume?" – and Emlyn presented his mother with a real fur from Harrods to replace the well-worn tippet she had displayed for years immemorial at Sunday chapel. Her face went scarlet. "There you are," said his father, "your Mam was always a lady and now she looks one as well." For the first time in his life Emlyn kissed her.

At six o'clock one morning a hired car arrived at the door and took him to British Lion Studios at Beaconsfield where Michael Balcon was filming *The Frightened Lady*. He was to repeat his rôle of Lord Lebanon with Cathleen Nesbitt again as his haughty mother and Gordon Harker as the lugubrious detective-sergeant. In those days the sound film was but a few years old, and plays were photographed with little change to the original dialogue. Emlyn knew his words already and was able to concentrate on adapting his performance to the new medium. In the theatre the raising of an eyebrow extended no more than a quarter of an inch. On the screen it could stretch over a foot or so. Everything had to be scaled down. The expansive gestures of the stage needed drastic reduction, and whereas in the theatre emotion was conveyed on a broad canvas, in the cinema a curve of the lip or a narrowing of the eye sufficed. Emlyn was young enough to appreciate this, and, unlike older-established actors, could smoothly translate from the wide brush strokes called for in a play to the miniature effects demanded in the cinema. *The Frightened Lady*, on release, went to Connah's Quay, where, on the hoarding he had so often dreamed over as a boy, a poster screamed: EMLYN WILLIAMS!!! SEE YOUR LOCAL FILM STAR!!! Emlyn told Miss Cooke: "My father after a lot of thought has decided to go to Chester, as he has heard the 'machines are better' there." His mother wrote to him, touchingly: ". . . when I see you in the pictures I feel I want to go and tell you something and you seem to be looking at us . . ."

Bill was one of the stage cast who had not appeared in *The Frightened Lady*, his part having gone to another actor, a professional hazard which, veteran that he was, he accepted with resignation. He still had not lost his capacity to surprise Emlyn. At supper one evening he revealed that he was the father of twin sons. He had met the girl who became their mother while on tour. Later, he heard, the family emigrated to America and some years afterward she sent him a photograph of the identical boys he had never seen, very beautiful American sailors. He had thrown the photograph away. "My beautiful American brothers," Emlyn thought to himself. Would they, he wondered, grow old one day, their features coarsened with middle age like their father's? "By now they're just your age," said Bill mischievously peering over his glasses as he prepared to read the evening paper.

All passion was not entirely spent between them, although Emlyn's feeling for him had solidified into a placid affection. Bill had long ago given up his attempts to cut down on smoking and drinking, and his sessions in clubs and bars extended each night into the early hours. Emlyn became increasingly irritated by the trembling hand, the perpetual cough, the watery eye. One night, asleep, he was abruptly woken by Bill staggering in drunk. In a moment of fury, outraged at this snub to the months of devotion he had offered, he sprang from his bed and hit him in the face. Bill lurched, his face reddened with murderous anger, and stumbled towards him. As he struck out Emlyn ducked and fled from the room, slamming the door behind him and pushing a wardrobe against it. Bill pounded on the door, a cannonade to awaken the dead. It certainly awoke a flustered landlord who enquired anxiously what was the matter. Just an old friend who'd had a couple, explained Emlyn, there'd been trouble getting him down the stairs. Next morning he packed his case and moved out to stay with friends. That night he saw Bill again, hung-over, nervous but friendly. He approved the new arrangement. "See you later, old boy." Emlyn watched him move off up the street, alone, rejected, yet, curiously, an object of love still.

Professional engagements helped to keep his mind off Bill. In the summer of 1932 he was in Oxford shooting a film on location, £12.10s. a day with a guarantee of twenty days' work and at least £250 at the end of it plus all expenses paid. As he wrote to Miss Cooke: "Exactly nine years ago a timid little *rustic lad* crept into Oxford in fear and trembling in search of fame and fortune, *George Williams* by name; this week that glamorous favourite film star *Emlyn Williams* drives into Oxford with a flourish of trumpets to make his very latest film. (Extract from imaginary press.)" The film was *Young Apollo*, later re-titled *Men of Tomorrow*, based on a novel by the then popular writer Anthony Gibbs. It was to be directed by the German Leontine Sagan, mannish, autocratic, who had gained notoriety with the vaguely lesbian film *Mädchen in Uniform* and who later emerged as the unexpected colleague of Ivor Novello in the production of his Ruritanian extravaganzas. Merle Oberon, of the exotic Indian looks, had been chosen as the heroine and would doubtless have engrossed the attention of Fraulein Sagan had she not already been the mistress, afterwards to become wife, of Alexander Korda who planned *Man of Tomorrow* as a starring vehicle for her. The actors included Robert Donat, half Polish, half Mancunian, whose North-Country vowels had been planed away through learning the business in Sir Frank Benson's Shakespearean company.

It was an eerie feeling, made-up, begowned, to sit in Christ Church Hall and then in Schools where, so short a time before, Emlyn had struggled with real examination questions. The re-creation of university life for the film sometimes made him uncertain where reality ended and illusion began. There was an occasional diversion, as when he attended a grand party at the home of Lady Lavery, wife to the fashionable portrait painter, ". . . where were also," he reported to Miss Cooke, "Mrs Belloc Lowndes, Cynthia and Oswald Mosley, the Editor of the *News Chronicle* and Lord Beaverbrook's daughter. So there! It was quite amusing but the essence of exquisite artifice. She is like the more frivolous type of salon-keeper (not saloon-keeper!) of Louis XIV's time."

After location scenes were completed the studio work remained to be done: ". . . incredibly boring – the other day I was made up at 9.45 in the morning, and did nothing till 8.30 in the evening . . . Everybody seems to be going slowly mad. You have no idea what goes on, the criminal waste of thousands of pounds. Yesterday they spent five hours shooting a scene which they had more than half decided not to use before they started to shoot it. Everybody has a finger in the pie, nobody knows what is happening, everybody bullies everybody else, nobody thinks the film is going to be any good . . ." His pessimism was justified: when the film had its première reviews compared it unfavourably with *Mädchen in Uniform*. The best things about it, they said, were the impressionistic atmosphere of Oxford and Emlyn's "whimsical humour" as "the silly ass" of the picture.

Since shooting had taken longer than expected (it usually does) Emlyn was able to bank £400. Another film, *Sally Bishop*, with Isabel Jeans and Kay Hammond, which he made almost immediately afterwards at Beaconsfield, brought five days at £20 a day. He was so busy in the studios that he had to turn down the flattering offer of a part in the new Haymarket play starring none other than Marie Tempest. At Miss Cooke's suggestion – "See here George, have you thgt. of life Insurance? In yr. profession surely invaluable, think abt. it" – he took out a large policy. He converted his war bonds from five per cent to three and a half per cent and, on her advice, invested heavily in Shell and Marks and Spencer, years before those stocks became legendary blue chips. At this rate he could afford to buy his parents half a dozen bungalows. He airily told them to burn all their decrepit furniture, and, cuddling his cheque book, went to a department store in Wrexham and bought a complete new set of beds, chairs, tables, cutlery, china, carpets, wardrobes, lamps, electric fires, wastepaper baskets, blankets, eiderdowns, hot-water bottles and even a large box of kitchen matches. 314A Connah's Quay was gone, expunged, obliterated, demolished. Except in the memory.

CHAPTER THREE

(i)
Fess

Emlyn's passport identified him. "Height: 5 feet, 9½ inches," it declared. "Eyes: Blue. Hair: Dark. Cut on finger next to little finger of left hand." In September, 1932, a few weeks before his twenty-seventh birthday, he took a train at Waterloo on the first lap of a journey to America. Five years earlier, in 1927, he had travelled the same route as a lowly member of the *And So To Bed* company. Now, Mr Emlyn Williams, rising young actor and playwright, was going to repeat his triumph as the decadent Lord Lebanon in Edgar Wallace's *The Case of The Frightened Lady*. For the New York production it had been re-baptised as *Criminal At Large* to avoid competition with the film lately released, and the director was to be Guthrie McClintic, famous man of the American theatre and husband of its leading lady Katherine Cornell. Bill came to see Emlyn off at Waterloo. As they shook hands he said: "Goodbye, my dear boy, look after yourself won't you, and write every week?" Those were the words Emlyn's father had spoken when he set off to France at the age of fifteen.

The few first-class passengers on the RMS *Berengaria* were not especially congenial except for the boyish-faced Frank Lawton who had recently played the hero in a much talked-of *Young Woodley* and was soon to marry Evelyn Laye. His destination was Hollywood and the film of Noël Coward's *Cavalcade*. As the three-chimneyed floating palace approached New York Emlyn felt nervousness. Reporters jostled him on landing. What was the latest about the Prince of Wales? What did he think of Mae West? Was he married? He booked in at the Hotel Bristol for old times' sake, felt woefully homesick, and moved out soon after into the more friendly Hotel Saint Hubert in West 57th Street. On the first day of rehearsal at the Belasco Theatre he made his entrance with carefully studied modesty. The jovial but sharp-tongued McClintic threw wide his arms and, in a mock English accent, welcomed him with: "Aw, our B-r-ritish staw!"

Letters from home and, more specially, from Miss Cooke began to trickle through and he cheered up. She told him, to his delight, that this parents had at last settled in at the new bungalow. "But my word!" she added, the old acerbity breaking out, "you can't say they have a great range of conversation . . . they didn't talk about 'George' but about 'He'." There was sensational news of Tom who had resigned from the Salvation Army because his Captain treated him "something cruel". Brother Job was about to marry a local girl and live and work on the farm that belonged to his father-in-law. Emlyn sent them fifty pounds as a wedding present. He was earning eighty pounds a week in *Criminal At Large*, royalties of ninety-nine pounds on *A Murder Has Been Arranged* had just come in, and he felt generous towards the brother in rural Wales who, until his wedding day, had never spent a night away from home.

The Wallace play, tightened and sharpened by McClintic, impressive in a manorial set of solid oak panelling, looked destined for a long run. Emlyn's agent relayed film offers from England and even noises off from Alexander Korda. Once *Criminal At Large* settled down Emlyn had time to look around at a New York vastly different from the one he first knew. He met, on equal terms, the celebrated Katherine Cornell, her black hair tousled, her sallow face untouched by make-up, rather like a "jolly and intelligent governess with a great sense of humour." The playwright George Kaufman (*Dinner At Eight*, *You Can't Take It With You*, *The Solid Gold Cadillac*) gave a party for Constance Collier where were the impresario Gilbert Miller, Irving Berlin, Edna Ferber and the English dramatist Dodie Smith, the last-named "a quiet mouse-like little women with an air of quiet amusement – she was the only real person in the whole galaxy . . . So you see I'm just 'going places' as they say here," he confided in Miss Cooke. "One side of me revels in the superficial gaiety and more than surface wit of it, the other is acutely embarrassed by the shameless artificiality. To see one leading lady greeting another with shrieks of 'Darling' is an education in theatrical etiquette. They are more shameless here even than in England." Then he met "the great Noël Coward for the first time, which I must say was rather a thrill." He had lunch with Lillian Gish, legendary heroine of silent films, and there was talk of his playing Hamlet to her Ophelia. The last time he saw her he had been a Welsh peasant boy gaping at the screen of the little picture-house in Connah's Quay.

There were other parties he did not describe to Miss Cooke. One such, in a large luxurious house, introduced him to a squirming mass of shrill-voiced men with rolling eyes and the gestures of schoolgirls.

Amid the turmoil he glimpsed a pair of sweet young US Navy sailors. The chatter was high-pitched and relentless, the atmosphere stifling. There was nothing for him in that room. He fled back to his hotel. He preferred to hunt alone, in bath-houses decently dim and in quiet corners where real men were to be found. And there was always, near the surface, the thought of Bill, to whom he wrote tenderly, the early passion now muted into a tranquil affection. "Bill – thank Heaven – is rehearsing Maugham's new play, very good part he says," he told Miss Cooke. "I do hope he keeps well for it." When *For Services Rendered* opened Bill cabled that "he has made a personal success in a very good part. Needless to say I'm immensely pleased and relieved, he has been getting very low lately." And again: "I'm terribly pleased, he was getting awfully depressed." But the play, one of Maugham's rare failures, closed within a week despite the presence of Cedric Hardwicke, Flora Robson and Ralph Richardson. Bill had only had three months' work out of twelve.

Although Emlyn voiced prim disapproval, chiefly one suspects for Miss Cooke's benefit, of New York's theatrical parties, they had their uses. Gilbert Miller remembered him from George Kaufman's *soirée* and asked him to anglicise a play by Sydney Howard (*They Knew What They Wanted, The Silver Cord*) which he had bought for presentation in London. It was called *The Late Christopher Bean* and, when Emlyn saw a matinée performance, he found it typically American and true to life. Only on receiving the script did he learn that it had been adapted from René Fauchois's *Prenez Garde à la Peinture*. Fauchois was an actor, a prolific boulevard dramatist and a charming raconteur who in old age delighted his hearers with memories of Sarah Bernhardt opposite whom he had played, of Beerbohm Tree who mounted his biographical play *Beethoven* at His Majesty's Theatre, of composers like Fauré and Saint-Saëns with whom he had worked, of Sacha Guitry who had been his boyhood friend. His play *Boudu Sauvé des Eaux* was made by Jean Renoir into a classic film, and it turned up again fifty years later in slick Hollywood dress as *Down and Out in Beverley Hills*. Fauchois brimmed over with ingenious ideas, not the least of them being *Prenez Garde à la Peinture*. The title is an equivalent of the warning "Wet paint," although it can also mean, the pun being untranslatable in English, "Watch out for the painting", that is, a painting by an artist.

A sleepy village is abruptly invaded by a trio of rival art dealers. The startled inhabitants awake to a realisation that the drunken layabout who once lived among them and who aroused their contempt for his "appalling" daubs has been acclaimed, now he is dead, as a great painter of canvases that fetch large sums. The doctor's family who grudgingly lent him their old cowshed as a studio search frantically for any pictures he may have left behind. One of them, they remember with horror, has been used to shore up a dilapidated hen-coop for protection from the rain. Others are discovered and money changes hands, although the biggest prize eludes them all: a large portrait of their humble maid. She will not sell it. Moreover, in the last act she reveals that, having been the layabout's mistress, she had also become his wife and has a ring to prove it. All the valuable pictures, and the money, thus belong to the modest little drudge and not to her overweening employers. The play emerges as a good humoured Molièresque satire on hypocrisy, cupidity and the wiles of the art market.

The most important character, Emlyn decided, was the maid. He turned her into Gwenny, a Welsh countrywoman, barely literate but shrewd and economical, an amalgam of all the Welsh housewives he had known as a boy and also, predominantly, a portrait of his own mother. He transferred the action to a Midlands village near the dour city of Chester and finished his neat adaptation within a week. His few days of work were handsomely rewarded by a fee of $250 (£70) on account of two per cent of the weekly gross. Edith Evans, he suggested, would be perfect as Gwenny, and Gilbert Miller agreed. She was then in New York playing *Evensong*, and after reading *The Late Christopher Bean*, she reacted enthusiastically. Miller had Cedric Hardwicke under contract, and he, they concluded, should play the male lead. Bill, Emlyn thought, would also do well in the play since "his Welsh accent is very good . . ."

By the Christmas of 1932 snow lay heavy on Central Park and *Criminal at Large* was only wobbling along at the box office. The cast agreed a cut in salary which kept it going until February, 1933, when it closed after a respectable run of twenty weeks compared with twenty-five in London. There was time for Emlyn to see "the first matinée of *Design for Living*, Coward's new play. It's a riot, a very frothy and completely amoral polite farce most wittily acted . . . It was really great fun." He added an envious postscript: "They were sold out for six weeks before they opened, and the reason they didn't sell further was because there were no tickets printed!"

He came back to England on the SS *Majestic* and saw Bill waiting for him at Southampton. Any adventures? asked Bill. Not many, Emlyn replied, for he'd chiefly been preoccupied with his writing. "All these weeks?" said Bill. "What a waste." They set up house again at 71A, Ebury Street. Here, the following year, Emlyn applied for a driving licence. He soon found the daunting arcana of gears and brakes and steering beyond him and quickly gave up driving – which is just as well, since, in those days, there was no driving test, and his attempts at navigation recalled those of Mr Toad.

The Late Christopher Bean made its debut at the St James's in May, 1933, with a first-night ovation that continued for a very long time. Cedric Hardwicke was good as the impecunious, family-ridden village doctor, but Edith Evans as Gwenny was even better. So musical was her accent, so rounded her vowels, that few people believed she was a daughter of Westminster rather than of Wales. After a run of nearly five hundred performances in the West End, the play went on tour. It brought good fortune to everyone. For Edith Evans it put her finances on a stable foundation at last. While on the tour Cedric Hardwicke received his knighthood. For Emlyn it earned, from tours and repertory, at least £7,000 and his name and photograph in the newspapers as author of "the greatest hit for months". Amid all the *réclame* he often thought guiltily of Sydney Howard, whose version he had adapted without consulting Fauchois's original. He was brought down to earth by Mrs Patrick Campbell, fat, throaty-voiced, long past her best but still capable of the deadly dart. John Gielgud introduced them to each other and mentioned Emlyn's latest success. "*Do* tell me more," she exuberated, "but you look a *child*, did you write it all by yourself?" "He's adapted it from the French," interposed Gielgud, helpfully but incorrectly. "Oh, you poor dear, a *translation?*" Plump fingers were raised in shock, rings glittered malevolently. "Now I've got a *spiffing* idea," she trumpeted at the embarrassed author. "Why not write a play out of your *very own head*, for a penniless old harridan who can still act? Goodbye dear John . . . and goodbye you naughty *cribber*, goodbye . . ."

While Edith Evans was drawing full houses at the St James's and earning her reputation with the Williams family as "that Miss Evans who is making Emlyn so much money", Emlyn himself returned to the London stage also. At five days' notice he took over from Brian Aherne in Cochran's production of *Wild Decembers*, a play about the Brontës by Clemence Dane. Both he and his fellow-player Ralph Richardson were "very fine", said Agate, although the piece did not last long, partly because another drama on the same subject was running at the same time. Pleased with himself at having learned and rehearsed his rôle at such brief notice, Emlyn happily took his place at the curtain-call and thought he detected cries of "Emlyn . . . Emlyn!" from the gallery. He had already moved forward to take a suitably modest bow when he realised with a thrill of horror that the shouts were directed at Beatrix Lehmann who had played Emily. Adroitly he turned and ushered her forward.

More reliable, and lucrative, were the offers of film work that poured in. He went out to Shepherd's Bush where the chromium-plated headquarters of the Gaumont-British film studios twinkled cheerily amid the dun surroundings of a lugubrious suburb. At breezy conferences he discussed the plot of *Friday the Thirteenth* for which he had been commissioned to write dialogue. Just before midnight one unlucky Friday, a London bus crashes in a storm and two of the passengers, as is revealed at the end, meet their death. The film tells, in flash-back, the stories of the six individuals the bus had been carrying. Emlyn would write his dialogue, try it out at conference, then go home to peruse and rewrite. The process gave him further lessons in the importance of economy and incisiveness. The cast list of *Friday the Thirteenth* is a glorious roll-call of nineteen-thirties British actors. Gordon Harker was a leery stockbroker and Robertson Hare a timorous Romeo, Wally Patch a Cockney policeman and Gibb McClaughlin a camp florist, with Jessie Matthews as a chorus girl and Ralph Richardson as her unlikely schoolmaster lover. There was even Max Miller as, well, Max Miller. Emlyn played the part of the crook who blackmails a shrinking Frank Lawton, the voice threateningly toneless, the pallid face taut with menace. Only in one scene did he falter: some clumsy business extracting a cigarette out of a case distracted attention from his smirking villainy. Otherwise he convinced, and the nasty little criminal deserved, you felt, the death that stormy night which released poor Frank Lawton from torment.

Having shown his mettle at Gaumont-British he was given a free hand with the screenplay for *Evergreen*, the classic nineteen-thirties musical in which Jessie Matthews, as sprightly a dancer as she was singer, made "Dancing on the Ceiling" and "Over My Shoulder" her own. He also provided what is known in the trade as "additional dialogue" for the George Robey version of that ancient stage hit *Chu Chin Chow* ("Thine eyes, beloved, have the bloom of the fresh fruits of Paradise"), and steeled himself to furnish the same service, though in a different idiom, for Alfred Hitchcock's *The Man Who Knew Too Much*. Give it "zing", they asked him, and "zing" he duly supplied.

As an actor speaking lines written by someone else, he pretended to play a dummy piano in *My Song For You* which featured Jan Kiepura and the omnipresent Sonnie Hale, who in those days seemed to have a clam-like grip on every British musical. In *Evensong*, the film of Beverley Nichols's weepy romance, Emlyn was the young musician who elopes with Evelyn Laye. *The Iron Duke* found him bowing to the exquisite George Arliss who added Wellington to the many great characters in history whom he impersonated with fame and profit. The knighthood he narrowly missed had been bestowed in all but name, for an atmosphere of impregnable dignity already surrounded this now forgotten star to whom even the highest executives of Gaumont-British respectfully deferred. Emlyn had an opportunity for demonism when he played the mad king Christian VI in *The Love Affair of a Dictator* and, according to some, stole the picture. Then he went back to juvenile lead again with *The City of Beautiful Nonsense* founded on an elderly best-seller in which he was a poverty-stricken composer. In that same year of 1935, when he seemed to be spending most of his time in film studios, he also appeared with Gordon Harker and Vi Loraine, George Robey's old co-star, in *Road House*, a melodrama about a singer from a low-life road house who becomes a star. All those early calls at a gruesome hour in the morning, all that waiting around on draughty sets and all the discomfort of blazing Klieg lights seemed worth it, however, when in June, 1933, he won the Best Performer award in a ballot held by *Film Weekly*. His popularity, according to the vote, was greater than that of Leslie Howard, Herbert Marshall and Jack Hulbert who came far behind. The magazine interviewed him and asked what were his favourite films? *King Kong* and *The Sign of the Cross*, he replied. Who were his favourite actresses? Greta Garbo, Kay Francis and Helen Hayes. Favourite actors? James Cagney, Herbert Marshall and Charles Laughton were the names he cited.

Amusing and profitable though the cinema was, it did not offer him the fulfilment to be had only in the theatre. Once he had completed his film chores for the day he would turn eagerly to ideas that had been germinating for plays. Plots were outlined, lists of characters drawn up, drafts made. *Up at Cardinal* was a three-act attempt to portray undergraduate life at some ancient Oxford college. A headline over a crime report in an issue of *The Times* seventy years ago gave him the title of *Shocking Fatality*, a murder mystery which inspired some ingenious ideas for staging, though he left it unfinished after two acts, other more urgent ideas having in the meantime clamoured for expression. He toyed also with *Celebrity* which took place at "a flat in Saint Martin's Lane, in the West End of London". This, again, did not go beyond the stage of typescript and pencilled notes.

Someone had once said to him, "You might write a good costume play." The suggestion resonated when he came across an article about the theatre in Shakespeare's day, the contemporary actor Richard Burbage, and the boys who played the female characters. He went to the Reading Room at the British Museum and made hurried notes about the Globe Theatre and life in Shoreditch. The connecting thread would be the heroine, a pretty girl who dresses as a boy and runs away from the prospect of a boring marriage in the country. She comes to London, falls in love with Burbage, and creates Viola in the first performance of *Twelfth Night*. What was the date of the play? Around the beginning of the century. The title, then, would be *Spring of 1600*, which finally became *Spring, 1600*. He completed it while playing Lord Lebanon in New York. American colleagues to whom he spoke of his new play thought he was quoting a Manhattan telephone number. One evening, after a dinner with much brandy to follow, he read his script aloud to Guthrie McClintic. By the time he reached the end of the first act, hoarse-voiced, McClintic was sound asleep.

Miss Cooke, on the other hand, was ecstatic. "Perfect, beautiful," she wrote to him after he had sent her the manuscript from New York, ". . . fresh, youthful, atmosphere ideal – the atmosphere of Spring and Youth . . . nothing riotous, yet a bubbling over of vitality: simple outlines, simple colours, everything just ready to bud forth, to burst forth . . ." And then she remembered she was a schoolmistress and added primly, though correctly: "The historical atmosphere is most attractive." Her remarks sum up the play admirably. As for the historical atmosphere, that is achieved most subtly. How, for example, was Emlyn to write a play about the troupe which gave the first performance of *Twelfth Night* without falling for the temptation of making Shakespeare himself a principal character? His solution demonstrates a pretty wit. At the close of the first act "A Visitor" calls. "Is Master Burbage at home?" he asks. "Yes, sir – in the kitchen, eating," replies the cook. The visitor goes off into the kitchen. "Who was that?" says a character. "A fellow that writes plays. William Shakespeare." The curtain falls.

The portrait of Richard Burbage shows that the nature of the star actor has not changed over the centuries. When a player threatens to leave him and join the troupe of his rival Edward Alleyn for a higher salary, he erupts magnificently. "Then go to Alleyn, and leave me to peddle ballads in Shoreditch! For what am I but the scum of the earth . . ." No, his wife assures him, he is the greatest Englishman living. He will not be calmed, and, intoxicated by the sound of his own beautiful voice, he enjoys himself in a cloud of rhetoric: "Get me candles, get me fresh straw, and strew it on the stage of my new theatre, and if I am not blinded by my tears, then let me light the fire that will burn my life's dream to ashes, and let me paint in the London sky the words 'Burbage and his men play no more,' for am I not the scum of the earth!" Hugely satisfied with the effect he has created, he stops automatically for applause. The tricks of the trade have not changed much either, for an actor who protests at the smallness of his role is told: "It is larger than it looks, Master Phillips, there are cries and looks galore that are not on the paper." Burbage, too, has the typical star's disdain for the mere scribblers who produce the words he utters so splendidly. He glances at the script of the new play he is to put on with his leading lady/boy/lady heroine. "What have we here . . . 'To die, to sleep; to sleep . . .' (*Suddenly interested, more slowly*). '. . . To sleep, perchance to . . .' Hm . . . Some idea of Will's, may come in useful . . . Can you see, my little ploughboy, to what golden heights this new play can rise, with you and me together?"

Ann the heroine is supposed to be the daughter of the composer William Byrd. This is the perfect excuse for incidental music to complement the lyrical nature of the dialogue. Towards the end of the play, by which time the sweetheart from her native Ongar in Essex has come to reclaim her, Burbage tells her that, despite her success on the London stage, she belongs to Essex: "Where the English earth is tilled and the orchard soberly tended, where even the smoke rises with a steadfast air, and knows its way to heaven." Ann will, he promises her, get over her infatuation with him when she turns back "into a maid" in the country again. He has had many women, but his only true mistress, the only one he is ever faithful to, is the theatre. The curtain begins to fall, very slowly, as, "silhouetted darkly against moonlight and candlelight, there sails slowly in, between her two swains, the legendary Elizabeth of England: tall, gaunt, over-painted, but graceful as a ship on the bosom of her own Thames." The opening lines of *Twelfth Night* are heard.

Emlyn sent the typescript to John Gielgud who was then charming the town in another costume play, *Richard of Bordeaux*. Soon afterwards he was bidden to the famous flat in Upper St Martin's Lane and climbed up a narrow stairway to the top floor. The sound of Bach on a gramophone, austere and measured, resounded throughout a room that was cheerful and crowded with books and scripts. "Emlyn, how nice to see you again," smiled Gielgud, whom Emlyn had only glimpsed twice up to then from a respectable distance. "I loved your play, how d'you feel about the last act?" He had suggestions to make, tactful, courteous. Once that last act was strengthened all would be well. He was already thinking of people for the cast. Rewriting, Emlyn knew, would be easy. Happily he picked his way down the steep stairs while Gielgud's eyrie above filled with the moody strains of César Franck.

With costumes and sets by "Motley", a team of three young girl designers soon to become well-known in the theatre, *Spring, 1600* opened at the cavernous Shaftesbury Theatre on January 31, 1934. Outside in the street it was cold and foggy. On stage the "Motley" sets depicted an idealised vision of Elizabethan Essex, elegant and fresh as out of a band-box, though later to be followed by the majestic disorder of Burbage's house in Shoreditch overlooking the busy Thames. Gielgud directed the production with a sensitiveness that brought to life a long-lost spring of centuries ago. "I'm happy to have done it whatever happens," said Gielgud. "You've been so patient, it's a lovely play." On the first night Emlyn skulked nervously high up in the flies amid ropes and pulleys. From the distant stage below he heard the swirl of the curtain, the faint snatches of music, the murmur of voices speaking lines he knew by heart. A sudden desperate need overcame him and he relieved it in a dusty old wash-basin. "You must," said Gielgud later when he told him, "be the first playwright who's peed over his own play."

They needed good notices to help the run of a play with a large cast of over twenty characters, music and expensive scenery. Agate helped in a review headlined "Love's Labour's Gained". *Spring, 1600* was, he said, a superb *divertissement* written with "the nicest dramatic sense". If dramatic carpentry was not its strongest point, "the best of this play is its wit . . . It is certainly choice entertainment for the fastidious." There were, Gielgud decided, *longueurs*, and Emlyn, gritting his teeth, cut some of his favourite lines. Audiences were appreciative but small after a deceptively welcoming first night. Within a very short time the box-office was faltering and the play came off. Motley's beautiful sets were consigned to a damp warehouse and the lovely dresses sold off in job lots to theatrical costumiers. "Oh dear, I am sad for you," said Gielgud, "we don't seem to have quite got away with it, all that work and love and then it just evaporates . . ."

Bill congratulated him, was proud of him. "Little did I think when I saw that quiet kid rehearsing *On the Spot* . . ." They no longer lived together at Ebury Street, for Bill drank as heavily as ever, was unbearable when ravaged by alcohol and hang-overs. Yet they still had a deep affection for each other. After months of unemployment – how did he live? Emlyn asked himself, how did he keep going? – he had finally obtained a good part in C. B. Cochran's big new production of *Escape Me Never* with Elisabeth Bergner. One evening, blithe and hazy with drink, he appeared at the flat in Ebury Street " 'Lo, ole boy, I brought a pal, all right?" he said, indicating a tall young man at his side. The pal, twenty years old, was Welsh. He had dark hair, grey eyes, and thick voluptuous lips. A top tooth missing at the side emphasised the lazy charm of his Welsh voice. "Emlyn, this is Fess," said Bill. Curtains were drawn, glasses filled and chairs drawn up. The fire crackled cheerily. "God, this is good . . ." Bill exulted, breathing fumes of nicotine and whisky. "My dearest boy, you've had a disappointment which has brought me luck, and I love you very much . . ." The night dissolved into a pleasurable threesome, intense and blissfully mindless.

At the Long Bar a few days later Emlyn saw Fess again. Banalities were exchanged. Fess had problems with his landlord, who, at first content with an occasional grope, was now demanding the rent in hard cash. Why not, Emlyn impulsively suggested, come and stay with him until something turned up? Fess gave an indolent smile. They collected his sparse belongings from the boarding-house and took a taxi to Ebury Street, Fess with the ever-present cigarette drooping from his plump lower lip. They slept in the big bed. Next morning Emlyn woke at ten. The door opened, and, to his surprise, he saw Bill, who was rarely up before twelve. "Who's that in the bed?" snapped Bill. A tousled head emerged. " 'Lo Bill, how's tricks?" The scene recalled a French farce. Bill reddened, unhappy and bewildered. "I see," he remarked slowly. "I certainly did start something . . ." He turned and walked heavily down the stairs.

The Fess type was, and is, immemorial. He is street-wise and charming. He is often to be found as the companion of elderly gentlemen, or of persons older and richer than he. Wealthy stockbrokers take him away for the weekend to Boulogne, although he readily sleeps with women too, sometimes for pleasure only. His speech is monosyllabic and his background obscure. There may be an orphanage, or a broken home, or Borstal somewhere in the past. Occasionally he surprises with a native witticism. He likes to smoke other people's cigarettes and graciously accepts when a drink is offered. He is unfailingly obliging. He might not be above driving away an unminded car or making off with a bag left at a railway station. To date that is probably the worst thing he has done. What will happen, though, when his looks fade and his charm is gone? There is a hint of danger about him that makes him irresistible.

The Welshness of Fess, his looks and the spice of danger attracted Emlyn. He was tired of working on *Spring, 1600*, of concocting film dialogue, of worrying about Bill and his recidivism. Gaumont-British could do without him for a month, so he decided to go abroad. He bought a car with advice from Fess, who stood by in silent admiration as he watched him write a cheque for a large sum. They would take the ferry from Southampton and tour through France. The Welsh boy already, to Emlyn's surprise, had a passport. He had been taken abroad before. They drove out of Le Havre, Fess at the wheel, confident and relaxed. From time to time, at his request, Emlyn lit a cigarette for him and put it between his lips. He whistled and sang pop songs. Emlyn suddenly remembered that he had not said goodbye to Bill, although the intention had been at the back of his mind all through preparations for the trip. It was too late now. In any case, there would have been embarrassment, as Bill would surely have asked who his companion was going to be.

When they came to Rouen Emlyn reminisced about the threesome he had enjoyed there as a nineteen-year-old student with the Breton sailor and the whore. Fess was intrigued, but not in the way Emlyn expected. He'd never had a woman until he was *nineteen*? Such a thing was incredible. They went to the brothel Emlyn remembered from his last visit. Nothing had changed, and even the girls, though different this time, looked the same. While Fess disappeared upstairs with one of them, Emlyn sat quietly over his beer feeling very adult. Yet for all his world-weariness he knew that Fess, sharp and down-to-earth, was the more mature.

As they drove south the weather grew warmer. The dying days of *Spring, 1600* in fogbound London seemed an eternity away. They put up at a hotel in Gibraltar where Fess, lifting the curtain a little on his past, revealed that he had once been in the Navy. He knew Gibraltar, he said, and asked with a sly grin whether Emlyn had ever heard of the Alameda Gardens? Fess went off on his own while Emlyn decided to explore the broad avenues with their spacious flower beds under shady trees. In the daytime respectable nannies wheeled their charges here and British officers took the air with their families. By night, the Alameda Gardens were full of elusive shadows that glided furtively among the trees. Emlyn saw in the moonlight a British sailor alone on a park bench. The sailor – *"Buenas noches, Señor"* – asked for a light.

Emlyn apologised and explained that he did not smoke. Oh well, sighed his companion, he was just going through the motions. There was a titter from behind the bushes. Don't mind them, remarked the sailor glancing backwards, they were the local Spanish queens, and they did not approve of English people trespassing on their beat.

Emlyn walked on, his footsteps echoing along a deserted avenue. Suddenly, accompanied by shrill giggles, a stone flew out from the tangled bushes around. It landed a yard behind him. Another flashed by his ear. Determined not to panic, he went forward at a regular pace. Stones now descended all around him during the last hundred yards, and the venomous chatter continued. At last he reached the gates. How amused Bill would be when he told him about the rent boys of Gibraltar who had stoned him out of the British Empire's treasured possession!

At the hotel an urgent telephone call from Gaumont-British summoned him back to write some more additional dialogue. In London, on their return, the flat looked cold and unwelcoming. Among the letters that piled up untidily on the floor was an official envelope addressed to "The Executors of the late W. Cronin Wilson". Emlyn chuckled. The Inland Revenue had not heard from Bill for so long that they had obviously given him up for dead. He laughed again as he looked forward to seeing the expression on Bill's face when he showed him the envelope.

There was also a message to ring a friend of Bill's. He dialled the number. "Emlyn, we did everything we could to find out where you were, nobody knew," said the voice at the other end. "I'm awfully sorry old chap, but Bill died two weeks ago."

(ii)
"London's the mischief!"

A cold had developed into pneumonia when Bill insisted, against all advice, on playing his part as a stolid German in the evening performance of *Escape Me Never*. By the following night he was dead, two months short of his forty-seventh birthday. He left nothing behind him, except, perhaps, for the twin sons, unknown and far away, whom he had produced by accident. Emlyn remembered the last time he saw him, framed in the doorway as he turned unhappily away from the bedroom. Why had not Emlyn telephoned him before he left with Fess? He kept reproaching himself for his thoughtlessness. It was his fault that Bill had died without the presence of the one human being who loved him. Already the body that Emlyn knew was beginning to rot and disintegrate in the cold earth.

He could not weep. All night he lay half-awake, his arms twined desperately around Fess who tried, in his clumsy way, to comfort him. The cast of *Escape Me Never* had sent a wreath, he learned later, and Cochran, generous as always, contributed a cheque. Nonetheless it had been a pauper's funeral. The only mourners at the cemetery were a remote cousin and a long-time drinking companion of Bill's. The latter, who had known Bill for many years, gave Emlyn the details. There were still expenses, of course. Emlyn wrote out a large cheque for him. It was conscience money, he told himself. Was there anything else, he asked? Did Bill say anything while he was on his hospital bed? Oh, he'd fallen into a coma and rambled on about his duty to Cochran. Then he'd said something that made the nurses giggle despite themselves. "Where's Ralph Lynn?" he'd mumbled. Why should Bill have begun talking about the star of the Aldwych farces? Emlyn walked slowly home. "Where's Ralph Lynn?" Just before he reached the flat he stopped. It was not "Where's Ralph Lynn?" that Bill had been saying. It was: "Where's Emlyn?"

In the leaden days of mourning that followed he turned again to an acquaintance he had made at a party after the first night of *A Murder Has Been Arranged*. She was Mrs Carus-Wilson, the wife of a barrister some fifteen years older. Jack Carus-Wilson, tall, slim, good-looking, very popular with ladies, nicknamed her "my little Mole". The teasing affection that existed between Molly, as she was called, and handsome Jack, intrigued Emlyn and made him a trifle envious when he contemplated the strange ways of married life. She had been on the stage herself, urged by an ambitious mother who, while Molly was still a nine-year-old child, had dragooned her into giving recitations before an audience. Molly's older sister Polly had also been through the same mill. After elocution lessons from Dame May Whitty, Molly, at the age of fifteen, toured in *Chu Chin Chow*, played the Hull Palace in *Mam'selle Kiki*, and came to London where she took a small part in *Battling Butler* with Jack Buchanan. Afterwards came more plays with titles like *Clo-Clo*, *Riki-Tiki* and *Enter Kiki*. A photograph in the *Illustrated Sporting and Dramatic News* at the time featured "Miss Molly O'Shann" under the legend "A Cabaret Soubrette", eyes ringed with mascara, hair cut in a dark fringe. A caption explained that her favourite pastime was sculling. Her ambition, it added, was to play Ophelia and Juliet.

The latter statement was not quite true and sprang, perhaps, from the imagination of a journalist. She never considered herself as good an actress as sister Polly, and she left the stage with some relief when she married Jack Carus-Wilson. Although she did indeed love the theatre, she preferred to do so as a member of the audience. Jack did not earn very much, and she took a part-time job in a shop. It depressed her. They rented a cottage by the Thames near Windsor and Emlyn joined them for a weekend. He thought how young she looked beside her mature and worldly husband. At the time he was writing *Spring, 1600*, and he arranged for her to play a small part in it. She was grateful to be released for a while from her job in the shop. Emlyn began to spend more weekends in the cottage by the Thames. Once he had introduced Bill to the Carus-Wilsons. What, Emlyn enquired eagerly, did he think of his new friends. Bill paused. He seemed a shade distant. "I thought he was bit smooth," he said at last.

After seven years of marriage, during which Jack had enjoyed a number of adventures, he suddenly left Molly for a small-part actress. Emlyn tried to console her and thought of taking her out to dinner. He decided against the idea, for he still did not feel entirely at ease with women. Instead, worried by her situation, he drew £30 from royalties on *The Late Christopher Bean* and sent them to her in an envelope. The money would help her through the days of waiting for her divorce.

"Where's Emlyn? Where's Emlyn?" With Bill's last words ringing through his brain he came home to find a telephone message from Molly. She called to see him, met Fess leaving for the pub, and sat down to drink sherry. Suddenly he was in her arms, the tears flowing freely at last, the dam broken, the self-accusations he had never dared articulate before welling up in a torrent of grief. He had let Bill die alone. He had condemned him to a pauper's grave. He could never forgive himself. "It's all right, darling," she said, "it's all right . . ." He remembered himself as a six-year-old being comforted by the little Welsh maid who had drudged in his father's pub.

Molly went down to Brookwood Cemetery with him. Together they picked their way through an undergrowth of grey stone slabs and found Bill's grave, a long mound of freshly turned earth damp in the chill of a March afternoon. While he stared at the slab of soil she discreetly looked the other way. The spirit of Bill was exorcised.

It was Emlyn's turn now to act the comforter. One afternoon Molly had sounded so desperate on the telephone that he rushed to join her. Jack was still being awkward, her divorce and her liberty seemed as distant as ever. She was unconsoled by a woman-friend's assurance that once she had her divorce she would be free to marry again. "Oh," she said, "I don't think anybody would want to marry me even if I was free . . ." Emlyn made up his mind instantly. "Molly, if you do get free, will you marry me?" "Of course I will," she said.

Divorce at that time was a long, adversarial process. It was essential that Emlyn and Molly should not be seen publicly together until after the final decree was granted, for otherwise there would be further complications. Emlyn leased a bungalow on a small island in the Thames, primitive, shabby, run-down. It was near Staines and cost fifty pounds a year. Fess helped put it to rights, painting, distempering, running up cupboards and fitting shelves. Here Molly was to live in discreet seclusion until the divorce was complete. It was spring, and the curious *ménage à trois* sat on the lawn and watched the occasional punt or barge as it glided slowly by. Fess, in tight white briefs, dived gracefully into the river and swam around. When he emerged drops of water pearled down his slim hairless chest and clustered on the long muscular thighs. The black hair clung wet and shiny to his head, the lips stood out even redder against the exquisite whiteness of a profile chilled by the sudden shock of cold river water.

Fess remained an obsession. Emlyn's mind became a battlefield where the two sides of his personality clashed and warred. In Molly he discovered a fulfilment he had never experienced before with any woman or man. She gave him a unique tenderness and surrounded him with an affection that touched his innermost heart. And yet, even as he lay in her arms, he would find himself thinking of Fess, of his narrow hips, of his sultry look. Through the whole of one night he told her all about himself. "You're in love with him, aren't you?" she said. He was, he acknowledged, although he did not even like him, was bored by him, was hopelessly in thrall to his sexuality.

Fess would be twenty-one in a week or so. What would he like for a birthday present? Emlyn asked. The boy's eyes glistened as he pointed out an advertisement in the *Motor Cycle* which featured a shiny monster of a machine. He made enquiries at a shop and came back with a typewritten bill for £81.3s.9d. Emlyn offered to write a cheque. No, said Fess, a shade embarrassed, the dealer wanted cash if he was to take it away. He went off and later in the day proudly returned on his motor-bike, gleaming, powerful. With real love in his eyes, the first time Emlyn had seen him display such an emotion, he switched the engine into throbbing life. "Anybody want a go on the pillion?" Thighs tightly clasped around the saddle, he roared off exultantly.

After he had gone the post arrived. A letter addressed to Fess which Emlyn opened by mistake came from the motor-cycle dealer. It enclosed a pound note and pointed out that Fess had miscalculated and paid £52.3s.9d. instead of £51.3s.9d. Emlyn was puzzled. He took out the original typewritten bill which carried the figure of £81.3s.9d. After careful study with a magnifying glass he discovered that the original sum had been changed from 51 into 81: a profit representing thirty pounds. When Fess returned a confrontation followed. He stayed calm, nonchalant even. No, he hadn't committed a forgery – it was nothing more than an everyday fiddle. Only when Emlyn refused to let him keep the bike did his self-control break down. For a moment his expression flamed with anger, his face blanched. Deprived of the only object he had ever loved, would ever love, he turned and walked out.

With his departure, thought Emlyn, hoped Emlyn, would come the end of his obsession. It did not. A few weeks later he saw a pair of old shoes in the kitchen. They had belonged to Fess. He looked at them, picked them up, sniffed them. He took off his own, and with a secret exaltation, slipped on the shoes that Fess had left behind. After taking a few steps in them he found himself trying to imitate the cocksure bandy walk of their owner. Rather than throw them away he carefully stored them at the back of a drawer. "You must try and get him out of your system," he heard Molly say. He was startled. He did not realise she had known.

In his attempted flight from the enchanter he tried everything, even to the extent of imagining what Fess would look like thirty years hence, the cheeks puffy, the thighs flaccid, the eyes rheumy and bloodshot. It was Molly who suggested an exercise in aversion therapy. He must go and visit Fess and spend time with him, time enough to see just how unattractive a character he was. So he travelled to Gloucester where Fess lived at his parents' home. His father and mother, Emlyn discovered with surprise, were quiet, respectable folk. He invited Fess back to London where he could stay in his old room. Fess, unsurprised and casual as always, replied "OK." His mother, though sorry to lose "our Fess", was glad he had another job with "Mr Williams".

Back in London they had a drink at the Long Bar where Fess idly cruised the glances that flickered his way. They dined in a restaurant and Emlyn was bored while Fess chattered vaguely. When they returned to Ebury Street they slept in separate rooms. Next day Emlyn travelled down to the riverside bungalow, having arranged for Fess to join him by train the following morning. He left him a five-pound note, and on the journey found himself longing to be with Molly again. A day passed, and a whole weekend, but there was no sign of Fess. Emlyn telephoned the flat again and again without reply. The post one morning brought an envelope addressed in an unfamiliar hand. Inside were a five-pound note and a message from Fess. He had decided to go home and wished Emlyn "all the best". And that was that.

There was little time to brood, for an urgent invitation to appear in Hugh Ross Williamson's new historical play *Rose and Glove* swept away all thought of Fess with the preoccupation of learning lines and rehearsals. After a fortnight playing Piers Gaveston to Richard Ainley's Edward II and Alan Wheatley's Earl of Gloucester, he was caught up in another far more ambitious venture. Alexander Korda had commissioned him to adapt a German comedy about Napoleon's Josephine. The flamboyant Hungarian was more accustomed to the film set than the stage, his links with the theatre being usually confined to buying the film rights of a promising play during the interval after the first act and then of selling them at a much higher price to another entrepreneur in the interval after the second. On this occasion, however, he had decided to launch *Josephine* with scenery and costumes as lavish as any he commanded for his spectacular films. The cast, too, was equally expensive and included Mary Ellis as leading lady with such current West End stars as Frank Vosper, Lyn Harding and Sam Livesey, who was the father of Roger, later a prominent actor in the British cinema. Emlyn and Donald Wolfit also had small rôles. The first night, which opened with all the glamour of a film première, struggled through disaster after disaster to end in boos and hisses from the gallery. *Josephine* closed within days.

A month later, in the October of 1934, Molly confirmed that she was pregnant. Now they had a perfect excuse to hasten the divorce proceedings which, if Jack were complaisant, could be expedited. When approached in confidence he agreed, subject to a condition which, given his pecuniary state, was not unexpected. His request was, though, unusually modest: in return for £30 he was ready to "connive". Was she, Molly wondered ironically, worth no more than that? The cash was handed over, in pound notes as stipulated, outside Holborn underground station.

Molly found a house at 5, Lincoln Street, just off the King's Road in

Chelsea, and they took it on a seven-year lease at £150 a year. This was the first of the homes she created in the years to come, filling its rooms with carpets and furniture and pictures which she bought, with a keen eye for artistic harmony, in shops and auction rooms. She, unlike Emlyn, knew how to "offer" a painting, how to place a sideboard, how to match curtains with other fabrics, how to arrange ornaments and position bowls of flowers. The things he had bought at Maples with a bachelor's expensive carelessness would, she suggested kindly, be best consigned to a nursery. He looked around him at the silver candlesticks, the Persian rug, the Regency sofa table, the French chairs, the eighteenth-century tallboy, and meekly agreed. He felt, for the first time in his life, as if he had come into his own home, a home that had been expressly created for himself and no other.

Towards the end of May, 1935, the *News of the World* reported in an obscure paragraph that "George Williams" had duly been cited in the Carus-Wilson divorce case. From the riverside bungalow, which soon knew them no more, Emlyn and Molly set off for Slough Town Hall, where, in a bleak and shabby office, an austere Registrar laid out documents for them to complete. He raised a puzzled eyebrow when Emlyn filled in his father's occupation as "labourer", the description given on his birth certificate. After a short address on the sanctity of marriage, delivered with the boredom of a bad actor in a long-running play, a wedding ring was handed over. The newly married couple stepped out into the High Street as "Mr and Mrs George E. Williams". The first floor of Lyons Coventry Street Corner House known to habitués as "The Lily Pond", the Long Bar, the Tea Kettle, the Cavour and the Chalice Bar were left behind him. Or were they?

(iii)
"Two Lumps in a Throat . . ."

Marriage delighted him. There was a pleasant ring to the phrase "Mr and Mrs Emlyn Williams" and the flattering implication that another human being honoured him enough to assume his name. Every day he learned something new. When Molly said they would have to give up the bungalow on the Thames he was puzzled. The lawn, she explained, went straight down to the water, and it would be dangerous. He still did not grasp why. "For a baby starting to walk," she added.

On a brief trip to Glasdir the new Mrs Williams met her parents-in-law and was given a dignified welcome. Emlyn's mother proved, in any case, a trifle distracted, for her favourite son Tom was about to marry a girl who had enslaved him and whose family, moreover, had got him quite under their thumb. As Emlyn told Miss Cooke, his mother "did something I'd never seen her do before – cried when I left". Miss Cooke herself, now that Molly and Emlyn were released from what he called "the polluted atmosphere of out-of-wedlockery," was very pleased. "You know how I longed for you to marry," she wrote, " – I was certainly very afraid, tut, tut, tut. I'm so sorry for bachelors. We old maids have a much better time really. They have a good time till they are fortyish, but afterwards, it is usually very thin."

To the house in Lincoln Street, so artfully decorated and furnished by Molly, came actresses and actors, writers and dramatists, film people and theatre directors. Molly was a sympathetic hostess, as skilled at achieving the right blend of guests as she was at the correct matching of fabrics. Emlyn's sharp tongue and mercurial chatter were counterpointed by her gentle tact. John Gielgud was a frequent visitor at genial lunch parties. So was Robert Helpmann, a youthful Australian pixie who crossed the Williams threshold and, taking in vain the name of a distinguished and very respectable actress, announced: "Don't be silly dear, I didn't *land* on these shores, I was smuggled through in Margaret Rawlings' handbag. I'm Outback *and* Outrageous and I don't care who knows it."

Others who frequented the house in Lincoln Street included Rodney Ackland, the young actor and playwright who lately enjoyed much success with his dramatisation of Hugh Walpole's creepy novel *The Old Ladies*. Emlyn had known him in Fagan's company at Oxford and done him a number of good turns since then by procuring small rôles for him in various productions with which he was associated. Like Molly, and Emlyn too, Ackland was an ardent film fan with a passion for the work of D. W. Griffith. Often they would play guessing games as to who could recall given scenes and close-ups in *Way Down East* or *Intolerance*. This enthusiasm for Griffith led to a bitter disagreement. As we shall see, it was Emlyn who played the lead and wrote the script for the re-make of Griffith's *Broken Blossoms*. At first, however, Ackland had hoped to do both these tasks himself. Then Griffith decided Emlyn should play the part and should write the script in collaboration with Ackland. Even this consolation was to be denied the latter, for misunderstanding flourished and accusations of double dealing multiplied. For over a year a coldness subsisted between Emlyn and Ackland. When the film was released Ackland went, out of morbid curiosity, to see it. Behind him sat a man and woman who commented audibly on the action between muffled giggles. There was a scene where Emlyn, slit-eyed, moved into close-up to kiss the heroine, tears bedewing her lashes, a smile tremulous on her lips. From behind him Ackland heard a stage whisper: "Kiss me goodnight, sergeant-major!" He collapsed into uncontrollable laughter at this incongruous remark, turned round and saw Emlyn and Molly. They all had to leave the cinema, helpless with mirth. Good relations were restored. A few days later Molly invited Ackland to a party at the Lincoln Street house. He was, however, at a trough in his career, depressed and penniless. When he arrived he could see through the windows a crowd of prosperous and confident stars. He did not have the heart tö join them, so he turned on his heel and crept off into the rainswept night.

Another guest was Noël Coward, not now, as a year or so ago, the remote star to be observed in awe, but a benevolent companion who watched the rise of his slightly younger contemporary with amused encouragement. Emlyn gave him the typescript of a play he had just completed. From Gerald Road, SW1, came a verdict phrased in mock schoolboyese. "I say, Williams, that was no end spiffing of you to send me your little play. As one chap to another don't you think it's just the teeniest, weensiest bit unpleasant here and there? But I suppose you writer fellows use everything as grist to our mill. Love to you and the little woman. Coward."

"Unpleasant", at least in the Shavian sense, was a drama that featured a pathological killer, two murders and a hatbox containing a severed head. The play had been inspired by the real-life murder cases that so enthralled Emlyn. Indeed, it opened with a peroration from the Lord Chief Justice in full robes presiding over the Court of Criminal Appeal. "I cannot help but think," he remarks, "that the deplorable atmosphere of sentimental drama which has pervaded this trial has made the *theatre* a more fitting background for it than a court of law . . .", a disarming observation which brazenly invites the audience to collude. Emlyn was a connoisseur of murder trials which he fre-quented whenever he possibly could. His companion was often the writer Fryn Tennyson Jesse, wife of the fashionable dramatist H. M. Harwood with whom she collaborated on plays. She also wrote novels and books of a criminological turn which explored the reasons for murder. One of her favourite cases, and of Emlyn's, concerned the young man Sidney Fox who set light to his mother and burned her to death for the sake of her life insurance. He was a very commonplace person who lived in Margate and whose favourite beverage was a glass of milk.

In November, 1935, just before his twenty-ninth birthday, Emlyn began writing his play. At first he visualised the central figure as a man who, like Fox, killed his mother, but then he decided that the truth was too shocking. Other murders were examined for details – that, for example, when the assassin cut up his victims as did the German Haarman, and the one where the culprit lost his nerve and kept the dead body for weeks in his room. Who should the murderer in the play be? Emlyn thought of Fess with his dangerous charm, his ability to wheedle, his monosyllabic speech. What would this character look like? He put a cigarette-end in his mouth and looked at his own reflection in the mirror. The part would be tailor-made.

Within a month the play was drafted, revised, cut and finished. It went to J. P. Mitchelhill who had bought the old Duchess Theatre and launched there a number of successful plays by J. B. Priestley as well as T. S. Eliot's *Murder In The Cathedral*. Mitchelhill was a Cockney businessman from Holborn who had in his time been a wheelwright's apprentice, a navvy and a foreman of stables. As the manager of a wine merchant's firm he bought out his employer and set up on his own. The man who lent him the capital for this soon became his partner, and together they embarked on many lucrative property deals. Quite by chance, as a result of his partner's accountant buying Collins's Music Hall in a mistaken bid at an auction, Mitchelhill found himself involved with the stage. From booking acts at Islington Green he moved to the legitimate theatre and, in 1930, at a time of recession, daringly bought the shabby little Duchess. There the stocky entrepreneur who looked like a cigar-smoking Mr Punch laid out many thousands on renovating his jewel of a theatre and gave opportunities to dramatists and players who rarely let him down by disappointing his flair for artistic promise. Once he was satisfied that a play or player had quality, he gave the artists a free hand. He was, in private, a generous philanthropist and took under his wing a number of protégés, among them Kathleen Harrison. On one point, however, he remained inflexible. The moment a play began to falter at the box-office over a short period of time, be it ever so little and despite a good press and appreciative audiences, he took it off. There was no indulgent nursing. In that way, unlike Cochran or Thomas Beecham, he made and actually kept a lot of money.

Nonetheless, he like to pretend that the box-office did not interest him and that only the purest artistic ideals inspired his decisions. As he told Emlyn with the airy manner of a benevolent uncle, "Well, me boy, yer play's very 'orrible but it grips yer all right an' I'm one o' those funny blokes not influenced by the public, people ought to see things like that." The first half of his statement at least was true, for *Night Must Fall* was indeed "very 'orrible" by the standards of the time. After the prologue in which the Lord Chief Justice tells us who the murderer is, the curtain rises on a cottage in a remote Essex forest. Here lives Mrs Bramson, an elderly *malade imaginaire* confined to a wheel-chair. Her household includes Olivia her long-suffering companion, Mrs Terence the cook and Dora the maid. A woman guest at a nearby hotel has recently been murdered and, unknown to the inhabitants of the cottage, her decapitated body is buried in the garden outside. Dan, a page-boy from the hotel who has impregnated Dora, calls to discuss the affair with her employer Mrs Bramson. The selfish old woman is charmed by his captivating ways and takes him into her service. He flatters her, encourages her belief that she is a chronic invalid, and is soon indispensable to her. Olivia, meanwhile, although intuitively suspecting that he is the murderer, has despite herself fallen in love with him. She, like Mrs Bramson, is fascinated by him. As the police inspector who finally arrests him puts it: "Plenty of women get a bit hysterical about a lad in your position. You'll find 'em queuing up all right when the time comes. Proposals of marriage by the score." It is Olivia who, when the inspector demands the key to a hat-box discovered in Dan's luggage, pretends that it belongs to her and that it is full of letters. It contains, in fact, the severed head of Dan's first victim.

His second victim is the doting Mrs Bramson whom he eventually murders for her cash box. Since the audience knows from the start that he is the culprit, the suspense of the play relies on his skill at evading the detective who is on his trail. A sense of irony sharpens the atmosphere. "I feel dead," moans Mrs Bramson in one of her frequent self-pitying moods as Dan wheels her back from a little excursion. "Don't you be a silly old woman," Dan chaffs her, "you look as pretty as a picture – strawberries and cream in your face, and not a day over forty; and when I've made you a nice cup of tea you'll be twenty-five in the sun and eighteen with your back to the light, so you think yourself lucky!" As he digs her in the side, Mrs Bramson gurgles: "Oh, Danny, you are a terror! He's been at me like this all the way. I must say it keeps me alive." "But you feel dead, I get you." "Oh, you caution!" says Mrs B, all kittenish. "You'll be the death of me!"

The two bravura parts in the play are Dan and Mrs Bramson. The latter is a monstrously self-indulgent creature, vain, avaricious, but an easy victim of Dan's wiles. Casting her was difficult. The obvious choice would have been Mrs Patrick Campbell. Fortunately she was not available, since, although she would have given a dazzling performance, her wayward habits would have destroyed the balance of the play. The name of Dame May Whitty was put forward. She was an actress of daunting experience, old enough to have appeared with Irving at the Lyceum and on his American tours in the eighteen-nineties. As a veteran exponent of Barrie, Milne, Pinero and Lonsdale, she tended to overshadow her husband Ben Webster who was of a similar vintage. Damehood had come her way thanks to an insatiable gusto for committe work, much of it devoted to the founding of Equity, the actors' trade union. Hitchcock's film *The Lady Vanishes* brought her a much wider audience as the absent-minded Miss Fray. In 1939, at the age of seventy-four, she left England permanently for Hollywood and enjoyed a new career into her eighties as a dithering old lady, plump-cheeked, very British, tremulous-toned, and given to clutching capacious handbags of an unfashionable design. She was an accomplished executant, as sure and formidable in her way as Marie Tempest. With not much enthusiasm she accepted the part of Mrs Bramson. The director of *Night Must Fall* was to be Miles Malleson. He was a prolific dramatist and actor whose face was his fortune: hair tousled, nose sharp as a parrot's, mouth gaping like a fish, jowls a-quiver, voice gabbling nervously. These attributes made him an ideal Shakespearean comic as Andrew Aguecheek, Silence, Lancelot Gobbo, Quince and Snout. His private life was as busy as his professional career, for on the way he acquired and discarded three wives. Malleson had been asked to direct because Emlyn himself was playing the major role of Dan. When Emlyn had made up with his blue pill-box hat, uniform trousers and bicycle clips, rather too small jacket and fag-end dangling from his lips, he felt there was something lacking. On a visit to the Thames-side bungalow he found in a drawer the old pair of shoes Fess had left behind. He wore them for the run of the play. Fetishism became realism.

For Dan was Fess, even unto the rough Welsh accent. He had the charm of Fess, the worldly wisdom, the nonchalance, the aura of danger. He was what Fess might easily have become, graduating by way of petty theft and forgery to the worst crime of all. Reviews of Emlyn's performance, chill and menacing, described it as "a study in schizophrenia". He had to look the word up in a dictionary. The other rôles, except for that of Mrs Bramson, were for stock characters but well written – Olivia's suitor, for example, was Basil Radford, round-cheeked and avuncular, incarnation of the very English cricket-loving chump. The cook was Kathleen Harrison, Mitchelhill's protégée, a diminutive Cockney with tightly curled hair inaugurating her series of low-comedy barmaids and serving-women. The heroine Olivia was played with tact and sympathy by Angela Baddeley, sister of Hermione and wife of Glen Byam Shaw, who became a special friend of Emlyn. As Mrs Bramson, Dame May Whitty soon realised that her part offered a unique opportunity to be grasped with all the skill of which she was mistress. She even subdued the recalcitrant wheel-chair in which she spent the whole of the play and learned to manoeuvre it with virtuoso ease around chairs and tables. On one occasion, though, an unexpected slant in the stage sent her careering down to the footlights. Only at the last minute was she able to apply the brake as the chair slewed round, and she played the rest of the scene with her back to the audience. She could be as domineering as the character she impersonated. Claiming to have a weak heart she demanded for herself the star dressing-room on a level with the stage so that she could avoid a wearisome climb upstairs. The Dame knew, and Emlyn knew, that her heart was the strongest thing about her. Emlyn reminded her that he had written the star part for himself and that she was not Mrs Patrick Campbell. Steel clashed on steel. Emlyn won.

Night Must Fall went on a short pre-London tour. It opened at the King's Theatre in Edinburgh and earned a modest weekly return of £437. In Newcastle the week's takings fell to £321, about a seventh of total capacity. Glasgow did no better. Would Mitchelhill change his mind? At the last minute a telephone call reported that Priestley's *Cornelius* was closing after only a few weeks' run at the Duchess and that Mitchelhill had no choice other than to book *Night Must Fall* into his theatre.

They opened on May 31, 1935. The dire omens of the provincial tour were immediately contradicted. In this case, as Emlyn wryly noted, what the provinces thought today London certainly did not think tomorrow. His play was an instant triumph, for himself as author and actor, for the Dame, for the whole cast. It ran at the Duchess for over a year and then transferred to the Cambridge Theatre for another six months. In Paris, as *l'Homme qui se donnait la comédie*, the part of Dan gave to Pierre Brasseur, that sinister, peaky-faced master of villainy, a ripe occasion for his disquieting talent, while Bernard Blier, the classic good-natured fool, was a perfect Gallic counterpart to Basil Radford. *Night Must Fall* went out on many provincial tours, emerged unexpectedly in far-off Scandinavian townships, could be seen from time to time in places as far apart as Poughkeepsie and Toronto, was revived on many occasions, and eventually subsided into a long and lucrative existence in repertory. Throughout the years Emlyn received a procession of young actors who called to pay their respects in his dressing-room and to tell him reverently of how their first big chance in the theatre had been the rôle of Dan.

One discordant voice, however, rang out amid the general acclaim. It belonged to Sean O'Casey. In his time he had suffered much from critics, and his book *The Flying Wasp* assailed the whole tribe of them with hearty invective. How, he asked, could the critics have been deceived by the rubbish that currently occupied the London stage? His "laughing look-over at what has been said about the things of the theatre by the English dramatic critics" devoted three biting chapters entitled "Coward Codology" to demolishing the author of *Private Lives*. Another, which he called "Murdher In The Theatre", attacked the enemy, among them Agate as "the dear old dean of the English critics," for having hailed the "brilliant matter-of-factness" of *Night Must Fall*. Where was the brilliance, and where the realism, demanded O'Casey, of a play that had less of life and real people than *A Midsummer Night's Dream* or Strindberg's *The Dream Play*? Which of us carries a human head around in a hatbox? Do women always fall for "insane young ruffians". As a working dramatist himself, O'Casey had no trouble in exposing the various theatrical tricks which had been used to forward the action. For O'Casey the real masterpiece of modern English theatre was *Murder In The Cathedral*. It is clear that he was not comparing like with like. Sullivan is not Mozart, John Buchan is not Dickens, Samuel Palmer is not Titian. Emlyn's entertainment on this subject of "murdher", as O'Casey jestingly termed it, was not meant to rival *Othello* or *Macbeth*. As Emlyn once remarked: "I aim to tell a story that interests the audience, that entertains, arouses, fascinates and if possible moves them . . . I see myself as a storyteller."

Night Must Fall was among the biggest successes of 1935. Old friends shared in the triumph. Charles Laughton saw it twice, as did Noël Coward. Lloyd George and his daughter Megan, whom Emlyn had once tutored in French, watched a matinée. To Emlyn's dressing-room came Laurence Olivier bringing with him the young actress Vivien Leigh whom he had just met for the first time in the audience. After the show they went out to Lyons Corner House in the Strand where Olivier, in despair at his own lack of success compared with Emlyn's brilliant début, remained hopeless and depressed. At three o'clock in the morning he was still protesting: "I'm washed up – I'll never make it!" Nothing Emlyn or Molly said would cheer him up.

Early in the afternoon matinée of August 28 a prearranged signal from the wings told Emlyn the news he had been waiting for. As soon as he made his exit he learned the details: his son Alan Emlyn had been born at 12.45 that day, 6lb 10 oz, nineteen inches high. Never had a matinée seemed longer. At the fall of the curtain he dashed off to the nursing home at 27, Welbeck Street and found Molly sitting up in bed filing her nails with supreme nonchalance. "It was the most peculiar feeling!" he told Miss Cooke. "He's (apparently) very like me – with quite a lot of black hair, and apparently very big blue eyes (which he's hardly opened yet) – the biggest in the nursery . . . I would have been *terribly* disappointed if it had been a girl – but daren't say so – even to Molly . . ." He went out and bought her a diamond clip, the first piece of jewellery she'd ever had. Noël Coward and John Gielgud bearing flowers joined the cast on stage for champagne after the evening performance, and the Dame proposed a toast to little Alan. "It was tactless of the boy not to arrive in the middle of the 100th performance," Emlyn joked to Miss Cooke, "but you can't expect his publicity sense to be developed quite so young." Later that year, on October 3, Alan was christened at Chelsea Old Church. His godfathers were Noël Coward and John Gielgud. The occasion, Gielgud recalls, was "hilarious".

The play ran on and on, interrupted only by the death of King George V in January, 1936. The Dame caused annoyance again. Not only was she a belligerent Christian Scientist, she was also ". . . a Socialist and has shocked everybody by her callous bad taste – she wanted the theatre open the night of the King's death *and* the funeral," Miss Cooke was told, "in spite of the fact it was the late King who gave her the Dameship which has made her a lady, succeeding where Nature has so signally failed. I say she's a Socialist, but it doesn't prevent her making her chauffeur call her 'your ladyship'. Isn't it incredible?" Emlyn and Molly watched the funeral procession from the window of a restaurant in St James's and saw the new King looking "so small and bewildered, in an overcoat and shoes that seemed much too big for him". Noël Coward treated Emlyn to lunch and a matinée of *Romeo and Juliet*, which helped to ease irritation inspired by the Dame – though it returned when Emlyn heard that, unlike *Night Must Fall* and all the other West End attractions, Noël's *Tonight at 8.30* was the only play to continue with packed houses throughout the week of the funeral.

Night Must Fall soon picked up, however, and other projects tempted him. Would he accept the post of BBC Programme Director for Wales? He remembered a broadcast he had done recently, "live" as all broadcasts were then, of Clemence Dane's *Will Shakespeare*. It was a paralysing experience in a windowless dungeon before a grey metal robot of a microphone. The actors turned the pages of their script as if they had been made of spun glass, fearing the slightest rustle, terrified by the unwinking eye of the baleful red light. This, Emlyn thought, was not acting. He did not enjoy broadcasting and he never would. He decided not to become BBC Programme Director for Wales. He did, though, as we know already, write the scenario and dialogue for a British re-make of *Broken Blossoms*, the old D. W. Griffith film. In addition he played the Richard Barthelmess part in an unconvincing "Chinese" make-up. Among his fellow players were Kathleen Harrison and Basil Radford with whom he acted each evening on stage in *Night Must Fall*. His was a chance piece of casting. While showing an unknown actor at auditions how to play the part of the romantic young Chinaman, he had so impressed Griffith that the famous director insisted he do it himself. If the film as a whole failed to improve on the original, the dialogue at least captivated audiences with its natural quality, despite the Célinesque emphasis on savagery and squalor.

By the autumn of 1936 *Night Must Fall* had completed its West End run and Emlyn, with Molly, set off on the *Queen Mary* for the New York production. Alan and nurse joined them later on the *Aquitania*. When Emlyn landed and saw his play billed as "The Spine-Chilling British Melodrama!" he felt misgiving. His premonition was correct. The play ran only for eight weeks. Consolation appeared in the shape of a Hollywood offer. The actor Robert Montgomery had seen *Night Must Fall* three or four times while in London and wanted it for himself. He had wearied of the glossy films in which MGM insisted on casting him, usually as a foil to glamorous properties like Joan Crawford. In the role of Dan he saw an opportunity to break away from his stereotyped image with some raw, powerful acting for once. He persuaded MGM to buy the film rights, and the management, with whom he was not popular, agreed to do so in the secret hope that the unsympathetic part might damage his reputation and rid them of an awkward employee. In the event he made a success of it, with Rosalind Russell as Olivia and the Dame playing her original part. But afterwards MGM still did not know quite what to do about him, and he languished as before. Emlyn, for one, had no doubt about Montgomery's excellence as Dan, and was flattered that so handsome, so elegant an actor should have trodden in his footsteps.

As *Night Must Fall* trickled to a dismal closure on Broadway Emlyn looked elsewhere for light relief. On his dressing-table stood a photograph of Alan, quite the most beautiful baby ever born, and, certainly, a genius: would he not be walking in a week or two? What other baby had ever done this before? Depression at the failure of the play was lightened by an invitation to a party at the Riverside Drive home of a billionaire. The house resembled the British Museum, with real Gobelins tapestries, real Rembrandts, and real gold taps in the bathroom. Pencils studded with rubies and pearls lay on tables. There were false book-fronts which dropped down when you pressed a button to reveal bottles of drink. By contrast, the Marshall Field home on Long Island represented the triumph of "old" money: to ensure there were no minor lapses of taste, a whole panelled room had been brought over bodily from Paris and reassembled on the spot.

John Gielgud was also in New York playing *Hamlet* and, despite a personal success, longing to be back in London and to start on a new venture he planned with Emlyn. Before he went to New York, while making up as Noah in André Obey's play, his face aureoled in a massive beard and his eyebrows bushy as thickets, he looked at Emlyn in his dressing-room mirror and said: "Why don't you write a play for me?" Soon afterwards Emlyn happened to read a book called *The Son of Marie Antoinette*. It cost 15 shillings, which he thought cheap for the idea it gave him, that of a drama about the lost Dauphin who would have become King XVII of France had he survived. "*Il est ńe gai*", said Marie-Antoinette of her child, a remark which suggested the title of his new play, *He Was Born Gay*. ("Unfortunate title, I fear," as Sir John Gielgud says nowadays.) Emlyn wrote it during the run of *Night Must Fall* and looked forward to repeating the happy collaboration with Gielgud which they had enjoyed in *Spring, 1600*. Calmly, reasonably, he had made with the best of will all the cuts and alterations Gielgud tentatively put forward. Once, Gielgud suggested, a scene was unduly encumbered with the names of flowers which held up the action. Might they not be cut? "By all means," Emlyn cheerfully agreed. "We don't want James Agate to head his Sunday article, 'Herrick, or little by little!' "

The same harmony informed their preparations for *He Was Born Gay*. They chose the beautiful American actress Carol Goodner to play the heroine.[1] Gielgud would be the Dauphin and Emlyn the sinister agent who encompasses his death. For the part of an eccentric old noblewoman Gielgud remembered an actress called Ada King. She was short, red-faced and sandy of hair. When not acting she wore gold-rimmed pince-nez jammed on her large nose. In *Henry VIII* she had been pure Holbein, and in *Cyrano de Bergerac* she looked, with her feathered hat, as if she had just stepped out of a Callot etching. She read the script of *He Was Born Gay* and arrived clad in her pince-nez and a fur tippet secured by a glum fox's mask. Flattered she was that the young men should remember her, and interested by the part. "But my memory is no longer as good as it once was," she finally added, "and I am afraid I could not dream of accepting an engagement nowadays unless I had several weeks beforehand to study and memorise my lines." Whereupon she picked up her umbrella, fur tippet a-jangle, and swept out of their lives into Shaftesbury Avenue.

He Was Born Gay went off on a short tour of those very towns where *Night Must Fall* had done so badly. Unlike its predecessor it played to record business. Emlyn's mother asked how it was doing in Manchester. "Sold out," Emlyn proudly replied, "standing room only." "Ah," said she, "London's the mischief." She was right. *He Was Born Gay* ran for twelve performances at the Queen's Theatre and closed abruptly.

The year is 1815 and the setting a house on the cliffs near Dover. The period is adroitly evoked – somebody says à propos of *Childe Harold*, "I hear it's a dirty book" – and the atmosphere of Regency England just before Waterloo is neatly captured. Problems begin once the maze of complications is embarked upon: Mrs Dell's provincial home is invaded by not one Dauphin claimant but, as the action develops, three of them. Two are obvious imposters, and the audience knew immediately that only one of them, that played by Gielgud, could be the real Dauphin, so truly royal were his gestures, so commanding was his voice. What Agate called his "exquisite Gielgudry" throbbed out nobly in a purple patch like: "A great murmur of voices, in low concert, like the leaves of the forest under the wind, and all breathing

---

[1] In a restaurant one evening James Agate was holding forth as usual about Sarah Bernhardt. "There", he said loudly, "was a personality. You would have recognised Sarah at the bottom of a coal-mine. Modern actresses have no personality. I suppose I have seen Carol Goodner and Constance Cummings twenty times at least. But if they were to walk into this restaurant now I wouldn't be able to tell t'other from which!" Two ladies at a nearby table, whose beauty he had already noted, sat up like offended rattlesnakes. "Those," whispered his companions simultaneously, "are Carol Goodner and Constance Cummings."

one name . . . Mine . . . A million faces watching as a coach is drawn by white horses through the cities and along the country roads . . . down the avenues of poplar trees . . . up the great steps . . . through the hall of a thousand mirrors . . . past the lackeys . . . past the regiment of proud faces staring from the drapes in panoplies of gold . . . past the panels, the dolphins and the eagles . . . the tinkle of the little harpsichords, the gleam of the needle, the rustle of embroidery against the skirts, the scent of powder, mother, *Maman*. This is my kingdom."

What went wrong with *He Was Born Gay*? First, Emlyn and Gielgud were young and successful, reason enough for critics to pounce with delight. Had the occasion been a first play it might have been treated more kindly. Second, and more substantial reason, the "romance in three acts", as Emlyn described it, offered too rich and varied a mixture of elements: poetry, comedy, tragedy and even dabs of farce. "He was most generous and sweet about the failure," says Sir John. He did not repine, either. Two months later, in August, 1937, he went to Buxton Opera House and played Oswald in Ibsen's *Ghosts*. There, as well, he was Angelo in *Measure for Measure*, a performance which he repeated at the Old Vic later that year. James Agate was struck by the "strange perversity" of the production. "Mr Emlyn Williams," he wrote, "unbelievably cast as Angelo, extricates himself from a fake position with diabolical ingenuity, playing throughout with the fervour of a man possessed. This is a feat of sheer acting, and promises well for the future. If Mr Williams can impress like this when he is unsuited, what will he do when he is suited? In addition, he speaks the verse beautifully . . ."

At the Old Vic, too, he was Richard Duke of Gloucester in *Richard III*, "a synthesis of cat and goblin, with a startling first pounce from the back of the stage to the footlights," recorded J. C. Trewin. Alan Dent wrote: "Here is the man of blood, and the satirical rogue, and the malformed gnome with a grouch against good health. He smiles and smiles, but we know him for a villain whose villainy those pale peers and prelates on the stage can conceivably not disown. Vocally the performance is all a shade too light, and in the earlier scenes the intonation is now and again too distinctly Welsh. But the right conception is there . . ." Emlyn's interpretation was, James Agate decided, "Quite rightly, Saturday-nightish, since a lot of the part is obviously written to be ranted. But the ranting is beautifully done, and throughout we hear every syllable of every word . . . what we are privileged to see is a fine player in the process of turning himself into a fine Shakespearean player." Such was Agate's public opinion, deployed majestically across the pages of the *Sunday Times*. In private, however, his view was more succinct; the entry in his diary reads: "Emlyn good second-rate, for he terrifies only the audience, whereas a first-rate Richard frightens his fellow-players."

Films claimed Emlyn during the day when he was not acting at the Old Vic. In *The Citadel*, based on A. J. Cronin's best-selling novel, he was reunited with his old friend Robert Donat. *Dead Men Tell No Tales* gave him more scope as a murderous headmaster who doubles as a hunchbacked money-lender and connives at the suicide by hanging of a school teacher on his staff. At the end, supping full of horrors, he abducts the heroine and cuts his own throat with a piece of glass. The best film he made in 1938 was *They Drive By Night* in which he played an ex-convict newly released from prison who goes to visit his former girl-friend. He finds her strangled, and, fearing that he will be accused of the crime, takes flight. A lorry driver gives him a lift northwards and he hides in an empty house with the aid of a girl whom he has saved from rape. Together they track down the murderer of his girl-friend and, after many adventures, bring him to justice. The film was, Emlyn remarked, "Very nice, very sordid." It was tautly directed and exquisitely photographed to create haunting images of rainy streets, lorries roaring through the night, steamy little roadside cafés. Although you knew that Emlyn, edgy and unshaven, was innocent, the power of his acting was such that you felt he might, just might, have been guilty of the strangling. An excellent cast supported him, among them that magnificent gargoyle Ernest Thesiger, here displaying his talent for the Gothic as a crazed assassin. Every performance by Thesiger – and he appeared in scores of films and plays over the years until he reached a great age – was a *tour de force* made memorable by his cadaverous profile and shrivelled stature and mincing diction. He was just as baroque off-stage. One day, on a visit to his old school Marlborough for dinner with the Senior Master, he could not keep his eyes off a particularly well-built sixth-form lad. He afterwards confided in his host: "I'd give *anything* to be that boy's mother." In London, much encumbered with parcels, he was about to board a bus, one foot on, one foot off, when it suddenly started and began dragging him along. "Stop! Stop!" he fluted loudly, "you're killing a genius!" The conductor heard him and Thesiger was saved by the bell.

The most curious of Emlyn's film experiences at this time involved *I, Claudius*. He had already discussed ideas for films with Alexander Korda, among them a life of Nijinsky and an account of the

Rattenbury murder case. Neither of these came to fruition and he found himself engaged instead to play Caligula in the version of Robert Graves's novel which Korda had bought as a medium for his star Charles Laughton. This was planned to be a very great epic indeed. Together with Laughton as the stuttering, limping Claudius were Merle Oberon as Messalina and Flora Robson as the octogenarian dowager empress. Korda charged Josef von Sternberg with the direction. Born Jo Stern in a lower-class Viennese family, the megalomaniac director adopted the nobiliary particle for himself early in a career which he firmly based on the notion that actors were plasticine to be shaped by the genius of the director. After seven years devoted to creating an icon, Marlene Dietrich, he had reached a state of exhaustion. Korda's offer shook him out of the nervous breakdown in which he was currently luxuriating, and he rose from his bed at the London Clinic relishing the battle ahead. For battle it was, between a sensitive, vulnerable Laughton pining for sympathetic direction and a tyrant who regarded him and all other actors as trash. Emlyn found Sternberg (or "Mr Josef von Sternberg", as Emlyn always called him with feline courtesy), very polite and considerate. The noble German was kind enough to describe him as "a bright young man." When Merle Oberon was hurt in a car crash soon after work had begun, the film was abandoned. It would have foundered anyway, for there could be no reconciliation of two such different personalities as Laughton and Sternberg. The director marched on to the set adorned in lace-up thigh boots, riding breeches and a colourful turban. At other times he simply wore a dressing-gown. The melancholy episode ended with less than half an hour's footage completed. What might have been a great performance by Laughton, as is hinted by the fragments that remain, was aborted. Emlyn, too, distinguished himself with an exhibition of high campery as the epicene Caligula. His small pallid features were topped by dainty black ringleted hair, his full lips pouted and leered, his voice hissed pettishly, and he wore a brief toga which ended just above the knee, "my little cocktail party number", as he called it. There is a scene where he orders Claudius to marry Messalina and bursts into hysterical laughter. It is beautifully done, the giggle rising irresistibly from the lungs, then flowering into a high-pitched cackle to be on a sudden cut short by an ominous frown. Such moments were few, since, as usual, he spent most of the time lounging around the set in full make-up. The hours were not wasted. During the long waits he covered page upon page with dialogue for a new play he felt welling up inside him.

He went on writing it at Kitzbühel where he holidayed with his family. Another holiday, this time at Dymchurch, the little seaside resort on the Kent coast near Folkestone, was spent in the former Georgian rectory where he completed the bulk of the first draft while Alan played on the lawn outside. Finishing touches were added in Monte Carlo. Holidays, film sets and waits between entrances on stage proved to be ideal occasions for serious writing. It had all begun when Molly said to him one day: "Why don't you write a play about Miss Cooke?" She was, after all, the largest single influence in his life, the woman who had sensed his promise, taught him, encouraged him, subsidised him, helped him in every possible way. He still wrote to her several times a week, always ending "Yours affectionately, George", in full, as she had instructed him to do when he was a boy. At first the idea had seemed too close to reality. Then it bodied forth shadowily in his mind. The manuscript went off to the typist in March, 1938. Apart from setting it well back in the nineteenth century, Emlyn told his own story in *The Corn Is Green*, a title which, despite sounding like a quotation from a poem, is in fact a phrase written by the young hero in an essay which for the first time convinces the teacher of his talent. This, then, is a stage version of Emlyn's autobiography, except that, for reasons of dramatic conflict, the boy is seduced by a local hussy who becomes pregnant and so jeopardises his chance of an Oxford career. The impasse is resolved by his teacher quietly paying off the mother and adopting the baby. For those who knew the real Miss Cooke, such a gesture would have been fully in character.

"It would be useless to pretend," Emlyn wrote to her enclosing the typescript of *The Corn Is Green*, "that the character of Miss Moffat is not based very largely on yourself, though as you'd realise there has to be a great deal of dramatic licence – as you yourself have so often said to me 'The essence of drama must be a struggle' and I had to invent a situation of combat and antagonism with the boy and girl, and of course the end is completely away from the original. I hope you'll find a great deal to amuse and please you and nothing to offend or annoy – if you do, I'll change it, but you may rest assured that anything that may offend or annoy is something brought in to make the play more effective and not based upon you! As you know, there could be no completely accurate representation of a real person on the stage; in the most realistic play you have to add and subtract. It is like highlights in a painting, I suppose." Not without trepidation, he sent off the parcel to Holywell.

A reply came very quickly. "Well, here I am writing – *but can't say anything*. Reading it gives me a most curious feeling. Of course you said nothing to hurt me. But what can I say? If I say 'far too flattering', it sounds as tho' I'm very self-satisfied. It is all so unreal in its reality that I can't believe it is there in black and white. Here are some *remarks*: several times I put it down to laugh heartily, that is the quips were so funny that I forgot everything in the sheer delight at the humour . . ." With a feeling of relief, he appended the dedication: "To SGC", that is, Sarah Grace Cooke.

The Corn Is Green was turned down by Binkie Beaumont, Emlyn's compatriot who by then had reached the height of his power and glory as arbiter of the West End stage. Beaumont's reason echoed, strangely enough, Miss Cooke's first reaction: the public was not interested in education. The play was taken up by Stephen Mitchell, a thirty-year-old producer from Aberdeen. Originally intended for the Bar, he decided instead, after taking his law degree, to go into the theatre where his energy and his *suaviter in modo sed fortiter in re* brought him high distinction. Later, despite his opinion of Binkie as "a bastard", he collaborated with him in presenting several other plays by Emlyn, although he was to find that Binkie, despite his rugged business methods, was in private matters a kindly and understanding man. After a "good" war in the Gordon Highlanders, Mitchell resumed his career and sponsored many famous productions. *The Corn Is Green* brought him his first big success. From his near namesake J. P. Mitchelhill he rented the Duchess Theatre, home of *Night Must Fall*, and cast Sybil Thorndike as Miss Moffat. It was Sybil of whom Emlyn first thought when writing the part. The role of the bright young scholar Morgan was difficult. Emlyn did not want it since he was directing as well. Eventually, and since Marius Goring was not available, he found himself, yet again, playing a part he had never intended to take. Mitchell was impressed by his attention to detail, his meticulous regard for planning the smallest moves, his unerring eye for effect. Another aspect of Emlyn emerged. The Kensington flat where Mitchell then lived faced a building frequented by a particularly vile murderer since despatched. On visits to Mitchell Emlyn would stand for long periods at the window, arms crossed, gazing in silent fascination at the place opposite.

The Corn Is Green had its première on September 20, 1938, after a brief provincial tour. It was an immediate hit. Alan Dent, a Hardy admirer, made a fruitful comparison between *Jude The Obscure* and "this tender little play". Emlyn's acting, he added, "at the head of a shining company whose other tower is Dame Sybil Thorndike, is full of inarticulate poetry. Both the chief players have an unusual range of emotion, and the skill and subtlety of their interplaying are fascinating to watch." James Agate considered that the evening belonged "to Dame Sybil Thorndike, who gives one of the sincerest and tenderest performances of her career, and to Mr Emlyn Williams to whom, as author and actor, must go the credit of staging a man of genius whose genius is manifest and unquestioned. The simplicity of the story can be relied on to throw the spectator into a mood of acceptance of make-believe . . . If anybody should want to know whether I really enjoyed this play I can only say that Mr Williams, aided by Dame Sybil Thorndike, served, so far as I was concerned, two lumps-in-a-throat and a half lump. And I suggest this is a very fine score indeed." Despite the encomium, when Agate came behind after the first night to greet his old chum Sybil, Emlyn refused to see him. He took the prudent view that actors should not mingle with critics on a social basis.

Whereas in *He Was Born Gay* the lyricism tends to purple patches, in *The Corn Is Green* it stems naturally out of the action. After Miss Moffat's whirlwind first entrance has been deftly prepared in advance, she announces her aim of founding a school in the Welsh wilderness to rescue the miners' children from their illiteracy and from "mining gold down there in that stinking dungeon for some beef-headed old miser!" She continues: "The printed page, what is it? One of the miracles of all time, that's what! And yet when these poor babbies set eyes on it, they might just as well have been struck by the miracle of sudden blindness; and that, to my mind, is plain infamous!" And then, when one of those very Welsh characters whom Emlyn delighted to portray is inspired by Miss Moffat's ringing idealism and exuberates: "We have the blessed opportunity to raise up the children from the bowels of the earth where the devil hath imprisoned them in the powers of darkness, and bring them to the light of knowledge – ", he is suddenly brought to earth by the maid who bears in a huge steaming teapot and calls out shrilly: "Tea!"

By the end of Act I Miss Moffat has established her school despite opposition from the local mine-owner, the pub, the chapel, and has got to know Morgan, the pitboy. An essay he writes on the subject of "Holiday-time" catches her attention. She reads aloud: "The mine is dark . . . If a light come in the mine . . . the rivers in the mine will run fast with the voice of many women; the walls will fall in, and it will be the end of the world. So the mine is dark. But when I walk through the Tan – something – shaft, in the dark, I can touch with my hands the leaves on the trees, and underneath . . . where the corn is green. There is a fresh wind in the shaft, not carbon monoxide they talk about, it smell like the sea, only like as if the sea had fresh flowers lying about . . . and that is my holiday." This is the work of an orphan who spells deplorably and who learned to write English from the Bible and *The Ladies' Companion*. The glimpse of talent enthrals her. She coaxes him out of his sullenness and, between shifts down the mine, starts an ambitious teaching programme for "the most brilliantly receptive brain I've ever come across." She even teaches him Greek by the classic device of keeping several pages ahead of him in the text-book.

Two years later Morgan goes to Oxford and takes his Viva. When he returns, he tells Miss Moffat: "I have come back – from the world! Since the day I was born, I have been a prisoner behind a stone wall, and somebody has given me a leg-up to have a look at the other side . . . *(vehement)* they cannot drag me back again, they cannot, they *must* give me a push and send me over!" The thought of failure appals him. He speaks of walking down the High and of his sudden vision: "I saw this room; you and me sitting here studying, and all those books – and everything I have ever learnt from those books, and from you, was lighted up – like a magic lantern – ancient Rome, Greece, Shakespeare, Carlyle, Milton . . . everything had a meaning, because I was in a new world – my world! And so it came to me why you worked like a slave to make me ready for this scholarship . . ." The beacon his teacher has lit burns with a steady flame.

The clash between learning and the devil in the flesh is skilfully handled to provide the climax of Act III. When the telegram arrives with news that Morgan has won the scholarship, there is a bitter confrontation between teacher and pupil. He wants to give up the scholarship and marry the girl for the sake of his illegitimate son. Miss Moffat argues him out of the idea and offers to adopt the child. The obvious condition, she points out, is that she, Miss Moffat, must never see him again. He finally agrees and leaves her. As the curtain falls she prepares to welcome the four-week-old infant to her household and mutters: "Moffat, my girl, you mustn't be clumsy this time. You mustn't be clumsy . . ." She has made the ultimate sacrifice.

The supporting characters are drawn from stock. Kathleen Harrison as the Cockney servant and Frederick Lloyd as the blimpish, anti-woman, anti-education squire, provided effective comic relief. The play depends, however, on Miss Moffat and Morgan. The undercurrents of their relationship are subtly explored. Miss Moffat, one feels, is Miss Cooke to the life, replete with her hearty slang – she calls the children "nippers" and is given, as her original was, to the mock exclamation "I dunno" – and her granitic personality. Morgan's character grows organically throughout the play, from his initial wariness of the strange new universe where Miss Moffat leads him, right through to his final conviction that he must not fail either her or himself. For the rest of his life, though, Emlyn had frequently to rebut various misconceptions. No, he would say, he himself had never been down a mine. No, the play did not have a "message", he originally described it as a comedy. And, above all, Miss Moffat was definitely not in love with Morgan, just as Miss Cooke had never cherished the least sexual feeling for her pupil George Williams.

CHAPTER FOUR

(i)
"Our eternal love for each other . . ."

The home in Lincoln Street, roomy though it seemed at first, had become too small. The reason for this was the arrival of a second son on January 22, 1938. He made his debut, as had Alan, at 27, Welbeck Street. The boy was christened in Chelsea Old Church on May 12 with J. P. Mitchelhill as one of his godparents. In a reply once to a newspaper questionnaire which asked Emlyn his favourite name, he had said that it was Brook. The child therefore became Brook and, as a gesture to his paternal grandfather, Richard.

All the details of this event were entered in a scrapbook which Emlyn had begun to keep. Scrapbook is too modest a word, however, to describe the large and capacious volumes into which he now pasted the ephemera of his existence. Volume I covered the years 1869, date of his mother's birth, to 1932, the time of his appearance as Lord Lebanon in *The Case of the Frightened Lady*. Like its successors, it stood several feet high, contained many pages of thick paper, and, when full, was luxuriously bound in heavy leather. Gold lettering on the spine proclaimed the legend "Emlyn Williams and Family". This first volume contained everything he could find out about his origins. Although he was to say that "my family tree is the shortest in the wood," the material he unearthed was considerable. Here were old snaps and photographs, ancient newspaper cuttings, genealogical diagrams, letters, advertisements, and a sheaf of birth certificates. As time went on he added, besides the programmes and notices of plays and family snaps one might expect, an unusual variety of things. There were out-of-date passports and builders' estimates, legal agreements and insurance documents, hotel bills and labels, press cuttings about the Royal family and receipts, invitations and Christmas cards, old envelopes picked up in the street and even bits of thirty-five-millimetre film. He could throw nothing away. Life, for the writer, is "copy". Everything that happens to him, everything he sees and experiences, is material for his work. Nothing is real, nothing exists, until he has converted it into the written word. These giant volumes into which Emlyn lovingly pasted every small scrap were both an assurance that life really existed and a source of ideas.

The scrapbooks, unwieldy to the extent that only an able-bodied person with a strong pair of hands could carry them, were among the possessions transported from the Lincoln Street home which Molly had decreed was not large enough for a growing family. She found a house in South Kensington near Onslow Square, tall, high-windowed, at 15, Pelham Crescent, a fashionable ellipse which stood discreetly aloof from the bustle of Fulham Road. In 1939 vans drew up outside bearing the furniture she had gathered together during the four years of their marriage. It was still not enough to fill their spacious new home, so she embarked on another agreeable series of expeditions to antique shops and auction rooms. Georgian tables materialised, and gilt mirrors and swagged curtains and sideboards of mellow mahogany. Sunshine sparkled through the elegant windows and lit up vases of flowers. *Homes and Gardens* came to interview and remained to praise.

While Molly puzzled out where to hang an aquatint or how to choose the exact shade for a sofa cover, Emlyn tapped away undisturbed at his noisy little typewriter. He had been brought up in a home where the lavatory was an outside earth closet and where he cleaned his teeth with soot. It had taken Molly a long time to understand his Welsh roots and background. There had been, and there were to happen again in future, cross words over money. But they neither of them approved of long silences, and they were not, as Molly put it, "the china-throwing kind, so when we *do* disagree, we seem to have violent sulks that never last long." Their views about money were different. Although he was not mean, his Welsh background imposed simplicity, whereas Molly wanted to conjure up a setting of beauty as well as comfort. Miss Cooke came to her rescue and made him understand what she meant. Had he not quoted Miss Cooke verbatim when in *The Corn is Green* he gave Miss Moffat the lines: "Anyone can squander money, and anyone can hoard it. But the most difficult thing in the world is to know how to spend it"? And even though he at last saw Molly's point of view, he remained impervious to the constant flood of begging letters which fame brought him. One such, from a member of the Royal Air Force, demanded a loan of twenty pounds to buy himself out of the Service because he had always wanted to be in films and theatre. "You are my last resort. It is a matter of life and death," concluded the postscript.

The "last resort" filed it without comment in what became "Emlyn Williams and Family. Volume III. 1937–1943." You never knew. It might come in handy for a play or a film, a bit of dialogue or a possible situation.

By the standards of his penurious childhood he was a rich man now. As a star actor he drew a star salary and a percentage of the takings. As a dramatist he was paid a royalty and an ever-growing income from a network of subsidiary rights. The bare little cottage of his youth was replaced by a graceful house in fashionable Kensington, and the society of miners' children among whom he grew up was succeeded by the friendship of distinguished names in theatre and cinema. He stayed, however, close to his roots. The flow of money was directed, on advice, into shares that were safe and solid enough to gain the approval of Welsh thrift. So long as Molly had her fling with lovely objects for the house, he was content with only a small amount for his personal needs. His frugal instincts dictated that in London he travelled by bus rather than taxi. On the train he always took a third-class ticket. If ever he went by chauffeur-driven car it was at the expense of a theatre management or because public transport could not function to time. Food and drink did not interest him. His favourite dish was poached egg on toast, and he could eat it with the same relish day after day. At the theatre, after a performance, he would allow himself, as a special reward, one gin and a lot of tonic water as he changed into his street clothes. No dresser attended him because other people fussing about distracted him and he preferred to dress himself. Theatrical superstition did not trouble his Welsh matter-of-factness, and he happily made up in front of a mirror which, though he failed to notice it for weeks, had an ominous crack at the side.

Writing was all that really mattered to him. In the midst of family uproar, against a background where the Hoover throbbed and children shouted, he clattered away with one finger at the Underwood typewriter on his lap, oblivious to everything except the world he was creating on paper. As a child, so as a man, he found that the private universe in which he lived was more real than what went on around him. The world outside existed only insofar as it gave him the raw material he needed. A change of scenery made no difference. On holiday in Monte Carlo during the Easter of 1939, he worked even more productively, for in the hotel the telephone did not interrupt him with calls from his agent, from theatre managements, from film companies, as it did at home. Yet for all his absorption in work, he savoured family life, watched with pride as Brook essayed his first uncertain steps, and took an exuberant lead in all their outings and excursions together. Although he was not what Dr Johnson described as a "clubbable" man, when elected to the Garrick he accepted more as an honour than through any desire for the company to be found there. The entrance fee, he carefully noted in his records, was twenty-one pounds, and the library fee one guinea. Half the annual subscription amounted to eight guineas. A total of thirty pounds and nine shillings was duly listed among his disbursements.

Other and more substantial expenses followed. For some time now Molly had been arguing that the family needed a home in the country where they could escape the fret of London and where the children could breathe fresh air. She made numerous enjoyable tours of the Home Counties and eventually, escorted by Messrs Knight, Frank and Rutley, fixed on a property at North Moreton, about two miles from Didcot junction, three from Wallingford and ten from Oxford. Park End farmhouse was tucked away off a quiet country road. It had been built some four hundred years ago and was ripe for Molly's attention. There were four bedrooms on the first floor, and, on the second, two more. The cost of the freehold was £1500. *Night Must Fall* more than paid for it. Many improvements were carried out, and many renovations. Walls were stripped and panels renewed. The superb herringbone brickwork of an ancient fireplace emerged in its pristine glory. Chintz decorated the leaded light windows and heavy oak beams criss-crossed the ceilings. Two overgrown gardens, sternly taken in hand, were dug up and replanted to flower in a profusion of roses and carnations. At Pelham Crescent Molly had created a model town house. At Park End she brought into existence its rustic counterpart. By September, 1939, the new house was ready. Unfortunately, that was the month when Great Britain declared war on Germany.

With Park End completed Molly discovered a patriotic outlet for her energy by obtaining her Red Cross Certificate in First Aid. Emlyn found desultory war work as a censor of prisoners' letters at Wormwood Scrubs until both the government and Equity decided that he would be more usefully occupied giving employment to actors through his own writing than in censoring that of others. A black-out now expunged the glitter of night-time London, street lamps no longer shone, the headlights of cars were dimmed, and curtains veiled windows that once threw a welcoming beam into the gloom. While Molly and the children lived for the time being at Park End, Emlyn carried on in London with performances of *The Corn is Green*. When he called one day at the house in Pelham Crescent he learned it had suffered from attentions inspired by the black-out. Under cover of friendly darkness thieves had broken in and stolen between five and six hundred pounds' worth of Molly's jewellery and furs.

Miss Cooke travelled up to see herself impersonated on stage by Sybil Thorndike. Between the acts she was introduced to her. Two strong-willed females came face to face. They decided that they liked each other. Miss Cooke reminisced about Emlyn's boyhood and produced some of his old exercise books to be admired by her new friend. The ladies waxed maternal as Emlyn chatted loquaciously. Sybil became yet another of his acquaintances added to Miss Cooke's mailing list as the recipient of long, vigorous letters scribbled in her sprawling hand. Sybil was to give as good as she got: the bold handwriting of her own missives rarely averaged more than forty words to a page.

Emlyn's days were spent in film studios, his evenings in playing *The Corn is Green* which ran for a year and achieved nearly four hundred performances before it was temporarily halted in the autumn of 1939. He made a rare excursion into comedy with the film *Night Alone* where he was a solicitor from the provinces who goes on the spree in London and ends up drunk in the flat of a girl. She happens to be the mistress of a crook, and the police arrive to arrest the innocent man of law. The subsequent complications and the way he extricates himself from the imbroglio comprise the remainder of an entertainment forgotten almost as soon as it was made. Emlyn was, more characteristically, a sinister pedlar for Hitchcock's version of the du Maurier romance *Jamaica Inn*, another occasion when his old friend Charles Laughton pitted his genius against a director who did not quite know how to handle him. In *The Stars Look Down*, Carol Reed's adaptation of A. J. Cronin's realistic novel about labour troubles in a north-country mining district, Emlyn acted the part of a small-time bookmaker intent on the downfall of the hero (Michael Redgrave), with whom he had quarrelled over a girl, (Margaret Lockwood). This was one of his more successful film rôles, well integrated, carefully thought out. Carol Reed also directed him in *The Girl In The News*, a romantic thriller again with Margaret Lockwood. And then there was *You Will Remember*, a film biography of the composer Leslie Stuart who wrote the operetta *Floradora* and those eternal melodies "Soldiers Of The Queen" and "The Lily Of Laguna". Robert Morley played Stuart, a man whose open-handed talent brought him from rags to riches and back to rags once more. As one goes through the films in which Emlyn appeared so industriously at this period one recalls that

Emlyn at the age of six or thereabouts. Stifled by the repressive atmosphere of Welsh chapel-going and the constant threat of poverty, he withdrew into a solitary life of imagination. Between the ages of thirteen and fifteen he had already written a novel, a drama and two unfinished romances.

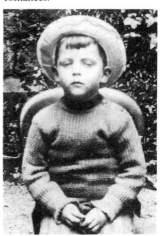

y Williams, lady's maid, deeply
s wife of Richard, whose
ken escapades revolted her,
gh she loved him still. Yet
never had a satisfactory
ionship with her son Emlyn.

Richard Williams, who in his time was ship's stoker, grocer, publican and labourer. Much given to drink as a young man, with increasing age he sobered up and lapsed into awe at the rise to fame of his eldest son Emlyn.

The White Lion inn, where Emlyn spent much of his childhood, still stands in Glanrafon, North Wales. Richard Williams was the licensee from 1906 to 1915 and drank away any profits. Here he stands outside with the infant Emlyn and one of Emlyn's aunts.

The young Miss Grace Cooke on her graduation day. She grew up into a formidable teacher who discerned the boy Emlyn's intellectual promise, helped him financially and encouraged him via scholarships to Oxford. For the rest of her life he wrote to her at least once and often several times a week.

Emlyn with an elderly Miss Cooke (RIGHT) whom Bette Davis (LEFT) played in the film of his autobiographical *The Corn Is Green*. A tough, strong-willed woman in the mould of Miss Cooke, Davis admired Emlyn and starred in *Miss Moffat*, the unsuccessful musical based on the play

Cronin Wilson, a solid, reliable actor of [se]rious origins, supposedly royal. Emlyn found [i]n the 'friend', the 'elder brother', he had looked [a]ll his life. Their deep emotional relationship [sur]vived the older man's alcoholism and frequent [quar]rels. Bill's death prostrated his young lover.

Emlyn in 1928 at his London flat. This was the year of his first London play, *Glamour*, staged at the Embassy Theatre. Two others, *Vigil* and *Full Moon*, had been produced by the OUDS while he was still at Oxford.

[Eml]yn the university student in drag for an OUDS [pla]ye. Miss Cooke disapproved and preferred him in [OU]DS productions of Shakespeare, Ibsen, Shaw and [vari]ous French plays. He also appeared in the OUDS [pro]duction of his own play *Vigil*.

Miss Molly O'Shann, reluctant actress, who after her divorce became Mrs Emlyn Williams. The happy couple started their married life in a curious *ménage à trois* which also included Emlyn's young Welsh lover Fess. Molly was a talented home maker and much adored by her husband and family.

Emlyn as Dan, the psychopathic killer in *Night Must Fall* (1935), his first great success. It was also the first of many roles in which he showed his talent for depicting villainy. His lifelong obsession with abnormal psychology was to culminate in *Beyond Belief* (1967), a detailed study of the notorious Moors murders.

One of the earliest of the thirty or so films Eml appeared in was *Friday The 13th* (1934), for whic he also provided an ingenious screenplay. Seen with Belle Chrystall, he played an odious blackma unctuous and menacing. Others in an all-star cas included Ralph Richardson, Jessie Matthews, Robertson Hare, Gordon Harker and Max Mille

The christening of Emlyn's first-born son Alan in 1936. LEFT TO RIGHT: John Gielgud, his hat partly obscuring Emlyn; Miss Cooke; Dame May Whitty from the cast of *Night Must Fall*, a prima donna whom Emlyn tamed nonetheless; the godfather Noël Coward; and Molly Williams.

Right Emlyn as Caligula in *I Claudius* (1936), Alexander Korda's ambitious attempt to film the Graves novel dire by the flamboyant Joseph von Sternberg. Although unfinished, this 'film that never was' might have been Cha Laughton's greatest achievement as the stuttering, limpin Emperor. Emlyn himself, in the few scenes that were completed, gave an eerily effeminate and vicious characterisation.

flections in a mirror: Emlyn (LEFT) as the spy
mbert and John Gielgud (RIGHT) as the Dauphin
He Was Born Gay (1938) – 'unfortunate title, I
r', says Sir John today. This drama about the lost
uphin of France was the second of Emlyn's plays
be directed by Gielgud, the first having been
ing, 1600 (1934), a lyrical episode about the
zabethan stage with a walk-on part for
kespeare.

The rising young star Mr Emlyn Williams in 1931,
soon after he had established himself in the West
End opposite Charles Laughton in Edgar Wallace's
thriller *On The Spot*. A few months later, in another
Wallace melodrama, *The Case of The Frightened Lady*,
Emlyn played what he claimed was his favourite part,
that of the insane Lord Lebanon.

Much impressed at audition by the gifts of his fellow Welshman the young Richard Burton, whom he took up as his protégé, Emlyn cast him in his new comedy *The Druid's Rest* (1944), Burton's first part on the West End stage. Though often exasperated by Burton's drunken escapades, Emlyn always forgave him for the sake of his talent. In this scene from *The Druid's Rest* Burton is second from left. Others (LEFT TO RIGHT) are Lyn Evans, Brynmor Thomas, Roddy Hughes and Gladys Henson, the last two being favourites of Emlyn who often wrote parts for them in his plays.

Emlyn as Will Trenting in *Accolade* (1950). Famous and much honoured in public, the Nobel prizewinning novelist Trenting leads a private life of debauchery with under-age Lolitas. Would he, the argument runs, be such a brilliant, comprehensive writer without this *nostalgie de la boue*? Some thought the play verged on the autobiographical.

Leading members of the ca in the first production of 7 *Corn Is Green* (1938), based on Emlyn's early career an his relationship with Miss Cooke. Circumstances obliged him to play the lea LEFT TO RIGHT: Emlyn as t young miner Morgan Evar Christine Silver; Kathleen Harrison, another of Emlyn's favourite actresse Frederick Lloyd as the peppery local squire; John Glyn Jones; Sybil Thorndi as the inspired and inspiri Miss Cooke; and Betty Jardine.

...nlyn as Shylock in the Stratford *Merchant of Venice* ...56). During the same season he also played Iago ... Harry Andrews' Othello and Angelo in *Measure ... Measure*. These, with Angelo and the Duke of ...oucester in *Richard III* at the Old Vic in 1937, ...re the sum total of his Shakespearean roles. ...everly profiting from his own physical and vocal ...aracteristics (and disadvantages), on each occasion ... inspired controversy.

Emlyn with Alison Leggatt in Harold Pinter's play *A Slight Ache* (1961). Instead of being outraged, as was Noël Coward, by the 'angry young men' who changed the face of the theatre Emlyn had grown up in, he was intrigued by, and a little envious of, their new-found freedom. The Pinter piece, one of a triple bill also featuring John Mortimer's *Lunch Hour* and N F Simpson's *The Form*, enabled him to give three virtuoso performances in plays entirely different from his own.

Family life was important to Emlyn. It was a haven to which he retreated from a hyper-active professional round and the strain of emotional pressures. Here, prematurely white-haired as all the Williams's were, he stands with his two sons Alan (front) and Brook. By a pleasing symmetry, they were between them to inherit his artistic gifts, Alan as writer and Brook as actor.

In later years Emlyn started a new career of one-man shows as Charles Dickens. His 'readings', in the flamboyant style of the great novelist, were actually performances in which he spoke from memory while using dummy books as props. Between 1951 and 1986 he gave 2,261 Dickens performances throughout the world.

All his life Emlyn had admired the witty short stories of 'Saki'. In 1977, under the title *The Playboy of the Weekend World*, he launched a series of one-man shows in which, languid and dandified, he despatched 'Saki's' heartless epigrams with elegant relish.

Emlyn's compatriot Dylan Thomas was a natural choice for a Welshman of exuberant eloquence. *A Boy Growing Up*, the one-man show he alternated with Dickens and 'Saki', began in 1955 and toured the world in over eight hundred performances. Though frankly admitting that he did not always understand the poetry, Emlyn spoke the words with a passion that convinced Mrs Thomas, the poet's mother.

the early Hollywood tycoons, who had to keep up an unremitting stream of movies in order to satisfy the voracious appetite of the cinema chains, rechristened the factories that turned out the product as "studios", a term which gave dignity to the manufacturing process.

The Corn Is Green went on a provincial tour after it closed at the Duchess. In Cardiff, naturally, it received an ovation. "This human and humorous play has done more to explain Welsh character and outlook to English folk than a thousand ballyhoo speeches and pamphlets," said the local newspaper. "Emlyn Williams has enhanced Wales in the eyes of the world." Emlyn, adopting his public face, declared simply: "I have described the life and the people I know." He took the play back with him to London where it re-opened in December, 1939, and ran for over two hundred more performances.

All this time, during intervals of *The Corn Is Green* and long waits in film studios, he was writing another play. He called it *The Light Of Heart*, which, like so many others of his titles, had a bardic ring but did not, in fact, come from Shakespeare or the Bible. His titles all sprang from within, and some arcane neurosis drove him to keep them, not always successfully, to no more than fourteen letters. In *The Light Of Heart* he returns to the milieu of his early play *Glamour*, the London theatre, but this time with much more expertness and confidence. The central character is a famous actor who, Emlyn said, he based on the then well-known figure of Henry Ainley and on "two other actors I knew well". One of them was certainly Bill, for Maddoc Thomas, as he calls him, is a master of his trade, but permanently flawed by drunkenness and haunted by his memories of war horrors in the trenches. The first act, set in the shabby Long Acre apartment house where Maddoc exists with his daughter, presents a series of beautifully written cameo parts. These provide a chorus for the tragedy of Maddoc Thomas, an actor who in his youth had shown glittering promise and earned the encouragement of Henry Irving for his Hamlet. Just when he reached the verge of greatness something, somewhere, went wrong. He started drinking heavily, his memory went, he became frightened. Today he is unshaven, disreputable, usually drunk, and he cannot even keep a temporary job as Father Christmas at Selfridges. His only support is his crippled daughter Cattrin who devotes her life to him, nurses him through his hangovers and keeps their pathetic household together. Yet even she, however eloquently she pleads, cannot cure his feelings of self-disgust and despair. He will never, he tells her, go back to the stage. "I haven't been inside a theatre for eight years. It was another life, and it's finished with."

Against his will he is tempted back with the offer of a small but well-paid part. He makes a success of it and more invitations arrive. His memory improves and he starts to drink less. Then the great C. B. Cochran engages him for a new production of *King Lear*, and, despite his protest that it is "unactable", he agrees to take the lead in it. Cattrin helps him study the part, and flashes of his early genius, inspired by nothing more potent than Vichy water, begin sporadically to appear. The atmosphere comes back to him as he recaptures the mood of curtain-rise. "The lights fade, the voices die into sudden silence, the pulse of the world is still . . . and then the drum. And like a cloud shaken from a sack, something spreads through the place from end to end. I don't know what it is, but it's magic, and there's nothing like it in the world. (*Unexpectedly, with a sob.*) Oh my dear, why have I wasted all those years – why . . ."

It is all too good to be true. Cattrin learns that she is a cripple because Maddoc fell down while carrying her as a baby in one of his drunken bouts. She decides that she has had enough and that it is time for her to live her own life, which she proposes to do with the young man whom she loves. Maddoc is desolated. Mr Cochran is obliged to announce the postponement of *King Lear* due to the star's "laryngitis", an excuse which veils a drunken relapse. Cattrin repents and decides not to leave him after all. He hears her decision in a benign mood. "Cheerful again, like the old days," he murmurs. "Very nice motto, y'know, blessed are the light of heart . . ." But he knows there is no way out. He leaves the room and commits suicide by throwing himself from a top-floor window.

Stephen Mitchell, who had sponsored *The Corn is Green*, was also involved with *The Light of Heart* which he presented in association with H. M. Tennent Ltd. Behind that simple statement lies a tangled history of negotiation and manoeuvre, since H. M. Tennent Ltd, of course, was Binkie Beaumont, who always preferred to deploy his skill in the shadows. His theatrical management was now the most powerful in London. He, like Emlyn, came from Wales, and the two men were to enjoy a wary friendship based on mutual respect for each other's determination (or obstinacy, as some might say) and flair. Having lost *The Corn is Green* through his mistaken judgement that the public was not interested in "education", Binkie had determined to claim *The Light of Heart* and to recruit one of England's most successful playwrights for his own company. The association of the two Welshmen turned out to be a wholly profitable one.

The Light of Heart opened at the Apollo on February 21, 1940. The part of Maddoc Thomas, a superb rôle for the actor lucky enough to play him, went to Godfrey Tearle, a very distinguished name and son of the equally distinguished Osmond. He had begun his career at the age of nine in his father's touring company and developed into a versatile actor at home in rôles both ancient and modern. He was also a fine Shakespearean and particularly noted for his Othello. In *Hamlet* he once played Horatio and was said to have out-acted Henry Ainley as the prince whenever they were together on the stage. Such *tours de force* were unhappily rare in a life which condemned him frequently to playing hearty clubmen and grave-faced bishops. He had dignity, a voice of mellow sonority, and a dominating presence. In time he was knighted, became the first president of British Actors' Equity, and was very much the elder statesman. After *The Light of Heart*, which he illuminated with a vivid pathos, he appeared more often in films than in plays. In a way this signalled a return to his beginnings, for he had made his first film in 1906 as the hero of a *Romeo and Juliet* much truncated for the purpose of the cinema.

There are inconsistencies in *The Light of Heart*. Would a great actor get drunk just before his triumphant return to the stage because his daughter proposed to marry her boy-friend? Would not Cochran himself have appeared and talked sense into him? These queries strike one, however, only after the curtain has fallen. While the play is in action one is persuaded by Emlyn's cunning stagecraft into accepting the unlikeliest incidents. His talent for characterisation was a powerful aid to drawing wool over the eyes of an audience. As James Agate put it: "Emlyn appears to write his plays in the way in which Mr Wemmick got married. 'Here's a church! Let's go in! Here's Miss Skiffins! Let's have a wedding!' Emlyn goes to Covent Garden and says to himself: 'Here's a staircase! Here's a flat full of Skiffinses! Let's have a play!' His talent, as I see it, is not for playwriting, but for depicting the Skiffinses of today, which he does admirably. Too admirably. His gift for eking out plays with amusing minor characters means that he needn't bother about his major drama, and he doesn't." On the other hand, as *The Times* pointed out, "none but an author who was also an actor could have written this distinguished play, for in its background there is a more authentic rendering of the magic of the stage than can be found in hundreds of plays which have dealt directly with theatrical life." One way of evoking the theatrical atmosphere was to sprinkle mentions of Cochran, Gielgud as producer of *King Lear*, and Edith Evans. Before taking Cochran's name in vain, Emlyn asked for his permission. Flattered and charmed, the impresario gave it, remarking that he was proud to be associated with a play by Emlyn but only on condition that the character depicted was not "an absolute bastard".

During his curtain speech at the first night Godfrey Tearle orated in his most senatorial manner. "I have been on the stage for a great many years," he observed, "but during the last five weeks I have learned a very great deal. Ladies and gentlemen, I commend to you Emlyn Williams. Cherish him. He is valuable to the theatre." *The Light of Heart* achieved over a hundred and twenty performances at the Apollo and then went on tour for a year, after which Tearle left the cast. It was rumoured that the venerable star wanted more time to fish the streams at his Cornish retreat. Emlyn himself took over, and, since he was too young for the part, turned Maddoc into Cattrin's brother. Despite this minor surgery which resulted in arrant miscasting, the play ran for another six months at the Globe. "Why," lamented James Agate, "if he wants to keep his company together, doesn't he write a new play for them? A natural and prolific wit, steeped in the theatre to his very lips, and brimming over with plots – he could easily run up a new play in a matter of three weeks or so." Later it was filmed in Hollywood as *Every Night at 8.30*. Monty Woolley played Maddoc Thomas, irascibility spiked with venom, and Ida Lupino his daughter. Emlyn discovered that Scott Fitzgerald had worked on the script. He remembered his own early chores as a hack at Gaumont-British Films employed to inject scripts with "zing" or "humour" as the case might be. Did the studio bosses, he wondered ironically, ever ring up Fitzgerald and ask him to put "warmth" or whatever into Miss Lupino's love scenes?

What was known as "the phoney war" had ended by now and bombs were falling in earnest. Emlyn was uneasy about his family. On June 26, 1940, then, Molly left England with their two small boys Alan and Brook. They were destined for the USA where Robert Montgomery, a close family friend ever since appearing in the film of *Night Must Fall*, offered them shelter at his house in the country. Bereft of his wife and children, Emlyn joined the Home Guard and paraded bashfully in the worst-fitting costume he had ever worn. More usefully, he wrote the screenplay of a patriotic film entitled *This England* and acted a leading rôle. Within a brief hour and a half it depicted the country's fight for freedom in turn against the Normans, the Armada, Napoleon and the Kaiser. It was full of fake beards and edifying attitudes. "We all look awful in the film," he wrote to Molly, "we've been Norman lords and serfs all the week in a grand hall, all in club wigs, looking like a series of Lesbian hockey mistresses who've lost their sticks . . ."

In the long letters he wrote to Molly throughout this difficult period he tried to keep her spirits up with London gossip and anecdotes. He reported that Ernest Thesiger had been observed hurrying down a side street and muttering: "I'm off to see if X Mansions is really razed to the ground, as I have an uncle who lives there and I know I'm in his will!" There was a new joke about Noël in circulation: the war was being fought to make America a country fit for Cowards to live in. Another reference to Noël's wide-ranging travels during the war inspired thoughts of sending him a prepaid telegram in California, where he had fleetingly come to rest: "Quite safe here awfully worried about you we hear heat very trying please cable." Merle Oberon's autobiography, he gleefully relayed in a jibe at her carefully concealed Eurasian parentage, was to be called *The Lives of a Bengal Free-lancer*. (A very popular film of the time had been *The Lives of a Bengal Lancer*.) Emlyn himself was categorised as being in a "reserved" occupation, that is his civilian work excused him from military service. Asked by an official what he would like to do if he were called up, he replied: "Air Force Intelligence." "There is no such thing as intelligence in the Air Force," responded the official austerely. His despatches to Molly blended humour with the macabre. On a visit to Glasdir and his parents he read in a letter from his brother Tom: "They buried the airman who crashed yesterday, a coffin and everything but a waste of money as they only found two fingers." His mother said: "Quite right, what a waste!" as she rushed to the door in a panic for fear of missing the butcher.

But Molly remained anxious. She hated the separation and feared for his safety in air-raids. Worse, even, was her ill-concealed alarm at the thought of him on his own and faced with many temptations. "It is such an impossible situation for us," she wrote. "I was hurt at your saying ours is not an ordinary marriage . . . it made me feel it depends only on the children, which is not really true . . . I don't feel as hopeful as you about seeing an end to it [the war]. I feel so much we have at least another year to face, and that is a terribly long time for two people to be separated, however fond you are of each other, I'm afraid you must grow apart, and I'm so afraid of it . . ."

There were more films to be made. Emlyn was Snobby Price, a cameo part, in *Major Barbara* directed by Gabriel Pascal, another of those irrepressible Hungarians who haunted the British film industry at the time. Pascal had captured the biggest prize of all, George Bernard Shaw, and formed with the idiosyncratic Irishman an improbable alliance which brought to the screen four of Shaw's major plays. *Hatter's Castle* found Emlyn as a dissolute lover squaring the triangle with James Mason and Deborah Kerr as the mistress of Robert Newton. The photography, unusually inspired, was the work of a brilliant craftsman who had had the misfortune to be born Mutz Greenbaum, a name much honoured in the film trade. Since there was a war on he prudently arranged to be credited under the pseudonym of "Max Greene".

Broadcasting House saw quite as much of Emlyn in those days as did the film studios, notwithstanding his distaste for the medium. As a true professional he overcame his natural reluctance and soon mastered the technique to become an effective broadcaster. One of his most memorable talks, or "Postscripts" as the series was called, concerned the well-known actor Esmond Knight who was blinded in a naval action. Emlyn had taken part in an all-star Esmond Knight matinée at the Palladium chaired by Noël Coward on behalf of St Dunstan's. In his broadcast he evoked the association's work and spoken of Knight's bravery when faced with disaster. Eventually Knight was to recover enough to act on stage again and to enjoy his preferred recreation of falconry. "What a wonderful welcome for your postscript," wrote Miss Cooke, "which, along with everything else, I found most moving. Has St Dunstan's written you a special letter of thanks?"

He also took part in an immensely popular series called "The Brains Trust", a group of variegated wits and experts kept in order by a question-master who fed them with enquiries sent in from the listening public: how do flies contrive to walk upside down? is it better to have loved and lost than never to have loved at all? what is the finest gift a fairy godmother could bestow? Among the regular and much-loved performers on this programme was an ex-naval man, Commander Campbell, who invariably prefaced his tall stories with the remark: "When I was in Patagonia . . ." (or Antofagasta or Sarawak). Another was a bearded gnome called Dr Joad, a professor of philosophy whose insistence on the precise definition of terms before engaging in debate became a national joke. "It depends what you mean by . . .", he would squeak in high, meticulous tones. Alas, one day Dr Joad was detected travelling by train without a ticket, arraigned in court, fined and never heard of again. In the meantime he flourished as a national figure who, today, would have been a television star. Emlyn's nimble wit and quick tongue served him well in his duels with Cyril Joad. Miss Cooke exulted: "The only thing I've heard about the Brains Trust is that you put Joad in his place once or twice . . ."

Radio quickly emerged as a powerful weapon of propaganda.

Besides his talks in English Emlyn made numerous broadcasts in French and Italian to the occupied countries. He had always kept up his languages since the Oxford days, and now he found that his linguistic talent helped him contribute positively to the war effort. A broadcast he made in the late-night "And So To Bed" programme also had a direct influence on his later career. He chose to give a reading from *Bleak House*, long a favourite novel of his. The episode is that magnificent, superbly Dickensian passage where Mr Tulkinghorn, the sinister man of law, walks home through the dark London street after he has threatened Lady Dedlock with the revelation of her secret. "He passes out into the streets, and walks on, with his hands behind him, under the shadow of the lofty houses, many of whose mysteries, difficulties, mortgages, delicate affairs of all kinds, are treasured up within his old black satin waistcoat. He is in the confidence of the very bricks and mortar. The high chimney-stacks telegraph family secrets to him. Yet there is not a voice in a mile of them to whisper, 'Don't go home!'" The passage ends with Tulkinghorn arriving at his grim Lincoln Inn chambers by moonlight. The sound of a pistol is heard and blood trickles over the carpet while he lies ". . . face downward on the floor, shot through the heart." If, Emlyn told his invisible audience after recounting the episode, ". . . by doing so I may persuade any listener to read (or re-read) for pleasure that master of dramatic narrative I shall be most happy." At least one of his listeners was suitably chilled. "I liked very much hearing you bring out the macabre in Dickens," reported Miss Cooke, "it'll be quite a long time before I forget that scene!"

He was just as busy in the theatre. Binkie Beaumont asked him in 1942 to direct the London production of Lillian Hellman's *Watch on the Rhine* which had been a Broadway success. As a playwright himself Emlyn had up to then been wary of directing a play by someone else for fear of tampering with the text and being unfair to the author. Binkie, with persuasive eloquence, made him think otherwise. During the first week of rehearsals Emlyn sensed hostility from some of the actors and a tendency to ignore his suggestions. He confided in Binkie, who once again airily put his fears to rest. In the end all went well. The male lead was taken by Anton Walbrook, né Adolph Wohlbrüch, son of a famous Viennese clown. Having made a reputation for versatility in his native land, he came to England in 1939 and quickly established himself as a player of romantic rôles for which his exotic accent, caressing voice and wistful good looks perfectly suited him. He was to make a number of very successful films, among them *Dangerous Moonlight*, where he starred as a glamorous Polish pianist, (playing, of course, the insistent "Warsaw Concerto"), *Queen of Spades*, and, most notably, *La Ronde*, in which he was the elegant and cynical *raisonneur* who links the episodes of the film together. In *Watch on the Rhine* he had a closing scene of such poignancy that at the dress rehearsal everyone burst into tears, including Walbrook himself. A child actor in the cast asked him: "Tell me, Mr Walbrook. Are you going to cry like this every night?" "Certainly not," Walbrook retorted. "In rehearsal *I* cry, in performance it is the bastards in front who cry."

So worthwhile had been Emlyn's first experience of directing a play by another writer, and so successful , that he indited a friendly letter to Lillian Hellman and told her how much he had enjoyed it. No answer came from Pleasantville, N.Y. A year later he directed another play of hers called *The Little Foxes* which had been imported from Broadway where it ran a long time and which, as a film, provided Bette Davis with an impressive vehicle. The London cast was a piquant blend of youth and age. Richard Attenborough, who had lately won the Bancroft Medal at the RADA, made an early London appearance in a juvenile part. One of the leading players was Percy Marmont, a veteran who, as well-known in New York as he was in London, had made the first of his many films in 1913. He was partnered by Fay Compton, she of the melancholy face and perfect timing. None knew better than she how to calculate a pause in such a way that it contributed more to the action of a play than words. Her air of long-suffering, perhaps enhanced by the fact that she had four husbands in her busy career, made her rare smile all the more captivating. Again Emlyn enjoyed himself as director, and again there came no response from the inaptly named town of Pleasantville. Some time afterwards he met Lillian Hellman for supper at the Savoy. He was obliged to admit defeat and noted that ". . . while in her plays she was gracefully witty, her private personality lacked humour to the point of grimness. The conversation dried up . . . I am fairly outgoing, but I never got closer to her than one would to a telephone operator who might phone a wake-up call every morning for weeks on end."

After contact with the glacial Miss Hellman he turned with relief to directing one of his own plays. This was *The Morning Star* which opened at the Globe Theatre on December 10, 1941. It depicted the blitz on London as experienced by a middle-class family living in Chelsea. The play was dedicated "To my sons" who were then far away in America, doubtless as a testimony to events which they would only appreciate when older. The scene was quickly set by an exchange between Mrs Parrilow and her charwoman Mrs Lane.

Mrs Lane	Excuse me, madam . . . (*brushing*)
Mrs Parrilow	Something caught your eye?
Miss Lane	I was watchin' a dogfight, madam.
Mrs Parrilow	Pity they're always such miles up, nothing but a lot of smoke rings.
Mrs Lane	They'll never bomb London, do you think?
Mrs Parrilow	Why not?
Mrs Lane	Well, madam, a person in Barking evacuated 'erself to a little place miles from anywhere; she no sooner give up 'er ticket and bent down to pick up a bird-cage then a bomb fell on top of 'er. (*Brushing.*) They'll never bomb London.
Mrs Parrilow	What happened to her?
Mrs Lane	They never found a thing. It was one o' them nuisance raids.

Mrs Lane was played by Gladys Henson, a plump, maternal sort of body. Beginning as a thirteen-year-old chorus girl, she quickly grew up to become the incarnation of all the comic charwomen and all the working-class mums who ever lived, eternally washing up and brewing tea. She had been the second wife of the comedian Leslie Henson (though not the mother of Nicky, that privilege being reserved for Henson's third wife), and, rather to his annoyance, kept his name for professional purposes. Her performance as Mrs Lane won the sort of notice from critics which was to be repeated throughout her career: ". . . a true-born Cockney to the core," they said. This was high praise, for she was in fact a true-born Irishwoman from Dublin.

Gladys Henson had already provided low comedy in *The Light of Heart*. Another member of the cast, Angela Baddeley, returned as the beautiful heroine. Also from the same play was Elliot Mason, a specialist in stalwart middle-aged matrons, this time playing Mrs Parrilow in *The Morning Star*. The conventional exterior imposed on her by professional requirements did not repress, in private, a neat wit that she often exercised on James Agate, a neighbour in the block of flats where she lived. Emlyn himself, besides directing, took the leading male rôle as Cliff Parrilow. The family atmosphere of the production was completed by Molly who had created the décor: a typically comfortable drawing-room with curtains and loose covers of a mellow tint, antique furniture carefully disposed, and portrait miniatures attractively deployed on the walls.

As the play proceeds the setting becomes more and more woebegone. Doors are shattered by a direct hit across the street, windows splinter, furniture is piled up in dusty chaos, and the once trim drawing-room starts to resemble a makeshift air-raid shelter. From time to time sirens wail, bombs explode, the clangour of fire engines reverberates. By the final curtain each of the people involved has undergone a catharsis: Mrs Parrilow through the loss of her younger son on active service; her eccentric lodger, an elderly doctor, through the death of his Welsh batman; Mrs Lane through the destruction of her home; and Alison the heroine through desertion by her husband. The experience of the leading character, Cliff Parrilow, elder son of Mrs Parrilow, is the most striking of all. He is a gifted doctor who has temporarily deserted medical research to write a best-selling novel. When the play opens he is about to leave war-torn London for Hollywood where he has been offered a lucrative contract. What he sees of the blitz, however, and of the Londoners who are standing up to it, makes him change his mind. He decides to stay and to resume work on a new life-saving technique he had almost perfected. "And I started thinking, quite unashamed, about God . . ." he explains, ". . . and I thought, there *is* something, very high up, very far away, high up over the balloon barrage, high up over the Jerry planes, watched us, hard, and saying . . . 'Stop asking why it all has to be, you'll know in my own time, the only thing that interests me, is . . . are you going to lie down, or are you going to stick together and fight?' "

No one looked more startled than Emlyn when, at the fall of the curtain, he received an ovation from an enthusiastic audience. He had written *The Morning Star* as a tribute to Londoners in their ordeal and as a record of their endurance. The subject challenged an old convention in the theatre that a wartime public preferred light-hearted distraction and would not be interested in plays about the war. Binkie Beaumont and Stephen Mitchell had taken a risk in presenting Emlyn's new work. It was a very pleasant surprise, therefore, when *The Morning Star* achieved warm acclaim against all the omens. Today, despite its skilful theatricality, it would not bear revival. It was born of special circumstances, and when those circumstances had passed away it no longer had relevance. James Agate testily noted: "I don't think you can make a war play by writing a first-class part for Gladys Henson as a London charwoman, running up a Croninesque plot about a doctor, and trying to get home with prayers in the Welsh idiom. Tonight's audience obviously didn't agree with me, and I shan't be surprised if Emlyn Williams's *The Morning Star* runs a year." In the event it played 474 performances and remained at the Globe for rather more than the year Agate predicted.

Its predecessor, *The Light of Heart*, had meanwhile been produced in America as *Yesterday's Magic* with Paul Muni as Maddoc Thomas. Cablegrams from Molly charted its short life. "Muni being very difficult," she cabled. "I feel discouraged." When it opened in New Haven, she opined: "Not too good, darling. Muni and Jessica Tandy disappointing . . . Longing to come home. Sick of it all." Then she noticed a slight turn for the better: "Greatly improved. Most notices good for play. Muni terribly slow . . . Hope for the best." The best was not to be. In New York: "No good, darling. Critics very hard. Never mind. Think of *Morning Star* . . . please don't get depressed."

It was not so much the failure of *Yesterday's Magic* that lowered Emlyn's spirits at this time as the absence of Molly and his family. He missed her horribly, and he missed his two sons. He needed her companionship, her kindness, her loyalty. He felt he was being denied a father's right to see his sons growing up at one of the most delightful stages of their life when, physically and emotionally, they were changing almost as day succeeded day. From all this he felt miserably cut off. One day, looking forward to Molly's imminent return, he bought a present for her. He put it in an envelope and enclosed a note: "My darling, you probably won't be able to take this back to America; but in a way that makes it better as a present, because it is really to welcome you home where you really belong, and where you can leave it till you come back. It is meant for you to have always, as a token of our eternal love for each other. It's not necessarily as good as it looks, as it breaks up into two bracelets and a brooch. Emlyn."

(ii)
Family Reunion

In the summer of 1942 there arrived at last the cablegram he had so impatiently awaited. "Rehearsals start 7 June," it read. This was the coded phrase Emlyn and Molly had agreed in advance to outwit a censor ever on the watch for any mention of shipping movements that might help the enemy. It signified that Molly was starting her journey back to England on June 7. She arrived at Liverpool on June 25 and was carried off triumphantly to Pelham Crescent where, for the time being, life went on in the basement, the upper floors having been shaken and damaged by air raids. Then they travelled down to Park End where the garden flourished in a blaze of summer brightness. After brief accounts of how *The Light of Heart* was doing, he wanted to hear about what was far more important to him at the time: his two boys. Eagerly he studied the snaps she had brought back with her, and anxiously he asked after the progress of Alan and Brook. A decision was made. Within a very short time Molly travelled across the Atlantic again and returned with the evacuees in person. London was no place for children, so the family settled at Park End. Alan began his schooling at an establishment in the neighbourhood. Brook, who even at that tender age had the charm and sociability which make him such an agreeable companion, struck up friendly relations with the farmer whose property abutted the Williams's. In time he evolved a routine by which he rose at the streak of dawn and persuaded the farmer to let him operate the tractor on expeditions gathering kale, eyes frowning in concentration and arms taut as he pretended to himself that he was a racing driver. His way of life had the extra advantage that it provided him with two breakfasts: one at five o'clock with the farmer and the other at a more conventional hour when he returned to the family dining-room.

A few months after the boys' return *The Morning Star* opened in New York with a strong cast that included Gladys Cooper and Gregory Peck. This "tense drama of 1940 wartime London" was greeted respectfully but with no great warmth. Like Terence Rattigan's *Flare Path* and other English plays dealing with the war, it did not appeal to American audiences who looked on the theatre chiefly as a place of escapism. Emlyn was unsurprised, for he still could not help regarding the London success of *The Morning Star* as a fluke. He busied himself with an adaptation of Turgenev's *A Month In The Country* for Tennent Plays Ltd. This was an independent company set up by Binkie Beaumont who had at last discovered a way of circumventing the iniquitous Entertainments Tax which regularly plundered twenty-five per cent of the gross profits accruing to H. M. Tennent Ltd. The device, a wholly legal one, took advantage of a financial regulation which, so long as all profits were ploughed back into the company, exempted from tax the presentation of plays which might be deemed educational or otherwise edifying. It had, moreover, the blessing of CEMA, a wartime quango which took the shape, as its acronym suggested, of a council for the encouragement of music and the arts. Again with complete legality, Binkie was able to charge a management fee which went to H. M. Tennent Ltd, while Tennent Plays Ltd waxed fat on its ploughed-back profits. John Gielgud's *Macbeth* had already been a notable success under the arrangement. So, too, was *A Month In The Country* which Emlyn also directed. Peggy Ashcroft was to have played Natalia, but an injury in a bomb explosion put her out of action and she was replaced by Valerie Taylor. Michael Redgrave played Rakitin with exquisite judgement. *A Month In The Country* had an unusually long run of three hundred and thirteen performances. Not the least surprising thing about it was the presence of Ronald Squire, that polished exponent of the Hawtrey-Du Maurier school, who for once deserted the fashionable drawing-rooms of Frederick Lonsdale to give a characterisation instinct with what *The Times* praised as "dry good humour".

Once *A Month In The Country* was launched Emlyn went on tour with *The Morning Star* and *Night Must Fall*. At the age of thirty-seven he still had youth enough, aided by his actor's skill, to play the part of a murderous page-boy. In the spring of 1943 he travelled with his repertoire through Scotland, the Midlands and the West to end up in his home country of Wales. "Success has not spoilt him," said a Cardiff newspaper of the local hero. "He has no 'side'. Unlike some Welsh men and women who have 'got on in the world', he is proud of his modest beginnings and of being Welsh."

A sudden and poignant reminder of those Welsh beginnings assailed him in July. He learned that on the 5th his father had died while in the very act of proudly displaying to his wife a photograph of their talented son. Richard Williams was seventy-three years old. The episodes of drunkenness and improvidence which blighted his marriage in earlier days had long ago ceased, and the stricken atmosphere of Connah's Quay had been succeeded by one of mellowness. In the little bungalow Emlyn had bought for his parents Richard led an existence of quiet contentment, though his old wit still flared on occasion. Much of his time he devoted to assembling press cuttings about Emlyn's career. No longer, though, would he point out to his mates the name of his son on a film poster, and no longer would Emlyn receive those ardent missives exulting "My dear Son George, once more your name is on all lips . . ." Emlyn went down to Glasdir for the funeral, a modest affair attended by his brothers Job and Thomas and a few other members of the family, his mother tight-lipped and stoic. Miss Cooke wrote: "As far as we can judge, it is better for your father to go first, for he had no womankind, no daughter to look after him; but the first break-up of a family is always hard . . . there's something of the end of the world about it." It was indeed something like the end of the world for his grieving mother. "I feel very love sick for your dad the place is so empty without him," she wrote. "I try to be content but it is very hard to think how sudden he went and was not uneconcius at all I hope your letter is on the way as I am anxious about you."

In August there was a family holiday at Minehead on the Somerset coast. No person from Porlock, which is nearby, succeeded in disturbing Emlyn as he had disturbed Coleridge and broken his train of thought. Unmoved by the shouts of the children as they played on the sand, he drummed away at the little typewriter quivering on his knee, his thoughts far away from sunshine and blue seas. When evening came he would entertain the boys with bedtime stories, or, rather, epics which began soon after tea and which were by no means over when Alan and Brook had at last clambered sleepily into bed. They were fantasies, comedies, sagas, immensely long stories which unrolled in a series of incidents dramatic or farcical, pastoral-comical, historical-pastoral, tragical-historical, depending on his mood. One evening at Park End he began such a recital in the sitting-room watched by four fascinated eyes. There was a little gallery which overlooked the room from upstairs and on this gallery there presently appeared two house guests, the American producer Josh Logan and the Welsh actor Richard Burton. They had been in the process of shaving. The hypnotic sound of Emlyn's voice and the marvellous exploits he was relating had drawn them irresistibly from their respective bedrooms. While they listened they forgot all about shaving. Only when the story ended and the spell was broken did they realise that their chins were still embellished with shaving cream which had long since dried into a frigid crust.

By autumn Emlyn was out on the road again with *Night Must Fall*. This tour came under the auspices of a wartime organisation known as ENSA, initials which stood for the Entertainments National Service Association, whose aim was to provide plays, concert parties and music for servicemen at home and overseas. The quality of the fare provided varied considerably, and the comedian Tommy Trinder claimed that among the troops the famous initials spelled out "Every Night Something Awful". This, however, did not apply in Emlyn's case, for, with his usual meticulous professionalism, he made sure that

Night Must Fall was produced to West End standards. From the North of England he made his way down to the West, playing in theatres, halls, gun emplacements, fit-ups, and anywhere that held troops wanting entertainment. Eventually he and the company arrived at Badminton, home of the Duke of Beaufort, where, for the duration, Queen Mary, the then Queen Mother, had made her wartime home as a stately and fearsome evacuee. From here, a zealous collector of old china, she made sallies to the antique-shops of Bath. Her visits were especially feared in the homes of the neighbouring aristocracy, for it was her habit to comment, with meaningful emphasis, on the choicer pieces in ancestral collections. So enthusiastic would be her remarks that the unfortunate owner was often terrorised into offering her a valuable item as tribute from a loyal subject.

At Badminton Emlyn and company gave a performance of *Night Must Fall* before Queen Mary and an assemblage of local personalities. It was not the last, but was probably the most unnerving, of all his royal appearances.

In October he was still preoccupied with the tour and could not attend the retirement ceremony at his old School when Miss Cooke at last said farewell to a career which had brought her vicarious fame as the heroine of a long-running play. In the assembly hall which he knew so well, before an audience of parents and children who often had quailed beneath her imperious eye, she stood four-square on the platform and reminisced about the life at Holywell which she had first encountered as a young teacher in 1912. "Over and over I remember parents speaking to me of their long connection with this School – they had had children at School of twelve, sixteen, eighteen. I taught the youngest daughter of one family whose eldest brother was one of the first students – that family connection with School covered twenty-three years. Is it a record?" During her speech she defined the philosophy that lay behind her teaching at Holywell for over thirty years. "I think if anyone had asked me what was my aim in education, the answer would have been twofold: to train students to dare to say No; to dare to be non-conformists, to dare to be non-smokers, to dare to be non-drinkers, and to see that every student is *happy*. Oh! by 'happy' I don't mean pleased or satisfied, and certainly the very opposite of 'self-satisfied'. I mean something much more affirmative – for the happiness of school life should be such as to lay the foundation of happiness in later life, and I believe that happiness is founded on '*I ought*'. Many of you will remember, at any rate, I hope you do, that the first French verb I used to teach was 'I want', because it is the first verb babies learn, the first verb babies use. Life teaches the replacing of 'I want' by 'I ought', and I believe that happiness has passed by those who have never learnt that replacement, and that school must help students to begin to *say* 'I ought'."

With this vigorous declaration of faith Miss Cooke withdrew from the arena in which she had figured as a doughty protagonist and a champion of standards. She went back home to her native Yorkshire and set up house with her old friend and teaching colleague May Swallow. They lived in Roundhay, a suburb of Leeds, the third member of their household being a middle-aged dog of orderly habits called Tuppence. With so much time on her hands Miss Cooke's letters to Emlyn grew longer and longer. She enclosed with them little scenarios for films – one in particular dear to her heart and intended to prove that German militarism would always be a threat – and speculations about current affairs, often coloured by her raging distaste for Socialist politicians like Aneurin Bevan. In retirement, too, she would often look back on her life as a spinster: "When you come to Leeds, I could show you the exact spot where, at 19 years of age, I had my first proposal of marriage – repeated till I was 25, when it was decided on both sides 'No go.' " Sometimes her revelations came as a surprise: "*I've loved the theatre every bit as much as you have* ... Is it the greatest astonishment on earth to know that I would have *loved* to be an actress? Moreover I know that I should not have failed. My first love? No, I can't truthfully say that. My first love would have been – the law ... I have loved teaching; but then I would have loved family, indeed – most things." The theatrical ambition is not, after all, so astonishing: had she not established herself as a *monstre sacré* of the classroom? Is not teaching, like acting, a matter of projection? She had certainly achieved a vicarious fulfilment of her wish to be an actress through the success of her most brilliant pupil. He wrote her, by return, letters often as long as the ones she wrote to him. Wherever he was, in New York, in London, in Kuala Lumpur, in Athens, in Barbados, he replied promptly. They explored literature together as they had when he was a schoolboy of sixteen. In her seventies, still receptive to novelty and eager for experiment, she found herself enjoying the witty surrealistic word-play of Raymond Queneau's *Zazie Dans le Métro*. When she disagreed with Emlyn over a play he had written their arguments were hard-hitting but good-humoured. They were equally frank about money. If a member of her family had trouble with a mortgage or a business deal, Emlyn responded immediately. There were occasions, also, when her pension could not meet unexpected demands. He solved the problem by making over to her the subsidiary rights in some of his plays. Even so, as she wrote to him: "For the record, your weekly letters give me greater pleasure than £100 a week."

By December he had finished the ENSA tour of *Night Must Fall* and was preparing for the launch at Blackpool of a new play very close to his heart. Often, when asked what is his favourite work, a writer will surprise by mentioning an obscure title which has not known popular success but which he particularly cherishes, rather as a mother will have a special affection for a handicapped child. In Emlyn's case the favoured infant was *Pen Don*, "A legend in Four Scenes". It was set on Pen Don, a hill-top in the Welsh mountains sacred to the goddess Don, mother of the world. The time was the enchanted eve of May Day in an age far removed from the present, King Arthur's age, medieval and ghostly, whose tales are recounted in the *Mabinogion*, that ancient repository of Celtic myths. Here Emlyn looked beyond the fashionable surroundings of the West End and back to the childhood of his race. He imagined the tribe assembling on Mount Don and glimpsing, through the mist, the dancing golden banners of King Arthur in Avalon. They move off on their way to the promised city of which they have talked and dreamed so much. Behind them they leave Lan, the simpleton of the tribe, with his sister Annwen. He, shrewder in his simplicity than the elders in their wisdom, muses that they may not find Avalon all they think it is. Suppose the lovely vision turns out to be no more than a disappointing chimera? "What a heart-burn for them all, eh? Do you know what I think, Annwen? You and me may be the lucky ones, after all!"

Not much happens in *Pen Don*. It is, in effect, an extended lyrical meditation. As the tribe waits at "the highest and holiest corner of the world", they look everywhere for the sign that will lead them to Avalon. While the elders argue and pray Lan the simple-minded reflects on nature. "The things I see, and how they go on. About beavers havin' dark-blue eyes, an' starlin's more speckles on 'em than in winter. Lady, have you noticed that? . . . An' then I think how to get near enough to the birds in the long grass, without givin' them a fright . . . If I get near enough so I catch their eye, they hop on my finger. All in a different way. The titmouse he stands on one leg, the chiff-chaff he cocks his head on one side, an' the missel-thrush, he bites your thumb, for a game."

Emlyn played Lan the holy fool and himself directed at Blackpool's Grand Theatre. *Pen Don* was not a success, and he realised the justice of Alfred Lunt's remark when he had sent him the play in the hope that Lunt would agree to appear in it: "I could not *picture* it in such theatres as now exist." Emlyn, with regret, put away his script for the time being and wryly commented: "I didn't really understand what it was about."

Within a few weeks he was back in the conventional West End theatre and directing another new play which he called *The Druid's Rest*. The title is the name of the Welsh public house in which the action proceeds. The play is an amused backward glance through rose-coloured spectacles at Emlyn's boyhood in the White Lion at Glanrafon. Indeed, the landlord's small son Tommos could be the boy Emlyn, his head always in a book, his mind filled with daydreams, his imagination peopling daily existence with bizarre incidents. When he patiently explains to his mother that his current reading of *Adam Bede* persuades him to confuse fiction with reality, she accuses him of telling lies: "Books is made up, and what's made up isn't the truth." "Then, Mam," he answers, "there must be a terrible lot of liars in the public library. Oh no Mam, I'm not a liar, I got a terrible imagination." She inflicts a dreadful punishment: his books will be confiscated for the whole period of the school holiday and he is condemned to occupy himself with useful chores. "But Mam, I run errands with my feet, and while I'm busy with my feet, what am I goin' to do with my mind?" Give it a rest, Mam proposes. "But it's my imagination I'm frightened of, Mam – you see, with no books and an empty mind, worse than ever it'll be – gallopin'!"

There is something of Richard Williams in Job, the boy's publican father – when, that is, Richard was in one of his good, buoyant moods. Job treats his customers to drinks, joins in choruses with them, gaily takes on bad debts. His great passion in life is singing, and, a prominent member of the local chapel choir, he engages his staff according to their vocal abilities. Other Welsh types neatly lined are Issmael Hughes, the tramp, Zachariah the village policeman, and Sarah Jane Jehovah the dedicated chapel goer. These affectionately observed character sketches are linked by a slender narrative concerning a mysterious English wayfarer who puts up at the pub. It is the period of the notorious "Brides in the Bath" murders, (even in comedy Emlyn cannot forget his other preoccupations), and Tommos, with his "gallopin' imagination", inspires a rumour that the unknown lodger must be the villain Smith himself, who is, according to newspapers, on the run in Wales. In fact, he is an English nobleman, weary of the grand life, anxious to get away from it all, and in the habit of using the incognito of Smith. All this only emerges at the end of a pastoral comedy which is developed with many a deft comic turn and twist. The last scene finds Tommos writing a poem which will probably win a prize at the Eisteddfod and Smith agreeing to Job's enthusiastic request that he adjudicate as Chief Druid.

The Druid's Rest, presented by H. M. Tennent at the St Martin's Theatre on January 26, 1944, reunited two prominent members of what had come to be Emlyn's unofficial repertory company. Gladys Henson was cast as the publican's wife, phlegmatic, down to earth, impatient of the fantasies to which both her husband and her son were, in their different ways, addicted. Job was round-faced Roddy Hughes, a plump and chattersome Welshman irrepressible in his bubbling enthusiasm for beer and singing. Other roles were advertised in *The Western Mail* which announced that Emlyn Williams sought actors and actresses including "a Welsh boy actor". The advertisement was seen by, among many others, a schoolteacher called Philip Burton. He had taken under his wing a pupil by the name of Richard Jenkins, more or less adopted him and built up with him a relationship which echoed to a certain extent that between Miss Cooke and Emlyn. So close were they, though innocent of the slightest carnality, that the seventeen-year-old boy had taken Phil's own name and was known as Richard Burton.

The Sandringham Hotel in Cardiff where auditions took place was crowded with parents anxious to exhibit the talents of their offspring. The candidates paraded in front of Daphne Rye, the H. M. Tennent casting director, a young lady whose beauty was equalled only by her forceful character. She whittled down the applicants until there remained a short list which Emlyn reviewed one evening at the hotel. He was impressed, as she had been, by Richard Burton. The boy's skin was bad, pock-marked indeed, yet the cheek-bones had a sculptural look, the features were irresistible and the wide blue eyes sparkled with charm. Phil Burton explained how Richard had distinguished himself in various school plays and had acted the role of Higgins in *Pygmalion*, a piece of information Emlyn received with malicious amusement, for Higgins is a linguistics expert who teaches the Cockney Eliza to enunciate perfect English, whereas Burton had a Welsh accent as thick as mist over Snowdon. This did not matter. Burton, Emlyn decided, had ". . . startling beauty and quiet intelligence. He looked – as very special human beings tend to look at that age – he looked imperishable." Burton knew, too, that he was very attractive, and, once Emlyn had decided to engage him, he attempted cold-bloodedly to seduce Daphne Rye, though in vain.

Emlyn and Richard Burton had much in common: Welsh peasant roots, a mining background, theatrical gifts, and a schoolteacher who had recognised and patiently nurtured their talent. The ". . . most spectacular-looking boy" had repose, Emlyn judged, with nothing precocious or smart-alec about him. "Almost shy but *sure* of himself, you know." He was given the part of Tommos' elder brother Glan in *The Druid's Rest*, and one of his earliest speeches mirrors, by chance, the preoccupations of the young Burton himself. Tommos, deprived of reading by his mother, asks Glan what he thinks about "with no stories in your head" when he is working in the hayfield. "I dunno," says Glan. "Girls, an' what the sky is like for tomorrow, an' the taste of a pint. An' girls . . ." For Burton was a rampant heterosexual whose favourite pursuits were girls, beer and hooliganism. With his understudy, a fifteen-year-old actor called Stanley Baker also from a poor Welsh background, he went drinking, whoring and scrapping in towns where *The Druid's Rest* travelled on its brief provincial tour before London. There were fights in dressing-rooms, smashed windows and brawls in pubs. Emlyn was patient with him for the sake of the talent he saw and sensed. Burton always won forgiveness. For, as Gladys Henson remarked, "He was the most beautiful boy I'd ever seen."

There was another side to Burton. It came out in the long conversations he had late at night with Emlyn about art and the theatre. He was finely sensitive to the beauty of words and the mystery of poetry. One evening, as they walked down a blacked-out street in Soho, he recited some verse by Dylan Thomas. It was Emlyn's first hearing of the poet, and he listened with fascination as the melody of the phrases danced in the air. In more ways than one Burton was to influence Emlyn and his family. Miss Cooke, naturally, had to meet his discovery. "He's like you," said she, "but he has the devil in him. You haven't."

Although Brynmor Thomas as the bookish lad made a great success in *The Druid's Rest*, Burton in a much smaller rôle earned praise. He "showed exceptional ability", observed the *New Statesman*. At the end of the play's run, a respectable total of a hundred and eighty-two performances, he went on to Oxford and National Service in the RAF.

The part of the English nobleman was taken by Michael Shepley, often type-cast as a peppery colonel. Wittier off-stage than on, a frequent courtier in James Agate's late-night retinue at the Café Royal, he once described himself as the last of the gentlemen-actors. Gladys Henson was Gladys Henson, a part she played with delightful ease. Miss Cooke believed *The Druid's Rest* ". . . far the wittiest of your plays . . . *Druid's Rest* may be 'slight,' but I thought it a joyous riot and thoroughly enjoyed it . . . Honestly – I think it's the most 'perfect' play you've written. I can't see that there's a chink in it."

In April Emlyn embarked on an ENSA tour of Egypt. There he put up at Shepheard's Hotel, that notorious wartime rendezvous for spies, conspirators, playboys, and shady operators of every description. "I'm in uniform now, as you can't move a step in civilian clothes without being challenged, makes it feel more unreal than ever," he told Miss Cooke. At the Cairo Royal Opera House he played Rattigan's *Flare Path*, a wartime drama in an RAF setting. With Kathleen Harrison providing the low comedy he attacked rehearsals of *Blithe Spirit* – "it's going to be tough going, one of the most difficult plays to learn ever written." Inevitably, he posed for the traditional photograph of himself astride a camel, the beast lazily malevolent, the rider poised with nervous aplomb between shaggy humps. He went to see the Pyramids and the Sphinx by moonlight. "Have also seen Beverley Nichols," he wrote to Molly, "not by moonlight, but he looks as old – in a funny, mummified way . . ." One morning he opened his *Egyptian Mail* to see the headline: "Ivor Novello sentenced." The luckless Ivor had been sent to prison for an offence against wartime regulations governing the use of petrol for private cars. Emlyn commented to Molly: "I suppose his great song for this war will have to be called *Keep The Home Tyres Turning*."

From Egypt he went on to Italy after a crowded voyage with five other passengers in a cabin designed for one. At Naples, he wrote to Miss Cooke, the ". . . view is as lovely as it was from Sorrento 19 years ago, Vesuvius rather whiter down the sides of the head (from recent lava) but then so am I!!" Brindisi was "a filthy town but most picturesque" and redeemed, for Emlyn at least, by the plaque on a house which announced that here died Virgil. In an article Emlyn later wrote for *The Listener* he recalled his pre-war visits to Italy and ". . . the same brilliant Italian sunlight on vineyard and mountain road and deep blue bay, the same soft moonlight on cypress and terrace and ancient pillared temple." But his memories this time included a ". . . little Italian boy, with a face thinner and sadder than little Jo's in *Bleak House*, watching through the broken window of our billet as we have our army ration tea of bread and jam, and his delighted surprise when he is given a slice."

After playing *Blithe Spirit* at the Argentina Theatre in Rome and giving a fluent curtain-speech in Italian (the actor Tullio Carminati had coached him for a week), he flew back to "sitting in the garden at Park

End, it will be wonderful all being together . . . those two grown-up schoolboys." In the autumn he was off again on an extended tour of France, Belgium and Holland. During a matinee of *Night Must Fall* in Dieppe a telegram was handed to him: "Your mother very ill." At Amiens he learned that she had died on October 18. "I know that when I go into Glasdir I shall be smitten with sudden intolerable sadness as I wait for her to come round the corner of the door with a teapot in her hand – but at the moment of the news I could only feel poignant relief – she is released from her 15 months sentence of solitary confinement, cut off from all that she really had lived for . . . I feel she had really died when my father died, and it was unbearable to think she was left behind . . . I feel they are together, or at any rate that their fifty years together are making an eternal murmur somewhere in the universe like the echo of a very solid sound, such as a bell." The excruciating pain of a growth in the bladder and the onset of gangrene had been followed by a quiet, well-mannered dissolution. Miss Cooke reported on her last visit to his mother. May had said to her: "He's been a good son to you, Mrs Williams." She answered fervently: "He has. He's been a good son."

Miss Cooke added shrewdly: "It was always interesting to hear her talk of you, she was rather like a mother hen that having hatched out a duckling couldn't follow it on to the pond, but was always ready to tell it how it should behave when on land . . ." He had long since passed beyond her ken, and she watched his career with bewilderment, proud but for ever unable to understand this peculiar child of hers. Between mother and son lay a profound abyss, and although both dearly yearned to cross it they had never been able to make the final effort.

Molly was now officially credited as an "ENSA artist" and wore an army lieutenant's uniform. She scoured Paris for material to brighten up the set of *Blithe Spirit* which, on one charming occasion, was played in a Dutch monastery where the monks themselves painted the scenery with their own blessed hands. In Brussels – "Charlotte Brönte went to school here and wrote a novel about it" – Emlyn did broadcasts in French and Molly bought toys for the children. General Montgomery attended the performance of *Blithe Spirit* there and ". . . came round to see us on the stage after Act II – surrounded by military sycophants – colonels whom we had seen in the ENSA office as overbearing overseers, and now quite unrecognizable as hand-rubbing flunkeys hovering in the background. He himself was charming, unassuming and rather shy – quite different from his inferiors – quite short and not as foxy-faced as in his photographs." News from home was eventful:

Alan's headmaster had just died, and Alan wrote: "Mr Forster passed away suddenly last week so we had a concert yesterday!!" The word "memorial", opined Emlyn, would have helped. And as a final *bonne bouche* for Miss Cooke he quoted the legend he had seen scrawled outside a theatre: "Abandon all hope ye who ENSA here."

Christmas that year was spent at Park End. Nine-year-old Alan, the aspiring dramatist, mounted a production for which the programme read: "Park End Miniature Theatre Company presents TRAGETY (sic) and TREASURE, a play in 5 scenes by Alan Williams . . . Scenic Effects and Production by Auntie Jackie and Daddy. Cigarettes by Abdullah." In quieter moments Emlyn brought his scrapbook up to date. He had plenty of material. It included Molly's official citation as an ENSA lieutenant ". . . entitled in the event of capture by the enemy to be treated as a prisoner of war." There was also a treasured cutting from an Egyptian newspaper about a woman who had given birth to a dog. He captioned it: "An everyday item of Cairo news."

Early in the new year of 1945 came the film version of *The Corn Is Green*. Miss Moffat, on Broadway Ethel Barrymore, was played by Bette Davis. Miss Barrymore, passed over for the film rôle, flashed her claws briefly: "She's too young for it!" she snapped. Morgan Evans was John Dall, an exquisite young stage actor who, when not required on the set, was apt to vanish on assignations with the more handsome members of the Welsh choir which had been engaged to sing traditional songs. His habit of making somewhat languorous entries and exits was remedied when the director abjured him to "think of soldiers marching in manly fashion on the parade field." Later he was to act in Hitchcock's *Rope* where he fell in love with the virile Farley Granger before dying, forgotten and disappointed, at the age of fifty-three. Although Bette Davis was only thirty-six and playing the role of a sixty-year old-woman, she brought a sharp authority to her portrayal. Her greatest problem involved the bicycle on which she made her first entry. "God damn this goddam bike!" she roared as she struggled with the recalcitrant machine. But it had been Ethel Barrymore's trademark entrance, and she was obliged not to disappoint those who had also seen the play. Emlyn was pleased with the good notices she received. "The general verdict seems to be that Bette Davis is very good though not as good as darling old Sybil," he wrote.[1]

[1] Sybil and her husband Lewis Casson were much given to good works. One day a friend telephoned to speak to them and their daughter answered: "They are neither of them in. Daddy is reading Shakespeare Sonnets to the blind and Mummy's playing Shakespeare to the lepers." This is a true story – Emlyn *dixit*.

Miss Cooke was enthusiastic: ". . . superb, a flawless performance
. . . a lovely piece of work. I can't help feeling that it is perfect *acting* –
it hasn't that something that is acting *plus* . . . I should like to write a
fan letter to Bette D. – shall I?"

At Christmas he finished writing another play. The idea had struck
him while he was touring Palestine with ENSA. "Palestine seemed so
much like my Welsh villages. I was afraid of the idea and it had lain
dormant. It took me about a year from the time I started it until it was
produced," he told a newspaper. Miss Cooke was informed: "I am
finishing a new play, *very* difficult subject – Wales 1856 but not very
Welsh. Very serious, less comedy than in any play of mine yet,
religious subject in a way, called 'The Breath of Heaven'." Finally
entitled *The Wind of Heaven*, the play depicted a Second Coming
which takes place in a Welsh village. In Palestine he had been strangely
reminded of his own childhood. "As I walked the road into the real
Bethlehem, the goat-herds called across the little valleys, and the faint
phrases might truly have been Welsh," he remembered. "Darkness
fell, and the soft chanting of Arab voices stole over the hallowed air. I
shut my eyes, and I was no longer on a mountain road in the East, I was
a child in Glanrafon, sitting up in bed on Christmas Eve and listening
to a group of colliers from Point-of-Ayr gathered in the moonlight on
Pen-y-Maes, and singing in a way nobody else has sung for me since,
not even at an Eisteddfod. Standing there below Bethlehem, I found
myself in a special country of my own imagining, half Welsh and half
Holy Land . . ."

At the time of the Crimean War a wounded soldier returns to his
native Welsh village in the mountains and starts a cholera epidemic. A
thirteen-year-old local boy suddenly discovers miraculous powers and
heals the sufferers. A cynical and disreputable showman at first tries to
secure him as a fairground attraction but is overcome by the lad's
transparent holiness and dedicates himself to a life of good works, for
the miracle worker "has called me to be a servant of God." A "wind of
music" sweeps through the village as the boy dies and the converted
showman recites, in faltering Welsh, the opening sentences of the
Lord's Prayer.

The Wind of Heaven stands with *Pen Don* as an exercise in poetic
eloquence. It is, however, more effective dramatically. Only after the
curtain has fallen does one realise that although the boy miracle-
worker dominates the play he appears but rarely, and that we know of
his unearthly feats only through the reports of others, a device which is
used with skill. Emlyn took the part of Ambrose Ellis, the flashy

showman, glib, top-hatted, much be-ringed. "He speaks perfect English, but there is something temperamentally foreign about him", runs a stage direction which could serve as a good description of Emlyn Williams. Diana Wynyard, to whom the play is dedicated, played the mother ". . . in terms of Raphael-like contour and expression," James Agate reported. "As the travelling showman the author himself perfectly suggests the man in spiritual travail – a beautifully thought-out piece of acting. Add a soul-shaking performance by Herbert Lomas as the shepherd, a mixture of Isaiah and any inarticulate, fervent, good old man. Let our young playgoers bend their attention on every movement and every accent of this superb performance. Let them realise that here is great acting." Lomas was an actor of patriarchal mien with a sonorous voice that could fill a theatre and a flashing eye that could still an audience, however restless. In the part of the shepherd Emlyn had given him one of the best rôles he ever played.

Miss Cooke had no doubt at all about *The Wind of Heaven* and claimed that it ". . . will always remain your greatest play because you had a tremendous, so dangerous, theme and you *didn't fail*. Far from it." Others concurred. W. A. Darlington judged it ". . . a play which goes very near greatness and has moments which are undoubtedly great." Audiences appeared to agree since it ran for two hundred and sixty-eight performances at the St James's Theatre throughout 1945. It even formed the topic of a sermon preached at St Peter's Church in Piccadilly, a circumstance which must have amused an author who, scarred by the tedious hours he had been condemned to sit through as a boy in chapel, nourished little enthusiasm for organised religion. Even Binkie Beaumont, one of the least religious men who ever lived, had been very impressed by the play from the start. "I've read your new play, Emlyn, and I like it twice as much as your last," said he. Emlyn quickly replied: "Does that mean you're going to pay twice my usual royalties?" It did not.

Towards the end of the year *Spring, 1600* was revived at the Lyric, Hammersmith, by the Company of Four, an offshoot of the H. M. Tennent organisation. Once again it failed to attract audiences. The Lyric, remarked Emlyn stoically, housed the Company of Four and the Audience of Two. Yet, absorbed as he normally was in the theatre, he could not ignore the General Election of 1945 which followed the end of the war in Europe. The vote he cast went to Labour, not through any political conviction but solely because he disliked the smugness of government luminaries with whom he had come into reluctant contact during the war. Then on Christmas Day, together with his family in Park End, he assisted at the world premiere of *Death In The Enchanted Palace*, "A Christmas Play by Alan Williams." The cast included King Cecil The Twenty-Third of Fairyland.

Outside England Emlyn's plays continued their lucrative wanderings. *The Wind of Heaven* opened successfully in Pretoria with Gwen Ffrangcon-Davies as the female lead. Flora Robson went on tour with *The Corn is Green*, unaware of the smile which her exalted sentiments caused the author. During the war, "when such a high-minded single lady should have been home," Emlyn told Miss Cooke, she had written from America a letter to a gossip-writer which he copied into his scrapbook as a prize specimen. "Oh," she declared in the course of it, "Oh, I am longing for after the war when I can help rebuild the theatre in every bomb-scarred city and town in England." Emlyn, prematurely, referred to her as "Dame Flora" among his friends: "If she's not a dame she jolly well writes like one."

After Christmas he adapted and directed an American play called *Guest In The House*, tightened a shaky structure with sympathetic doctoring and built up a jewel of a part for his beloved Gladys Henson, to whom, as yet another cook-general, he gave this splendid exit line: "I've been called a madam, Madam, and I'm leaving." Two days later, on May 23, 1946 he made his return to the West End stage in person as Sir Robert Morton in Terence Rattigan's *The Winslow Boy*. The play was based on the Archer-Shee case, a *cause célèbre* early this century involving a thirteen-year-old naval cadet who had been dismissed on suspicion of having stolen and forged a five-shilling postal order. Convinced of the boy's innocence, his father waged a determined battle against Admiralty and government until, after two years of struggle and with the aid of the famous advocate Sir Edward Carson, he won the fight to clear his son's name. Rattigan, like Emlyn, was a connoisseur of trials and a fascinated spectator at court. In *The Winslow Boy*, however, he met the challenge of setting the action, not in a court-room, but in the home of the family involved. He also faced the daunting task of explaining complex legal issues in a clear but theatrically convincing way. This double dare he carried off brilliantly. At the same time he expressed a deep personal belief: the five-shilling postal order was unimportant in itself, but the principle it represented was paramount. Right must be done.

Both Eric Portman and John Gielgud had turned down Sir Robert Morton. Emlyn, however, realised that although the role was not large its importance much outweighed its size. He thus acquired, as he was later to remark, a part which supplanted that of Edgar Wallace's Lord

Lebanon as his favourite. Sir Robert is a cold and supercilious fish. A Conservative in politics, he aspires to the Establishment and sees himself as a future Lord Justice. How can such a man be expected to take up a hopeless case which, whatever the result, is bound to harm his ambition? He comes to the Winslow home and ruthlessly cross-examines the boy. In a long and gruelling scene he tears the child's testimony to pieces, makes him contradict himself, trips him up, and finally reduces him to tears by calling him a forger, a liar, a thief. At the end, while the family and their solicitor watch in amazement, Sir Robert coolly sweeps out saying: "The boy is plainly innocent. I accept the brief."

This devastating Act II curtain would alone make the part worthwhile. It is enhanced by the way in which Rattigan subtly develops character. At first the boy's sister, a girl with "progressive" political opinions, is suspicious of Sir Robert and his right-wing views. As the play proceeds she comes to respect him for his motives, and he, in turn, relaxes his severity as he gets to know her better. Perhaps, we feel, these two will continue their association after the curtain falls. In the meantime, Emlyn presented a figure of chilly aloofness. His first entry was unforgettable after an act in which he had constantly been talked about and expectation heightened. Clad in black overcoat and white gloves, he walked slowly to a chair downstage. There he paused, and, in unsmiling silence, took off his gloves, removing each finger with concentrated deliberation. The audience was gripped, and remained so all the time he spoke his words in those clear, exquisitely enunciated syllables. When he delivered the curtain line on that first night the whole house erupted in cheers.

"Mr Williams's advocate – with his wary eyelids and his cautious walk and his rare Machiavellian smile – is one of this Welsh wizard's best things," wrote Alan Dent. Kenneth Harris decided: "The play really got going with his magnificent entrance as the great Sir Robert, over-acted with just that touch of deliberate theatre which brought a coughing audience to heel." Thereafter, each weekday night and on matinée afternoons, Emlyn walked from Pelham Crescent to South Kensington tube station an hour before curtain up and took a Number 14 bus to Shaftesbury Avenue. From there he went on foot to his dressing-room at the Lyric Theatre. He was to follow this itinerary on nearly five hundred occasions, for that is the number of performances *The Winslow Boy* achieved. From Binkie Beaumont came an expensive book on the art of glass inscribed: "Dear Emlyn – Many thanks. Binkie. *The Winslow Boy*." And from F2 Albany came a note: "Dear

Emlyn, With so many thanks for your really magnificent performance, and every possible good wish for the future. Terry."

The war was over, and, too, though never forgotten, the nightmare
of bombs and shattered streets and sudden death. Molly set about 15,
Pelham Crescent with builders and decorators. Soon the façade
glistened again in fresh white paint and the box hedge at the side was
clipped and disciplined London fashion. The first-floor drawing-room
looked out through French windows and over the graceful ironwork
of a balcony on to the neat lawns and shrubs of a residents' garden. At
the corner of Number 15 – for it stands at the junction with Pelham
Place – a flowering tree exuberantly thrust its branches over the spiked
white wall that sealed off a little patio. In Pelham Place, a few doors
away, was Oliver Messel whom Emlyn had known as an undergraduate at Oxford. Now a very successful designer, notably for the
stage, Messel lived with his lifelong companion, a massive Dane called
Vagn Riis-Hansen. Vagn had fought courageously in the Resistance
during the war and escaped on three occasions from German
concentration camps. After the war he took British nationality, and,
when his English wife died at a tragically early age, settled down with
Messel as the practical, level-headed mentor whom the phantastical
artist badly needed. For the next twenty years they were hospitable
neighbours to the Williamses and the closest of friends. Spectacular
parties were given and plates and cutlery borrowed one from the other.
"Darling," Messel would say to Molly, "I've just finished my model
for the play at the Globe and I do think it's rather beautiful," seizing
her arm and rushing her off to his studio. Sometimes, when just the
four of them were together, Messel would slip to the floor and lie on
his back. "Oliver, you silly bugger," Vagn would say, "you've been
overdoing it again. Are you all right?" For Messel, unknown to most
people, suffered constant pain from arthritis. Once, commissioned to
design and furnish a colossal house, he remembered a pair of oval
side-tables in Emlyn's home which would perfectly fit the dining
room. They had been one of Molly's inspired *trouvailles* at auction.
Such was his charm that he persuaded her to sell them to him.

A new play now preoccupied Emlyn. *Trespass*, "A Ghost Story in
Six Scenes", was a return, though more adroit, to the Grand Guignol
atmosphere of his earlier work *Vigil*. It takes place in a Welsh castle all
turrets and stone stairs. The main character is Saviello, an Italian who,
supposedly, can speak no English and who is a spiritualist medium –
although, half-way through the play, he is revealed as a Welsh draper
and a fake. "I'm Welsh!" he confesses, "and not a peasant neither, I'm

just as much in the upper classes as anybody, I've got my own shop in Cardiff." What will happen next, for it seems as if the play is over? At this point Williams the master of technique performs a sleight of hand to such effect that by the final curtain, in a scene of blood-chilling excitement, Saviello turns out after all to be a genuine medium able to re-create the past and to call up the dead. Reality, shown to be false, is then proved to be real after all. Had Emlyn remembered his youthful association with Pirandello's *Enrico IV*? The blend of true and false is ingeniously handled. It gave him the opportunity of a virtuoso display as Saviello: "In this room and among these people, there is something unusual about him: he appears so primitive as to be strange. Is he acting any of this, or is it genuine? The people who are now meeting him cannot tell, neither can you the reader, neither can the audience," runs a stage direction.

The role of the widow who refuses to believe that her husband is dead was taken by Françoise Rosay, a French star of formidable power. She had, thought Emlyn, just the right touch of French accent for the part. After making a number of classic French films – *La Kermesse Héroïque, Drôle de Drame, Un Carnet de Bal* – she took refuge in England during the war and developed from *grande dame* into a character actress of international fame. The play was dedicated to her as a token of Emlyn's admiration. Two of his stalwarts also appeared with him: the ebullient Roddy Hughes and the phlegmatic Gladys Henson. He himself gave an eerie impersonation of the medium who, in the climactic scene, is possessed by the spirit of the dead husband and reproduces his last moments on earth. "On the Saturday, it had to be seen to be believed," wrote Miss Cooke. "The number of people sitting *motionless, immoveable* . . . they were just tensely *waiting, waiting, waiting.*" *Trespass* had no other aim than to make the flesh creep and to provide a thrilling night out. In that it succeeded. Some, however, did not agree. An outraged member of the Psychical Research Society protested to Emlyn that he had been ". . . bitterly disappointed, not to say disgusted, that such good acting should be thrown away on such inaccurate nonsense. It is so psychologically incorrect, from start to finish . . ."

Presented at the Globe on July 16, 1947, by the usual team of Binkie Beaumont and Stephen Mitchell, *Trespass* ran comfortably throughout the rest of the year and into 1948. When it came off Emlyn rewarded himself with a nostalgic trip to Paris where he browsed among the *bouquinistes* on the banks of the Seine and discovered new treasures for his collection of old postcards. His theatre visits included Louis

Jouvet's new production of Molière's *Dom Juan* and Jean-Louis Barrault's dramatisation of Kafka's *Le Procès*. Due tribute having been paid to art, he found less exalted entertainment in the Lesbian night club known as "Madame Arthur".

That summer at Park End Alan and Brook were home for the school holidays. One damp and rainy evening they sat around bored and wondering what to do next. They had played all their games, heard all the radio programmes, and Emlyn, for the time being, had exhausted his fund of stories. Suddenly he remembered his wartime broadcast of extracts from Dickens's *Bleak House* and picked up the book again. He opened it at the chapter describing Tulkinghorn's murder and began reading to the boys: "He passes out into the streets, and walks on, with his hands behind him, under the shadow of the lofty houses . . ." Four youthful eyes, at first blank, then quickened and shining, reflected interest. By the time he arrived at the closing words: ". . . lying face downward on the floor, shot through the heart", the two boys were captivated. They went on to read *Bleak House* for themselves and then *Our Mutual Friend*. If, Emlyn thought afterwards, he could grip and hold the interest of two small children on a wet evening by reading Dickens to them, what might he not do with a full-size audience? "From the moment when, like nine people out of ten, I first encountered Dickens in the schoolroom," he was later to write, "for years I thought of him as a favourite story-teller and a great writer of prose. But as nothing else; I assumed his dedication to the printed page to have been absolute. Then, through biographies, I gradually became interested by an extraordinary second career which ultimately dominated his life as powerfully as did his literary output . . . Charles Dickens, as surely as were Macready and Irving, was born with the theatre in his blood. And as over the years he sat toiling at his desk – bowed over a pen steadily forming, one after the other, a few million words – no amount of sedentary and ruminative hours could assuage a natural craving. For the footlights." He thought of the sensational public reading Dickens had given in the later years of his career, of the performances in which their creator had brought to life, with dramatic power and telling mimicry, Sam Weller, Bill Sikes, Mrs Gamp, Mr Tulkinghorn, Paul Dombey, Sydney Carton – four hundred and thirty-three readings in all, their popularity so great that they earned the then staggering sum of £45,000, more than half the total value of his estate. Why should not Emlyn, the professional actor where Dickens was an amateur, attempt to re-create the atmosphere of these occasions?

But before he could do anything further about Dickens a new idea was agitating for expression. He had been reading a novel by Joanna Godden, *A House by the Sea*, and conceived it as a film with himself and Edith Evans, his friend since *The Late Christopher Bean*, as the not-so-young lovers. The company which bought the rights thought Edith Evans too old and insisted on a film test. The test confirmed their fears, she was considered too "stagey", and the project aborted. Soon after that, however, she played the terrifying old Countess in the film *The Queen of Spades*, taken from Pushkin's novel, and proved that on the screen, given the right part, she could dazzle. Knowing her disappointment over *A House by the Sea*, Emlyn was determined to make a film with her. Soon he found the perfect subject in a news item that came his way about plans to flood one of the loveliest valleys in Snowdonia and to create a chain of reservoirs. The public debate was bitter and passionate. He decided he would make a film about a Welsh village in a valley threatened by flooding. Edith Evans would be the old Welshwoman who plays a vital part in the story. Emlyn himself would be the shady adventurer who, expelled in disgrace from the village when a boy, returns to seek his vengeance as agent of the company which plans to turn the valley into a reservoir. The romantic lead would be Richard Burton. For the role of the ancient nobleman, chairman of the water company, he engaged Allan Aynesworth, who was thus to make his first film appearance since *The Iron Duke* twenty years previously. When we see *The Last Days of Dolwyn*, as the film was called, we are also seeing a piece of stage history, for Aynesworth, then eight-four years old, had played the part of Algernon Moncrieff at the first performance of *The Importance of Being Earnest* in 1895.

Richard Burton had completed his National Service in the RAF and been employed by Binkie Beaumont at a small regular salary. He was now twenty-three years old, lacking the traditional regular features of a matinée idol but blessed with something much more interesting in Emlyn's opinion: "the face of a boxing poet". Emlyn gave him the main role in a live television performance of *The Corn is Green*. When he passed a screen test for *The Last Days of Dolwyn* Emlyn sent him a jubilant telegram that quoted a line from the play: "You have won the scholarship." Burton responded well to direction. For his love scenes with Andrea Lea Emlyn would first act out a lively impression of what was needed and then leave him to give his own interpretation. He never disappointed. His portrayal was gentle, moving and humorous. He even sang well and managed to get through a Welsh love ballad which needed several takes before it was right. He never forgot the words, and, years later, Emlyn heard him chant it in duet with Elizabeth Taylor who had made it her party piece. Already, though, he was drinking heavily and Emlyn did his best to dissuade him in long paternal discussions. At the end of one such interview, Emlyn told Melvyn Bragg, "He just stood there, looking so desperate that I gave us both an enormous gin and tonic!" In another attempt to help him settle down, Emlyn introduced him to the nineteen-year-old Sybil Williams who played a small part in *The Last Days of Dolwyn*. A few months later she became the first Mrs Richard Burton. Now he felt that his career was opening up he asked Beaumont for his £15 week to be increased to £20. Binkie compromised with £17.10s. Enchanted with his skilful (so he thought) bargaining, Burton told Emlyn the news. The latter was unimpressed: "Go back and ask for thirty pounds," he advised. Having fortified himself on the way with generous libations, the young actor confronted Binkie and, after a long and heated session, got his way. As he left the room Binkie fired a Parthian shot. "I suppose," he grunted, "that old Welsh pit pony put you up to this."

In July, 1948, shooting began. "The old Welsh pit pony", a nickname he ever afterwards delighted to use, knew a lot about films, having written many scenarios and acted in them. He was not, however, fully acquainted with the techniques of direction, and in this he was helped by an associate director, Russell Lloyd, a veteran of over thirty Korda films. They discussed each scene in detail beforehand. Then, while Emlyn worked on the script with the actors and later came in to rehearse them, Lloyd would take over the preliminary task of smoothing the general movement and layout of a shot. As usual Emlyn surrounded himself with favourite actors. Roddy Hughes exuberated as the village publican and Hugh Griffith gloomed majestically as the local minister all in black. A special role was found for that long-lived character actress Madoline Price, yet another Welsh discovery of Emlyn's. At the age of ninety-two she later played at the National in *Uncle Vanya*. When she was ninety-seven she made her final appearance with Emlyn in the BBC film *Caring*. She was to die, in 1990, just three days short of her hundredth birthday.

The Last Days of Dolwyn, beautifully photographed by Otto Heller, presents a lyrico-pastoral view of a Welsh village at the turn of the century. As in Emlyn's plays, that view is idealised and evokes a way of life that had already begun to vanish before he was born. The characters are drawn with loving skill. There is humour – "We've got to be deported to England!" says a housewife on learning that the village is to be evacuated and flooded; another laments: "They're sending us abroad – to Liverpool!" – and pathos, as when the aged widow Merri, played by Edith Evans, refuses to give up her humble cottage however much money she is offered. Through an ironic twist to the story it is she who finally opens up the flood gates and submerges her much-loved birthplace. Emlyn, sneering of lip, defiant of chin, was a thoroughly nasty villain and came to a melodramatic end: knocked out in a fight with Richard Burton, he was burnt to death and his corpse floated out of Merri's cottage on the rising tide of floodwater. Without a doubt, though, the star was Edith Evans, her Welsh accent extraordinarily musical, her eyes expressing every shade of poignancy and alarm and despair and happiness, her mouth wonderfully mobile – all completely natural, so it seemed, and all quite spontaneous as fine acting should appear to be. Such was her impact on the film, one critic remarked, that she looked as "disproportionate as a life-size Rembrandt in a one-room flatlet."

In *The Last Days of Dolwyn* one may from time to time glimpse the conscious manipulation of the puppet master – as, for example, in the fulsome geniality of the scene where the chairman of the water company is persuaded to change his mind by the guileful Merri – and one may, afterwards, feel that emotion is being cunningly exploited, as when the villagers march over the hill from their flooded village and intone "Land of Our Fathers". Yet, once again, these qualifications only come to mind after the film has ended. While the action is in progress disbelief is willingly suspended. *The Last Days of Dolwyn* has all the characteristics of Emlyn the playwright: vivid characterisation, an eye for the human quirk and comicality, the unexpected development, and, above all, the ability to make the audience want to know what happens next. Perhaps this last talent was responsible for a basic flaw. As C. A. Lejeune wrote: "I doubt if Emlyn Williams, except for a few lines in *The Corn Is Green*, has ever hewed more closely to the heart of poetry than he does in the first two acts of this film . . ." It was the third act, she complained, that detracted from the film's artistic unity with its sensational turn dictated by the exigencies of plotting. Nevertheless, *The Last Days of Dolwyn* merited a better fate than it received. After only a week's run at the Empire, Leicester Square, attendances were so small that it was hastily withdrawn and replaced with a new piece of routine musical rubbish.

If West End cinema audiences had proved fickle towards him, Emlyn's home country at least remained faithful. In April, 1949, he went to Bangor where the University College of North Wales conferred upon him an honorary LLD. Among the other graduands *honoris causa* who received their degrees from Prince Philip, newly installed as Chancellor, were Princess Elizabeth, the Prime Minister, Clement Attlee, and Lady Megan Lloyd-George who had once been Emlyn's pupil for Italian lessons. Said the Public Orator of Dr Emlyn Williams, robed and attentive: "In brief, holding, as 'twere, the mirror up to nature, he is, on stage and screen, the interpreter of Wales to many peoples, and for this we would do him honour." And Prince Philip ended his address with the ringing cry of "*Cymru Ambyth*," which, for the benefit of infidels, means "Wales for ever".

Later that year Emlyn was in New York once more. He had been offered the role of the villainous Izquierdo in Lillian Hellman's adaptation of the Roblès play *Montserrat*, a drama set in early nineteenth-century Venezuela at a time of uprisings led by the patriot Simon Bolivar. Unfortunately Miss Hellman was also to direct the play, but the part was so tempting that Emlyn ignored his earlier depressing experiences with her over *The Little Foxes* and *The Watch On The Rhine* and decided to accept. The decision was a sound one so far as the critics' reaction was concerned. Lean, sardonic, chilling, he gave a bravura study in smiling nastiness which, said reviews, expertly dominated the play. Later produced in London with Richard Burton as the hero, *Montserrat* failed to please New York audiences. It opened in October and closed on Christmas Eve after sixty-six performances. At rehearsals the atmosphere was unhappy, for Miss Hellman proved to be a director with little sympathy for actors – indeed, thought Emlyn, she must positively have disliked them, to judge from the way she lectured and bullied them. She was ill at ease, indecisive. When Emlyn made tentative suggestions about a piece of business or a difficult speech, her face turned to stone and her response was icy. Exasperated, he finally wrote her a letter in which he told her that she did not know how to handle actors. Her reply was vituperative.

He moved on to Hollywood and more congenial work as a departed spirit in the comedy *Three Husbands* with the vivacious Eve Arden and Billie Burke. On the day of the central character's funeral his executor hands a confidential letter to each of his three friends revealing that he had known all their wives rather intimately, whereupon the husbands react in their own way and the wives in theirs, all the time observed with glee by the departed mischief-maker in Heaven. It was a delicate subject, given the rules laid down by the censor Joseph Breen who at that time regulated the morals of the screen. "The Production Code," his office pointed out, "makes it mandatory that the intimate parts of the body – specifically, the breasts of women – be fully clothed at all times." As for a line in the script, "Marriage is a sacred institution", it must be delivered, said authority, "seriously and not with any flavour of being a comedy line." Despite these restrictions, an amusing film emerged and Emlyn played his part with enjoyably pointed malice. At the furnished bungalow he rented in Los Angeles for himself and Molly he spent agreeable evenings culling material for his scrap-books from Hollywood newspapers: an item about a mouse that imagined it was a kitten, another concerning a too-uxorious husband who hacked off his wife's hair to make her stay at home. Best of all, however, were the cuttings he took from *The Times* on his return to England. A correspondence was then raging on the conduct of birds. The headline read: "Badly behaved tits". It was followed by a nature article entitled "More bad behaviour by tits", which opened: "What will the tits be up to next?"

He went that year, unwillingly, to Ascot and sat restive in a private box with Molly, Vivien Leigh and Binkie Beaumont. Bored to death, as he knew he would be, he took some consolation from the knowledge that he had insisted on the bill of £6.3s.6d. for his morning coat and top hat being met as a business expense by H. M. Tennent Ltd. Why should his own pocket suffer the cost of boredom? Another tiresome situation arose when Oliver Messel, as an amicable gesture, painted his portrait. It was in a faintly pointillist style and at least, to one observer, caught the look of Emlyn's eyes. The subject did not think so, in fact detested the picture, and needed all his Welsh eloquence to disguise his true feeling from the well-intentioned friend. At some later date, probably after Messel's death, he quietly disposed of it through Christie's. Worst of all, though, was an incident compromising Molly. On her return from New York she had been fined £200 for, so the customs officer said, attempting to evade duty on a mink stole bought in the USA. "Never mind darling," said the telegram rushed off to her, "it could have happened to any of us, Emlyn."

CHAPTER FIVE

(i)
The Astonishing Glass Shade

It was E. M. Forster who drew attention to "the astonishing glass shade that interposes between married couples and the world." In public the couple seem contented, charmed with each other's company, going everywhere together, doing everything together, a single unit presenting a genial front to the outside observer. Convention sees two people combined as one, sharing intimate joys and disappointments and taking strength from unity behind the insulating glass shade. It is only when the husband elopes with a mistress or the wife makes off with a lover or the marriage crashes for unknown reasons that one realises the glass is not so much transparent as, in reality, opaque.

Emlyn and Molly were known to be a devoted couple. The glass shade around them positively sparkled with affection. During their extended separations, when Emlyn was touring in England and abroad, they wrote long letters to each other. Even at home they exchanged adoring little notes scribbled on the backs of envelopes or scraps of paper. If Molly had to go away for a day or so, she would find a message awaiting her: "All my love, my darling – it won't be long – enjoy yourself – I'll miss you. Emlyn." On Valentine's Day, every year, he never forgot to send a card with some such inscription as: "Longing to see you my darling. I'll ring between 7 & 8. Emlyn." If, for any reason, he was prevented during an absence from writing to her, he would cable: "My darling, I may not write to you once a week, but I do love you just the same. Emlyn." On their wedding anniversary he did not fail to send a card: "All my love always my darling. Emlyn." At a first night he would find in his dressing-room some small present with a note attached: "My darling, you know all I wish you tonight and always. Your loving wife." And when he came back after a tour which had taken him away from London, he would be greeted with: "Darling, I'm so happy you are home. I've missed you so much. My love, Molly."

The emotion, on both sides, was intense. It sometimes erupted, under the stress of events, with scenes of jealousy and recrimination. "My darling," wrote Emlyn after a disagreement, "I love you so much and that is the trouble, isn't it – but it is worth it, I long to see you again and keep reminding myself you will be there on the 1st. Emlyn." On occasion the barbs they hurled at each other recalled Edward Albee's play *Who's Afraid of Virginia Woolf?*, in which a couple lacerate themselves with unforgiving attacks – hence the note from Emlyn: "My darling, I love you very much and you love me very much and I don't think we mean what we sometimes say. Yours always, Virginia Woolf." The Albee play, filmed with Richard Burton and Elizabeth Taylor, had made a deep impression on them, and they often referred to it, wryly.

Molly knew only too well that an actor's life is rich in opportunities for transient affairs. Casual relationships blossom and as quickly wither in the time it takes for a play to run its course or a film to be made. "Tell me," said an earnest young actor to an elderly veteran once, "is Ophelia really in love with Hamlet?" "I don't know, laddie," came the reply, "but in the companies I toured with she always was." Ever round the corner is another play, another film, another broadcast, offering new faces and new personalities to be explored under conditions charged with nervous tension. Since Emlyn was often away for months at a time, in later years travelling throughout Asia and the Americas, Molly sat at home, in London or at Park End, anxious and worried. From New York, once, he tried to reassure her. "My darling," he wrote, "we know (in both countries) so many lone people. I realise more and more how wonderful it is that we have each other, and we must never let ourselves, via moods and irritations, lose sight of that. I think of you more and more as a warm and wonderful other half of myself. And I think that now is the time to say that when I am alone . . . I long to be in bed with you and call to you and talk to you (as I do) – I couldn't imagine anybody else. I know you must sometimes wonder about this and I know if anything awful happened to you and I lost you I would think 'Oh why did I never tell her these things?' . . . I could have affairs with women . . . but I would be miserable about you and wanting you instead any way . . . For instance, [x] is alone in New York and I know she would love a one-night stand with no complications (you know how one knows these things instinctively without anything being said) but I just couldn't – that sounds smug, but you will understand." There had, however, been a deeply-felt affair with an unnamed woman in 1940 while Molly was in America. That, he went on to assure her, was the only occasion to date.

As for the other side of his nature, she was fully cognisant of his bisexuality and knew that the tendency persisted. Had she not, indeed, shared him in the early days with his lover, the disreputable Fess? In the same letter Emlyn goes on to say: "Of course, I have the very occasional encounters of the other sort, but never more than once with the same person, and more and more half-hearted, a matter of expediency – cold blooded almost, with the heart beating (if anything) slower rather than faster." Perhaps he did protest too much. To judge from the testimony of those of his male lovers who are still alive, he must have been as ardent with men as he was with women.

A play Emlyn wrote in 1950 dramatised the contradictions of his private life. He visualised the protagonist as a famous writer, winner of the Nobel Prize for his realistic novels and lately recipient of a knighthood for services to literature. The novelist, however, has a dark secret: from time to time, impelled by his *nostalgie de la boue* and confined by the public existence of a celebrity, he slips away to the East End where he indulges in wild parties. The original version of *Accolade*, as Emlyn called his play, gave his hero a penchant for boys. Since the Lord Chamberlain at that time still had the power of censorship and would never have agreed to this, an under-age girl was substituted as the object of debauch.

The hidden life of Sir Will Trenting is revealed when a blackmailer calls on him. He produces incriminating photographs and announces himself as the father of the girl. Her birth certificate proves that she is only fifteen years old. The blackmailing father seeks an unusual reward. He does not want money. He is a frustrated writer himself and believes that without knowing the right people it is impossible to place literary work. Power and influence are what he is after. He therefore proposes that Trenting employ him as his confidential secretary. Punctuation, he adds, has always been his strong point, as has spelling – the only qualifications, it is sadly apparent, which he possesses as a writer. Perhaps, he slyly hints, he might in time handle Lady Trenting's correspondence for her?

But Lady Trenting already knows about her husband's escapades. As she explains to his publisher: "This side of his life, which you're finding out about now – however unattractive you may think it is – does not come from the attitude of a writer in search of copy . . . The thing about him is, that this side of his life springs inherently from his character as a *man*. He was like this before he ever put pen to paper, and he's stayed like it." She outlines her own attitude: "It's no good pretending I don't wish he were – otherwise . . . But if he were, how do we know he'd still have talent? And he might not even be human, in which case I wouldn't have wanted a thing to do with him . . ." So she has compromised, willing to condone the sleaze for the sake of his brilliant talent and the artistic and material success it has achieved. He tells her: "If I hadn't married you, I would not have lived. I trust you, and you trust me. You need me, and I need you." Then, glancing round him at the luxurious setting of their Regent's Park house, he remarks bitterly: "Cast your mind back to when we first met. I liked living in the mud, and I didn't care who knew it. Trenting the Tramp. But I was a physical wreck, it was killing my work. So I got married. And that gave me security, steadied me down. Damned useful. I had it both ways . . . A wife, a son, a home – how *could* I have thought I had a right to them, as well as to the other? If I liked the mud so much, the least I could have done was stay in it. (Looking round.) I don't belong here." His loyal wife replies: "Don't say that, you'll break my heart."

For a moment she wavers. As she tells his publisher, because she wanted to marry Trenting so much, perhaps she *made* herself not mind his adventures. Had she been firm, he might have reformed. "It was always understood," she adds, "that he should lead his own life side by side with his life with me." Did she make a mistake? They fall silent. The publisher, who plays the part of *raisonneur*, sums up: "Will, two things will help you to face this. First, that we all have one thing *we're ashamed of*. All those out there have. Even the judge, who'll be peering at you over his glasses, making you feel like dirt. His secret may be the nastiest of the lot. Only *you* have committed the sin of being found out . . . The other thing is, that whatever trouble you've got into, you have *lived*. And because you've lived, you've written. Think of the masterpieces round this room. If none of the men who wrote them had ever broken the law, half of the books would never have seen the light of day. That's no reflection on the other half, but it's true. So in the name of . . . François Villon, Thomas de Quincey, Oscar Wilde, Baudelaire, William Shakespeare, and quite a few others . . . take heart."

The blackmailer, rejected, informs the Director of Public Prosecutions. Newspaper headlines exult TRENTING OUT ON BAIL and revel in details of East End orgies, and the knight and the schoolgirl, and obscene photographs. A hostile crowd gathers outside the home. Boos are heard, and the crash of splintering glass as a stone hurtles through a window. Trenting, his wife and his son, now closer together than ever before, prepare to go into exile.

The problem is posed and the details are worked out with Emlyn's usual stagecraft. In the first scene the Trenting family celebrate the newly-announced knighthood, an award the writer has accepted chiefly because of the pleasure it will give his wife. All is sunshine and champagne while his publisher and friends crowd in to congratulate him. At the height of the merriment his butler takes a mysterious telephone call. The audience only hears the butler's side of the conversation and sees his face gradually cloud over. Something, obviously, is untoward, and the curtain falls on a threatening atmosphere. From then on the screw is tightened by an expert hand with revelation succeeding revelation to create a painful impact. Only towards the end does invention falter. The flaw in the immaculate construction emerges when Trenting makes a sudden and quite unlikely repentance. As he holds in his hand the stone which an angry crowd has thrown through the window, he says: "I thought I had the right to be free. But if you're a member of society . . . you have to conform, or crack. You can't have it both ways." The issue has, one feels, in the end been evaded. And in any case, as Emlyn himself knew, it was possible, if at a cost, to have it both ways, provided, unlike Trenting, you weren't found out.

Accolade went on a pre-London tour and scored five triumphant curtain calls in Liverpool. It opened at the Aldwych Theatre on September 18, 1950, and ran for a hundred and fifty performances with Emlyn playing the central character, his skill as an actor persuading the audience to overlook Trenting's abrupt recantation. Lady Trenting was Diana Churchill, dignified, believable. One of Trenting's disreputable companions on his journeys through the lower depths, a barmaidish Cockney, was personated by Dora Bryan, malicious as a kitten. Noël Coward, for one, thought they acted well, though he considered the play to be of "considerable expertness and horrifying vulgarity". Some of the critics agreed while unable to deny its considerable power. Miss Cooke, having read the manuscript, protested: "You'll never get away with it . . . No, George, this play misfires", a criticism which Emlyn stoutly rebutted in a long letter. John Gielgud also had his comment to make. As he left the theatre after the first night he was heard to murmur: "A jolly good play, but Emlyn made it rather too autobiographical for my liking." It was an opinion Molly shared in silence.

During the intervals of *Accolade* Emlyn was deep in Una Pope-

Hennessy's popular biography of Charles Dickens. He read that Dickens had once said: "Nature intended me for the lessee of a National Theatre. Have pen and ink spoiled an actor-manager?" And on another occasion, this time to an actress: "I should like to be going all over the country and acting everywhere. There is nothing in the world equal to seeing the house rise at you . . . One sea of delighted faces, one hurrah of applause . . ." Emlyn paused: a sea of delighted faces . . .

He visited the Dickens shrine in Doughty Street and wandered through rooms where the young writer, at the height of his talent, had lived, slept and worked. The texts which Dickens used for the public readings left him incredulous. Had he really spoken those words in front of an audience and got away with it? The only explanation was that his hearers must have mesmerised themselves into believing that every single word the great man penned was sacred. The mawkishness, the blood and thunder, appalled Emlyn. Mass hysteria on the part of the audience could have been the only reason for the sensational triumph of Dickens's readings.

He was pleased to find that copyright in the books had lapsed in 1920. This gave him the freedom to make his own selection, and with relief he shut up the text of Dickens's own readings. The *pièce de résistance* amongst them had been the murder of Nancy from *Oliver Twist*, an episode to which the author brought so much energy and passion that, a sick man already, he shortened his life. Emlyn would have dreaded the thought of even attempting it. Such was the difference between the instinct of the professional actor and the unwary self-display of the amateur in love with acting for the wrong reason. The amateur moved both himself and his audience. The professional moved only the audience.

After a long and careful reading of the whole canon Emlyn decided that Dickens the actor had not done full justice to Dickens the author in the material he chose for his public performances. He had, in short, neglected the richest vein in his books: the descriptive writing. Emlyn thought again of the passage that introduces the murder of Tulking-horn in *Bleak House*, its evocation of London by moonlight, the feeling it produced when he read it aloud to Alan and Brook. How thrilling it would sound if spoken from the stage! There was no comparison between such masterly writing and the cheap Grand Guignol effect of Nancy's murder.

Since Dickens wrote in newspaper serial instalments which followed each other like a soap opera with the fade-out placed at exactly the right question mark, the books fell naturally into ready-made sections. Cutting, however, was needed, though without harming the rich eloquence of Dickens's prose. This was not difficult, for, as Emlyn discovered, "the extraneous 'fatty tissue' stood out a mile, leaving the gold nuggets glinting bravely through, asking to be turned into speech." He must also remember that the people who went to Dickens's readings were thoroughly acquainted with his books and often knew passages in them by heart. He, Emlyn, should never assume that anyone in the audience was familiar with the book from which he had taken an item.

There remained the most teasing question of all: did the novelist, text in front of him, actually "read" the words or had he memorised them? None of the many eye-witness accounts tell us this. They speak, vaguely, of his being "word-perfect". If this were so he would have needed many hours of learning and rehearsal. As Emlyn the actor-playwright knew, it is far more difficult to memorise what you yourself have written than what someone else has, because the words you have put on paper are already familiar to you and cannot make a wholly vivid impact when you try to learn it. If Dickens had simply read his text, he was denying himself the most telling weapon of all in the armoury of actors, orchestral conductors and anyone who seeks to dominate a group of people: the eyes. How otherwise did he unleash the uncontrollable laughter, swoons and hysteria which accompanied his readings? Did he find, as reading succeeded reading, that he was beginning to half-know his text and then start paraphrasing? This seemed wholly improbable for an author to whom the exact placing of a word in a sentence was of supreme importance. Yet nowhere do we learn of Dickens asking a friend to "hear" him. Since there was no evidence, one way or another, Emlyn liked to think that Dickens, in the midst of all his whirling activities, somehow found time to sit down and "learn his part".[1]

Finally, what form should the presentation take? It should be the same as Dickens's own: a simple background of draperies or screens

---

[1] In the introduction to his edition of the Dickens reading scripts, Professor Philip Collins states that ". . . he [Dickens] recited, for he knew his scripts by heart, and often improvised, or improved upon his original version . . .", although he quotes no direct evidence for this. He adds: "Everybody was riveted by his eyes – eyes 'like exclamation points,' eyes of 'mingled kindness and sharpness,' 'a look of keen intelligence about the strong brow and eye – the look of a man who has seen much and is wide awake to see more,' eyes 'unlike anything before in our experience, there are no living eyes like them,' to quote from American accounts." Philip Collins: *Charles Dickens: Sikes and Nancy and Other Public Readings.* World's Classics, O.U.P., 1983. Emlyn was right in placing emphasis on the eyes.

with the "actor", not "reader", centre stage. There should also be a desk similar to the one used by the novelist and preserved in the Doughty Street house. It was a table with four long slim legs. Stage left, screwed into the top, was an oblong block on which the performer could rest his elbow while holding the book. It served also to rest the whole body. Stage right, the table had a small shelf to accommodate a carafe of water, a tumbler, and a handkerchief for mopping the fevered brow. At the front of the desk a wooden rail provided a welcome resting place for a leg that had begun to ache. The desk was, Emlyn concluded, "the invention of a true man of the theatre."

So now he was ready to emulate the author, "an actor to his fingertips", who once appeared in a play where he took six different parts including an old crone, a tetchy hypochondriac, a waiter and a doddering sexton, passing from one to the other "with marvellous rapidity." Emlyn also had to rival a man who trained his vocal register to produce, often within a single sentence, the gruff tones of Bill Sikes, the drunken drawl of Mrs Gamp, the shrill pitch of Quilp, the piping of children, the bluff roar of Peggotty and the piercing screams of Nancy.

From Morris Angel, the theatrical costumiers, he hired a Victorian evening dress, and from Wig Creations the necessary beard, moustache and hairpiece. An opportunity to try out his new idea came when he was invited to appear at Drury Lane in "Merely Players", a charity matinée organised by various theatrical benevolent societies. At rehearsals in that cavernous theatre he felt an arrant beginner. "More voice," he chided himself, "bigger gestures." He had never worn a false beard before, and as he pressed it to his jaw he wondered fearfully if the spirit gum would melt under the hot lights and reveal his shamefully naked face to a jeering public.

On February 4, 1951, he made up in his Aldwych dressing-room where *Accolade* was entering the last days of its run. Then he went round the corner to Drury Lane. Was he making a terrible mistake? In the deathly, ghost-laden silence before he went on he could hear his heart beating. His throat was parched, he had never in all his life felt so nervous. From the wings he saw a stage-hand nonchalantly position the hallowed desk borrowed for the occasion from Doughty Street. Item eight on the programme came up: "Mr Charles Dickens gives a reading." He strode on, ample of gesture, the Inimitable Boz to the life, and for a quarter of an hour enthralled his hearers with the murder of Tulkinghorn from *Bleak House*. His beard did not slip loose and he remembered all the words. An audience of two thousand had been as rapt by his performance as had his sons that dull and rainy day. The applause, when he ended, was massive.

While playing in *Accolade* he had suffered such pain from a kidney stone that he nearly collapsed on stage. After the closure of the play and his début as Charles Dickens, he felt it was time to despatch the stone for good. Once before, while undergoing agonies, he had moved into a hospital for the operation. The matron, on the eve, happened to tell him that the basic fees would be four hundred pounds a day. His notion of frugality outraged by so shocking an expense, he immediately packed his bags and went home. Happily, the pain soon subsided. This time, however, he did not escape so easily. The operation was carried out at the London clinic, after which he fled thankfully with Molly on a convalescent trip to Kitzbühel and then Taormina.

That Easter he was back in London where a film he had just made, *Another Man's Poison*, opened at a West End cinema. It was a grotesque salmagundi about a woman novelist in love both with her horse and a handsome young engineer. Her ex-convict husband inconveniently turns up and she disposes of him with the aid of a horse pill. Then her husband's accomplice materialises, and he, in turn, is slaughtered by the homicidal female with a cocktail of horse serum in alcohol. A veterinary surgeon unknowingly administers the same concoction to her, and she dies in close-up, laughing and laughing and laughing with maniacal hysteria. Emlyn, mindful of the large fee he was receiving, did his professional best as the horse doctor of the Yorkshire moors. His co-star was Bette Davis, who already knew and liked him from her filming of *The Corn is Green*. She penetrated into his circle far enough to consort with Miss Cooke, another tough woman in the same mould as herself and one of whom she entirely approved. She did not at all get on with the producer Douglas Fairbanks Junior. "The only thing decent that came out of that mess," she later declared, "was the wonderful friendship that evolved with Emlyn Williams. If only he and I could have worked on something decent!" In the hysterical closing scene she gave her party piece as a raving queen of the vixens, snapping and screaming as though she were doing a nightclub impersonation of herself. This was the sort of thing that won her the idolatry of gay admirers by the thousand. There was a joke at the time that featured two of them drinking in a bar. One said: "You must be in love with Bette Davis the way you go on about her so much." Replied the other: "*In love* with Bette Davis: I AM Bette Davis!"

Now Emlyn was free to carry on with his Dickens performance. On July 25, 1951, he began a provincial tour at the Cambridge Arts Theatre. His programme, lasting just over two hours with a pair of ten-minute intervals, was a mixed grill composed of "Moving in Society" (the Veneerings in *Our Mutual Friend*), "Paul" (*Dombey & Son*), "Bob Sawyer gives a party" (*The Pickwick Papers*), "Death of an aristocrat" (*A Tale of Two Cities*), and "Moving higher in Society" (*Little Dorrit*). A master carpenter had built for him an exact replica of the famous desk at which, negligently flipping the pages of a prop book, he performed against a background of black velvet drapes. In the course of his tour he received a letter of congratulation from a great-nephew of Dickens. Even more interesting, he heard from the son of a man who had actually been among the audience at the novelist's readings. Dickens, it appeared, wore heavy make-up and was framed within a gas-lit canopy. Instead of the red geranium Emlyn fixed in his button-hole, he had sported, showman to the last degree, a chunky cluster of diamonds and rubies. Miss Cooke was ecstatic. Had he, she asked, counted the number of characters he re-created on the stage? There were thirty-six. "George," she wrote, "you've never seen your face . . . you've never had the wonderful experience of *seeing* thirty-six characters come to life, some but for a moment, others slowly developed – we outsiders never had your thrill of creation, but we've had a thrill denied to you."

In London, after performing briefly at the Lyric Hammersmith under the aegis of Binkie Beaumont's non-profit-making company, he moved to the Criterion and then settled in at the Duchess. Weekly takings averaged well over £2,000, and since Emlyn's share in addition to his fee was eighty per cent of anything beyond £1,300, the financial arrangements were secure. *The Times* praised his "astonishing virtuosity". It could be nothing less, for he was, in effect, playing one of the largest stage parts ever written, a part which entailed learning more than fifteen thousand words. Each of them was Dickens's own, skilfully edited from the original text. The dandified little man walked on to the stage, bowed stiffly, and with mincing delicacy took off the white gloves which he placed to the side of his reading desk. A sip of water from the carafe, a flick of the pages, and he was off, as he once remarked, "playing the part of Dickens in a play, in the course of which he gives dramatic readings from his works. Only there is no play . . ." Despite the beard and moustache that obscured his features, he made his effect chiefly with eyes that sparkled, flashed, veiled over, brightened, and gleamed again. The timing was exquisite, the voice brilliantly adaptable and veering in an instant from high to low, from tears to laughter, from fear to bravado. "It was difficult," said one critic, "to know whom to admire more, Mr Williams or Dickens."

Next year, in January, he followed Dickens's footsteps by travelling to the USA. There he gave his Dickens "readings" in Boston, scene of the writer's own triumph some ninety years before. Under Sol Hurok's management he went on to New York and gained a reception as warm as he had enjoyed in London. "Magnificent," said Brooks Atkinson, a leading critic. Others praised his "eloquent hands". In March he left New York fortified with gross takings of £26,000. On the way back to England he stopped off at Geneva, another town where Dickens had lived and performed, and charmed a Swiss audience with what one of them described as "magic". The visit had a special significance. While in Switzerland he went to visit Mademoiselle Tardy, the friend whom Miss Cooke had sent him to stay with as a boy.

Saint-Julien lay just over the border in Haute-Savoie. He looked back over thirty-one years and saw the schoolboy George Williams arriving in the town. The place seemed little changed. Under the frigid March sunshine he recognised the old hospital where he used to go for his weekly bath. One side of the town square had been torn down to accommodate a hideous block of flats. The fountain, whose gentle plashing was the first thing he remembered about Saint-Julien, was now pushed into a corner to make way for traffic. At the Cheval Blanc, where he had sometimes eaten a pre-school breakfast, he ordered lunch and felt like a ghost amid the modern chromium plating. Carrying a bunch of flowers he'd bought in Geneva, he walked to Mademoiselle Tardy's house and pressed the bell. There was no reply. He rang again. He turned, and there she was coming down the street.

"I saw advancing towards me my own mother at sixty-five – small, broadened across the middle with the padded effect that slight people acquire when they get heavy," he wrote to Miss Cooke, "snow-white hair pulled back to a bun, dark woollen clothes, one of my mother's long buttoned jerseys – thick ribbed stockings, and flat country shoes, with on her head quite a saucy dark boater: still her rosy colour, and a springy bustling small walk . . ." It was significant that he spoke of his mother.

They chattered in French over tea and cakes. Her eyes danced with amused, cynical curiosity about "*le grand acteur*". She kept their exchanges on a level of ironic banter. How long could this profession of "*artiste*" be expected to last? "So you're alone on the stage, are you?

Is it a lecture you're giving?" No, she would not come and see him perform as Charles Dickens, even though he offered to send a car for her. She shook her head and laughed as if he were suggesting she do a cabaret act at a private party. He was relieved to see that she had no feeling about him beyond inquisitiveness. Sitting in her old country kitchen she looked like a real Savoyard peasant-woman touched with the mischievousness of a Parisian hostess. Perhaps, she conceded, she might come and see his act next year. The sentimental journey had not been so sentimental after all.

He came back to London and a spectacular party given by his neighbour Oliver Messel who was celebrating the first night of a play for which he had designed the scenery and costumes. Overtones of Manet and Renoir predominated. In fact the play, an adaptation of Henry James's *The Reverberator*, was almost stifled by the exuberance of Messel's inspiration. Six flamenco artists flew in from Spain to enliven the party, and Messel's house was decked in the manner of a Spanish fiesta. Ambassadors were there, and writers and artists and actors and members of what was then London's gilded society. They watched the flamenco dancers pirouette into the night and well into the morning. Emlyn went to bed early.

He needed his sleep because each morning he had to be off at an appalling hour to the film studios. He appeared in an American film, *The Scarf*, about an escapee from a lunatic asylum who sets out to prove himself innocent of the crime for which he was immured. It was glum and leaden. More worthy and determinedly well-meaning was *The Magic Box*, a celebration of the cinema pioneer William Friese-Green who died in poverty after heroic efforts to invent the film camera. Headed by Robert Donat, the all-star cast comprised in effect a roll-call of British actors and actresses of the time. Emlyn played, with fussy precision, a disbelieving bank manager. Finally, hair tousled, clad in peasant's rags, he capered blithely as the fey Wamba in a Technicolor version of Walter Scott's romance *Ivanhoe*. This was probably his first encounter with the actress who played Rebecca, a woman who in future was to cause him vexation and to inspire some of his most barbed comments as the wife of his protégé Richard Burton: a young woman called Elizabeth Taylor.

At the Edinburgh Festival of 1952 he acted thirty-five characters in his three-part adaptation of Dickens's *Bleak House*. He brought it to London at the Ambassador's Theatre in September and gave seventy performances. One evening Charlie Chaplin and his wife, in England for the première of *Limelight*, were among the audience. Emlyn paid a nicely phrased tribute to him. "He also is named Charles, and he more than any other man of our time expresses and typifies", with a bow towards Dickens's reading desk, "the spirit of these books."

After touring Germany with Dickens he set off, early in 1953, on extensive travels throughout Canada and the USA. From a one-night stand in the Masonic Hall, Wallingford, he voyaged on to Montreal, Ottawa, Toronto, Boston, Philadelphia and Indiana, not forgetting Baton Rouge and Cedar Falls. Dallas was to know him, and Oklahoma as well. In all he visited some thirty big American cities. It was an exhausting itinerary, though light relief would insist on breaking in. At the Bob Jones University in Greville, North Carolina, visiting artists were warned in a message whose earnestness overcame the rules of grammar: "As a Christian institution, our students and faculty neither smoke nor drink; and we request that all of our artists refrain from either in our buildings and on our campus . . . if an artist appears in backless evening dress, or one with too extreme décolleté, she will find that for our audience she is improperly attired."

By road and by rail he criss-crossed immense distances charted by Sol Hurok's efficient office. Trains were timed to the minute, cars were always punctual, hotel reservations slotted into the jigsaw with unfailing smoothness. In Beverly Hills he stayed at a crazy bungalow owned by the Richard Burtons – "very Golders Green". On the set of *How to Marry a Millionaire* he was introduced to Marilyn Monroe, "the sweetest demurest sexiest little girl you ever saw." In another studio where *Rain* was being shot he met "a very demure shopgirl ('Pleased to meet you') who turned out to be Rita Hayworth." He went to a preview of her new film *Salome*, and when John the Baptist's head was carried into the banqueting hall, a voice at the back of the audience shouted: "Man, get that cr-r-r-azy dessert!"

The first week in April saw him emerge from the Cabbagevilles of middle America and arrive in San Francisco. From there he travelled on for a three-week season in New York at the Shubert Theater. His opening night was the twenty-fifth anniversary of the date when he began his duties as call-boy and assistant stage manager on *And So To Bed* in that very theatre. Now he was the solo star, his name in flashing lights on the marquee and dominating the posters in big fat capitals. Now, too, he was performing his version of *A Tale of Two Cities* on television at a fee of £100 a minute compared with the £12 a week he had earned as assistant stage manager. In New York he brought himself up to date on the gossip he adored. Laurence Olivier's marriage to Vivien Leigh was crumbling, and Emlyn purveyed to Molly the sort of juicy story which lurked in the background during Olivier's lifetime and was to persist long after his death. "The whispered rumour is that Larry is in Italy with a BOY!!! I simply can't believe it; has it penetrated to your side? If it hasn't, for heaven's sake don't breathe a word (except to [X] of course, and to [Y] so he can tell Bobby). I do hope the news is better about Vivien, it still seems incredible."

The New York season brought full houses and critical praise. He returned to London, and, after a holiday in Italy, to new honours. The Royal Society of Literature made him a Fellow. In August he was elected President of that year's Eisteddfod. Wearing Druid's robes as a member of the Gorsedd, he delivered in impeccable Welsh, his first language, a touching address.

During his Italian holiday he had written a new play. It was based on a favourite murder case, one well known to criminologists and featuring a victim known as Julia Wallace who was killed by her husband in 1931. As usual, he wrote it backwards, getting the climax right first and then working in reverse through the events that led up to it. *Someone Waiting* is perhaps the most ingenious of his thrillers and the most tautly constructed. The opening scene is a model of economical playwriting. In four brief pages of dialogue, with seeming effortlessness, Emlyn conveys essential information and sketches characters indelibly in the mind of the audience. We learn that John Nedlow is a pompous tycoon whose loveless marriage to his wife Vera is camouflaged by a display of false affection; that they are both exasperated by their rebellious adopted son Martin; that Nedlow is having an affair with his secretary; that there has recently been a mysterious murder in the Nedlow home; and that for this reason the Nedlows have put the flat on the market. All these facts are established with perfect naturalness in a brilliant expository passage.

The groundwork having been established, a maid reports that there is "someone waiting" in the hall. The "someone" is a Mr Fenn, a dim little tutor engaged to "cram" Martin for his law exams. Gradually the nondescript Mr Fenn is revealed to be the father of a young man executed for the murder committed in Nedlow's flat. When he discovers that Nedlow himself is the murderer, he plans a complicated scheme to avenge his son's death. It goes horribly wrong, for in carrying it out he kills an innocent girl and then organises his own suicide in such a manner that Nedlow will be found guilty of murdering him. "Will you ring the nearest police station," says Vera

Nedlow, the long-suffering wife who now foresees release from her unbearable husband. "Tell them there's been a murder."

Emlyn played Fenn, a bespectacled, shabby creature in worn raincoat and baggy suit, nervous, unsure of himself. As the play goes on the sinister undertones of his character begin to emerge: he is obsessed with an urge to kill the man who encompassed the execution of his beloved son for a murder he did not commit. When he takes Martin into his confidence and outlines his maniacal plan, the Nedlows' adopted son says to him in horror: "You've crossed a frontier. Into a different world." "Haven't *you*?" asks Fenn. "No, replies Martin, "you've left me behind. I've no passport." "What would you call my new world?" "Madness. You're utterly mad." "You're utterly mistaken. My world is a magic place. The air is fresh – I'm released – I've just been born – but as a full-grown man – no, a god. A god . . ." This was Emlyn the dramatist writing words he knew Emlyn the actor would deliver with chill intensity.

Someone Waiting opened its provincial tour in Liverpool, scene of the Julia Wallace murder some twenty years before. The play went on to Cardiff and took well over £2,000 in a week. Emlyn was happy to be back again working with other people, for the Charles Dickens show, rewarding though it had been, was a lonely business. It was good to be a member of a cast once more, reacting to other players and responding to cues. With him were Gladys Henson, ripely convincing as an ex-barmaid, and another old friend, Adrianne Allen, Raymond Massey's ex-wife and here playing the unfulfilled Vera Nedlow. They opened at the Globe Theatre in November and had a run of a hundred and fifty-seven performances, about the average for Emlyn's later plays. Miss Cooke reserved her judgement: "Oh! don't say I didn't appreciate *Someone Waiting*, I didn't and I don't think of it as a thriller, though I felt that part was very ingenious; but the father fascinated me, you've done some very interesting characters, never one more interesting . . . You wrote it very quickly, didn't you, and Molly said she complained that not a single character was sympathique, and you softened down the wife a bit, if only we could have felt full sympathy for that father, but somehow or other, – well! well! It was like going into a most attractive room, and there was something not quite right – and Molly puts her finger on the spot, I canna." Later, she was to decide: "I'll own it's a box of tricks." She was right. *Someone Waiting*, like *Trespass*, was a box of tricks artfully designed by a skilful actor-playwright to create suspense and to give himself a plum part.

Someone Waiting achieved the commercial success which always evaded *Pen Don*, that ugly duckling of his apparently condemned never to turn into a swan. Tyrone Guthrie, a friend at Oxford and now a well-known director, became interested in it and Emlyn, once more, revised his mythic play drastically. Immensely tall, like "a maypole" as Emlyn once described him, Guthrie was a cousin of the American film actor Tyrone Power. He was also a man of vivid enthusiasms and the only theatre director known in history to have run a jam factory. He established it in the disused railway station of an Irish village where he had spent his schoolboy holidays. The signal box was transformed into an office, the freight shed became a kitchen and refrigeration plant, and the waiting-room served as a laboratory. "No artificial colouring or flavouring is added," said the label proudly, "and no chemical preservatives whatsoever are added." The financial problems this foolhardy enterprise caused were to plague Guthrie until he died.

Pen Don became as dear to this lover of lost causes as the jam factory. A current passion for mythology had led him to take up Emlyn's play, and in 1954 he quixotically turned down other important commissions for the sake of staging it in Swansea. He assembled a cast of amateurs and lovingly directed three performances in the Natural History Museum of that city. There was no scenery, the action took place on an oblong rostrum, and through a leaking roof there dripped water in a steady, lugubrious pit-a-pat. Yet those who saw this production considered it a miracle of staging "with utterly magical moments". Among those moments for the American actress Ruth Gordon, who never forgot it, was the one where the boy Lan refuses to join the others on their journey to Avalon and remarks simply: "I don't think I'm goin'." With that moment of magic Emlyn had to be content, and the typescript of *Pen Don* went back into a drawer again.

He holidayed in Venice that summer and was invited with Molly to a reception for the Duke and Duchess of Windsor at the Besteguy Palace, restored at vast expense by its Mexican millionaire owner. They were presented to the Duchess, shorter than expected and with a tiny tiny waist. "I *love* the Welsh," said she, "and my favourite is Aneurin Bevan, perhaps because he's controversial and I've been a figure of controversy myself." Her fan fluttered, her vivacious metallic smile clicked on and off. (If there was an Iron Duke, Emlyn said afterwards, she'd certainly be an Iron Duchess.) The Duke was called over, "small, preoccupied, a wizened schoolboy of sixty, lost, lost". He spoke with cordiality but with the unmistakable royal tone of clipped authority. "Are you a painter?" "Don't you remember, darling," the

Duchess broke in, "one of your greatest actors, from *your* country, darling." "Ah! Wales," said the Duke, adding in perfect Welsh: "The land of my fathers is dear to me." It was very jauntily done. "I saw Megan last year," Emlyn ventured." "Oh," the Duke replied, "they tell me she's gone rather funny lately." They wandered off. The last Emlyn saw of the man whose story had made such an impression on his and Molly's generation was a tiny figure in a vast empty salon talking with a large American woman. The Duke looked around in a haunted way. "Where's my wife? I must find my wife."

(ii)

Emelett, Emden, Emmelin, Emiline, Amlyn, M. Lynn, Emilio, Dmly, Mnmlyn and Others

One day, under the caption "A household name – Emlyn Williams", he pasted into his scrapbook a selection of envelopes addressed to him bearing twenty-five variations on the spelling of his Christian name. They ranged from MLYNN to EMLYON, from EMILIO to MNMLYN, from MELYN to EYLYA. The stamps they bore came from all over the world, including South Africa, where, in the autumn of 1954, he took the Charles Dickens recital on a long tour from Johannesburg to Gatoona. His repertory was different this time and included extracts from *David Copperfield*, *Little Dorrit*, and a grotesque Mrs Gamp episode from *Martin Chuzzlewit*. Entirely new was a piece from the lesser-known *Battle For Life*, an item he was unfamiliar with until, of all people, Vivien Leigh brought it to his attention.

In South Africa he renewed acquaintance with Molly's mother and sister who lived in Cape Town, and there met, for the first time, his brother-in-law, manager of a mine at Filabusi. He also appeared in a testimonial advertisement for Albany Filter Tipped Cigarettes. "I utter nightly nearly 20,000 words," he was reported as saying under a beaming picture of himself. "I dared not smoke until I could find a cigarette I knew would soothe." The copy went on to state that this was "certainly a deserving tribute from a great man to a great cigarette, Albany." Other personalities visiting South Africa who testified to

Albany included Richard Burton, Claire Bloom, Eric Portman, Lilli Palmer and Bobby Helpmann. It is unlikely that Emlyn received his fee in kind. He never, all his life, smoked a cigarette for pleasure, and it was a habit he disliked in others. But the money was attractive.

After South Africa he made a film with Vivien Leigh, a version of Rattigan's *The Deep Blue Sea* in which she had appeared on stage with Kenneth More. She had, Emlyn told her biographer Alexander Walker, "an odd, funny-peculiar turn of mind". He remembered a location scene with the two of them in a car driving past the camera and turning a corner. At the third take, as they climbed back into the car once more, she said, almost as if she wanted it to happen: "Wouldn't it be funny if we drove off now, and nobody ever saw us again?"

As a play *The Deep Blue Sea* is a well-built piece of theatrical construction. The dramatic interest never flags, the scenes are developed with finely graded control, and not one word could be cut from the dialogue without harming the fabric. It is based on the simple theme of A who loves B who loves C, none of them being loved in return. William Collyer (Emlyn) loves his estranged wife (Vivien Leigh) who is desperately in love with the irresistible but weak and feckless Freddie Page (Kenneth More). In the end, after two suicide attempts, she resigns herself to his departure for Canada where he has been offered a lucrative job. The plot does not sound much, but in the hands of a craftsman like Rattigan it thrums with life. Emlyn, as the high court judge who vainly attempts to win back his wife, gave a softened version of Sir Robert Morton in *The Winslow Boy*, precise and pinstripe-trousered yet at the same time much more human and at the mercy of emotion. Although Rattigan himself wrote the screenplay, the narrative does not quite seem to have the mesmerising effect of the stage original. Its main value is that it preserves the fine performances of Vivien Leigh and Kenneth More, and also gave Emlyn a chance to depict the well-meaning but dull husband – and dullness needs to be skilfully portrayed by an actor if he is not to bore the audience.

Once the film was out of the way – he would have agreed with Dennis Quilley that the theatre makes you happy, television makes you famous, films make you rich – he turned back to his study of an author who was beginning to preoccupy him as much as Dickens. In 1954, shortly after the poet's death, he had appeared with Richard Burton and Edith Evans in a *Homage to Dylan Thomas* programme of poetry, music, and drama. It was presented at the Globe Theatre, and Emlyn read two short stories, "A Visit to Grandpa's" and "Just like little dogs". On a Sunday night at the Old Vic he also took part in a reading of *Under Milk Wood*, and savoured once again the wealth of language, the exuberance, the surrealistic humour, which had so impressed him when Richard Burton made the dark Soho streets ring with Thomas's lines. The more Emlyn read of his work, the nearer he felt to him. "What fun he *is*, in every paragraph of the prose . . . I went about reading line by line with the loving care of the dredger after gold. The limpid-clear imagination of a brilliant child, the devastating humour of the completely honest man – no, child again, for even when . . . the boy is grown up, you feel that essentially he is as much of a child as ever, and always will be." The emphasis is put on Dylan's prose. Much of the verse, Emlyn candidly avowed, was beyond him. He simply did not understand it.

He never encountered Thomas. One evening, in 1950, at Christopher Isherwood's house in Santa Monica when Emlyn was making *Three Husbands*, the poet was expected to call while on a reading tour. Typically, he did not arrive. "I'm glad he didn't," said Emlyn. "Hollywood . . . doesn't seem the right setting for a first meeting between two Welshmen. A Swansea pub on a damp night would have fitted better: fog smelling of dirty sea, yes – smog smelling of clean celluloid, no."

Why should he not do for his fellow Welshman what he had done for Dickens? He had had to call his Dickens performances "readings", since that was the term the author himself used, although Emlyn's trick was to bring the books on, "using them purely as a dramatic effect, and by looking at them at certain moments, mime the turning of pages where it was effective, and *never* use them for reading from." He would do the same with Thomas. But he refused to call his programme a "reading". "What should it be? "A one-man marathon? A solitary symposium? A monodrama of moods? A Cymric kaleidoscope? A farcical fandango? A lone-wolf welter?" He finally settled for "an entertainment".

Whereas he had made himself up to look like Dickens with beard and frock-coat and flower in button hole, he would not even try to impersonate Thomas, who resembled, in his own words, "an unmade bed", pop-eyed and bee-stung of lip. The style of presentation would be more informal: just a backdrop with the poet's signature scrawled across it and a Chippendale chair centre stage. At the Connaught Theatre, Worthing, on April 25, 1955, Emlyn introduced *Dylan Thomas Growing Up*, an entertainment which chronicled the boy's life from the ages of five to seventeen. He wore a formal lounge suit and a red tie. "I come on with a pile of manuscripts, say they are the stories, lay them on the floor, and never look at them again; thenceforth I sit, jump up, lie down, pull faces, walk, run, wink, laugh, cry, play the piano, and paddle in the sea." On that first night he was handicapped by a bout of influenza. The audience was small, and during the two ten-minute intervals a lady pianist bravely tinkled melodies from *There's No Business Like Show Business* while a shrunken house evaporated to find solace in the bar.

His influenza, and his audience, improved as he toured Bath and Cambridge to arrive at the Globe Theatre for his London opening on May 31. *Emlyn Williams as Dylan Thomas Growing Up* pleased the West End and ran at the Globe for nearly three months. The fifteen thousand words Emlyn memorised included seventeen extracts from Thomas's autobiographical writings, chiefly *Quite Early One Morning, Portrait of the Artist as A Young Dog, Adventures In The Skin Trade*, and several short stories. These were interspersed with a few of the more accessible poems: "Fern Hill", "The force that through the green fuse drives the flower", "The Hand", "Love in the Asylum," and "In my Craft or Sullen Art". Unlike the fiery Dickens readings, this was a more intimate performance with the emphasis on quiet humour. The audience felt as if it were eavesdropping on a private recital which Emlyn was giving for his own pleasure. At the end he trailed into the distance with the poet's words growing fainter. The curtain fell, then rose again as a spotlight picked out the chair on which Dylan's papers and notes lay mute.

"The recital is rich in fun, wit, pathos, poetry, characters, humanity, and an all-pervading, intensively attractive quality for which there is no other word but Welshness," said Alan Dent, echoing a general opinion. In the autumn, after a triumphant London season with eighty-five performances of *Dylan Thomas*, Emlyn went on a tour of Holland. At his return to Great Britain, in Swansea with some trepidation he prepared to meet Mrs Thomas, the poet's mother. He saw a merry old lady, white-haired, pretty, with Dylan's little nose. She hobbled in on two sticks and said: "When you came on stage and said you were Dylan, I didn't believe you, but by the end I did. I want to come again." He beamed with pleasure.

"Yes," she went on, "I lost him, and Daddy and his sister Nancy, *and* fell down and broke both my legs, all in one year. It wasn't a very good year for me, was it? If I'd had four legs I suppose I'd have broken the extra two as well ... Daddy was the English master in the grammar-school, you know, and every day Daddy and Dylan used to read Shakespeare together, he was Dylan's favourite author, with Dickens . . . People say to me, 'Mrs Thomas, where *did* Dylan get his brains?' well I think that's rude, don't you? I always answer back 'I can't imagine where, it can't be from *me*, so it must be Daddy!' . . . However did you learn all those words tonight? I don't want to sound rude, but you actors must have minds like sponges! I brought a present for you."

From a brown-paper wrapping she drew forth a gaudy cardboard box that once contained cheap ties. "Dylan always used to keep his poems in this when he stayed with me." Inside were several scraps of ruled paper which bore, in his tiny and carefully rounded hand, the first drafts of poems. In the margin were doodled sketches of the sort children scribble when they can think of nothing to write. Emlyn visualised the poet sucking his pencil, drawing another face, sucking the pencil again.

"Yes," said Mrs Thomas, "there wasn't an ounce of harm in Dylan, bless him . . . The piece you do about the two of them going to the sea-shore – I remember him and the other boy missing the bus home and having to walk fifteen miles and they hadn't had a bit of food and no money, so they climbed into an orchard and pinched some apples and the farmer chased them off – the state his clothes were in when he got home! but he enjoyed life . . ." She sighed – but smiled too.

Another journey took Emlyn and Molly to Sandringham for a miniature command performance in the Queen Mother's drawing-room. One mellow evening as he described it, they drove through idyllic woods and trees and lawns up to the hideous façade. A nervous young man received them – it was only his second day as aide-de-camp – and led them on to a terrace overlooking a sunken lake where cygnets placidly cruised. At dinner the Queen Mother explained that the Goya tapestries on the wall had been given to George V by the King of Spain. The plates, Emlyn noticed with amused recognition, were the same as his at home in Pelham Crescent. Conversation was informal. A royal personage made up her lips in the middle of dinner, and, before the courses were finished, smoked cigarettes through a long holder. After the ladies had risen and gone, the men sat round the dinner table. "Are you nervous?" hissed a courtier to Emlyn. "Do tell me – *are* actors nervous? Do you ever feel not in the mood?"

They joined the ladies in the drawing-room. With lights fixed to shine up on his face, Emlyn gave an hour and a half of Dylan. The audience played its part brilliantly and laughed a lot. Afterwards the royal personage put on records from her favourite musical, *Carmen*

Jones, which accompanied her everywhere on her travels. She told Emlyn how she remembered meeting Dylan Thomas. "He had china-blue eyes and looked absolutely splendid." Her teeth, Emlyn observed as she sat and made up her lips again before a little mirror, were whitely magnificent. Quite a little madam, he thought, and more like a film starlet than royalty.

At half-past midnight, while some drank whisky and others tea, the Queen Mother rose and said goodbye. They stood awkwardly, since etiquette demanded that one should wait for royalty to leave first. She resolved the situation with tact. "I think the car is outside, isn't it?" she said sweetly, and they left.

That December he came back to the stage as member of a cast with Dorothy Tutin and Michael Gough. She played Hedwig and he Hjalmar Ekdal in Ibsen's *The Wild Duck*. "Ekdal's hypocrisy is made extremely amusing by Emlyn Williams when, surely, it ought to be rather more horrifying," said one review. *The Times* remarked that he played "the egocentric photographer as though he were one of Dickens's self-conscious humbugs". This was a review that tended to recur more and more often whenever he appeared in a play with other actors. So much time spent in solo performances as Dickens and Dylan Thomas instilled habits which became difficult to shake off. There was a temptation to dominate, to stand out from the rest of the cast. There were problems of integration.

These reservations inhibited critical reaction to his three major Shakespearean appearances in 1956. Nineteen years after playing Angelo in *Measure for Measure* and earning high praise from James Agate for his "diabolical ingenuity" and beautiful verse-speaking, he agreed to repeat the rôle in the current Stratford season. He also undertook Shylock and Iago. As always he prepared himself in the finest detail. The text he used was the 1895 large-paper Cambridge edition whose many volumes marched in stately array across his bookshelves. Soon every available white space of the end-papers and pages, thickly sumptuous and deckle-edged, was blackened with hastily scribbled rehearsal notes. Scenes were analysed, difficult words spelt out, rhymes marked, stresses picked up. The prose passages received as much attention as those in verse. Iago's speech in Scene ii, Act IV, for example, was underlined in blue pencil, as was all his part, and broken down: "I grant indeed/it hath *not appeared*/and *your* suspicion is not without wit/and judgement. But, Roderigo (if thou hast *that*-in-thee indeed, (which I have greater reason to believe [now/than *ever*]./I mean purpose, courage and valour)) this-night/

show it: if thou (the next night following)/*enjoy not* Desdemona/take me/from this world/with treachery/and devise *engines*/for my life." In a marginal note Emlyn warned himself of the unexpected alternation between "you" and "thou", something which tripped him up if he did not take care.

His make-up preparations were equally detailed. For Shylock, the diagram specified black then red over the month, the upper lip and the lower eye-lids to be highlighted. There were black lines over the eyes and their ends were also highlighted. Shadows were touched in on cheekbones, under the mouth, with highlights over and under eyes, over mouth and on chest and neck. The nose was shadowed and nostrils were outlined with black pencil and highlighted. The dome of the forehead was highlighted. "Beard, moustaches, wig, eyebrows, dress, hands, nails," added the notes. Teeth were to be darkened with black pencil.

That was how he made his debut as Shylock at Stratford in April, cheeks pearled with sweat, nose razor-sharp and crooked, lips fat and gleaming between straggly moustache and wispy beard. Emlyn's particular gift brought a specially sinister flavour to the old money-lender, yet in the trial scene, malignant though the character was, he managed to gain the sympathy of the audience. Attention was held throughout by his abrupt switches from sardonic cunning to breast-beating hysterics. This, said one critic, was "a grey, greasy, shambling Shylock". Another complained that his interpretation, although consistent, had a precise but artificial accent suggesting a rabbi unable to forget his synagogue manner. What no-one could deny was the quality lauded by Agate so many years ago: the crystalline delivery of the words in which every syllable emerged with clarity. It was an object lesson in how to be heard and understood.

His Iago, inevitably, encouraged critics to evoke his manner as Dickens and Thomas. Here, Kenneth Tynan began, was an Iago who looked like "a swart boy mortician" and who, in a vein of bleak mechanical frigidity, delivered his lines with the sarcastic emphasis of a Latin master reading out for ridicule the latest prose composition of his most backward pupil. Encouraged by his triumph as a solo performer, Tynan concluded, Emlyn recited rather than played Iago. To compensate for his slight physique – although, as actors say, he always contrived to fill his space – Emlyn adopted a crouching stance as he circled around Harry Andrews' Othello, knees bent, fingers flexing, like a monstrous insect waiting to leap on its prey. This was a study in frank revenge, all black and white, and untrammelled cynicism.

In the years that passed since he first played Angelo, Emlyn's view of the character had changed. As a young actor he saw in the complicated Puritan a fair-haired libertine. Now, in his early fifties, he visualised a man for whom power was as desirable as sex. His reading of the part concentrated on the hypocrisy that results from the conflict between these two urges. Again the critics remained undecided. One of them, at least, did not let him down. His wife left him a present in his dressing-room. "Darling," she wrote, "I thought you were wonderful last night and am longing for tonight. We are all very thrilled to be here. These glasses and little box will add to your collection. All my love, Molly." Miss Cooke put things in her plain-spoken way: "I think of critics, and much as I detest their glib writing, I can see their-almost-annoyance! They can't get hold of you – what are you? – actor? writer? director? . . . if you could have 'felt' the intensity of Mrs Owen's pride [a Welsh friend of theirs] that you, Emlyn Williams, ever the 'nice' Emlyn Williams who was always helping, and yet the Emlyn Williams of Shylock and Iago, if you could feel the pride of the thousands of ordinary folk like her, – well! I think that perhaps you would pause a little and not always, always be driving yourself . . ."

After the last night of what had been an exhausting season he recited a farewell poem in the Memorial Theatre which ended:

"Once more the Swan of Avon folds his wing
To hibernate until the Ashcroft spring."

Following which he perpetrated even direr doggerel in an end-of-term cabaret for himself and other members of the company. His own lines included:

"I'm just an old White Welsh pit pony,
While Badel plays Hamlet, I in Dylan Thomas in Mentone,
And it couldn't matter *less* to me
How Redgrave played Shylock in Fifty-three."

After the rigours of five hard-working months it was a time for relaxation. Someone asked what he thought about Paul Robeson playing Othello at Stratford. "Look black in anger," he replied.

After Stratford he went on tour again with Dickens and Thomas. The turn of the year found him in South Africa. Molly was staying there in Cape Town on a visit to her mother, now frail with the after-effects of a thrombosis, yet, despite bad nights, in good spirits. She had been reading Hesketh Pearson's new biography of Beerbohm Tree, the witty Edwardian actor-manager, and one of the jokes made her laugh so much that it brought on another attack. Later, out of curiosity, she peeped at the end of the book to see the cause of Tree's death. It was a thrombosis. She hastily shut the book, turned off the light and tried to sleep.

The high point of this South African tour was Emlyn's Dylan Thomas entertainment at the Bantu Social Centre. "What a wonderful audience ... They listened like intelligent children, rapt, excited to quick laughter and to quicker silence. And one realised how Dylan, describing his dreams in sordid Swansea, could so easily have been a gifted coloured boy in Jo'burg dreaming of escape. Things like, in the opening passage – mention of a passport – they can't have one. The boys escaping "from the streets that owned us", "Abyssinia" for "I'll be seeing you". They screamed wildly at the schoolroom jokes. The only pleasantry they missed was the two boys discussing a girl: "Is she young?" "No, she's twenty or thirty." For them, a girl *was* old at twenty. At the end a black boy came on stage to present Emlyn with a book and quoted Dylan's poetry. During the interval another had brought him tea and remarked: "Sir, this is what we have been hungering for."

With Molly at his side the tour became a vacation as well. After lounging on the beach at Johannesburg in streaming sunshine he was interviewed by a journalist. Yes, he said, he was enjoying a splendid holiday. "Surely it isn't all holiday, Mr Williams. There's the show every night." "That's not work. It's fun, and I do it for fun."

He was back in London briefly for the premiere of *I Accuse!*, a film about the Dreyfus case directed by José Ferrer with a screenplay by Gore Vidal. Ferrer played Dreyfus, Donald Wolfit the war minister and Anton Walbrook the true culprit. Emlyn was Emile Zola, the crusading novelist who fought on behalf of the innocent Dreyfus. He read out, with silky conviction, the famous letter in which Zola accused the French government of injustice. He was, thought some critics, a little too smooth. That March he appeared as a guest of honour at the annual dinner of the Critics' Circle. He told them he had an idea for a musical version of *Oedipus Rex*: it would be called *Mum's The Word*.

In the autumn of 1957 he began a major tour of the USA with *Dylan Thomas: A Boy Growing Up* at the Long Acre Theater in New York. His two-week engagement there sold out. Critics wrote about "an evening of pure charm", "ribald, rose-coloured, runaway prose", "a wonderful world of wackiness". "Every phrase does a comic dance," said Brooks Atkinson. "It is not only entertaining. It is a revelation."

From Basil Rathbone, the South African-born English actor long since established in Hollywood as the personification of Sherlock Holmes, came an admiring letter: "The sheer magic of your performance will live with me for the rest of my life. I have seen and heard great artists accomplish great things – Nijinsky, Chaliapin, Caruso, Forbes-Robertson – you belong with them."

Emlyn was both writer and actor, like Dickens, and he needed an audience. He knew of few emotions that could compare with the feeling he experienced when, through the exercise of his technique, he dominated his hearers, could make them rock with laughter or shiver with sadness. "When Dickens went on tour and read from his own works," he told an American journalist, "he went through all the emotions involved at every performance. But the trick is to exhaust the audience emotionally – not yourself." And yet, in the midst of this triumphant exercise of his craft and art, there were moments, as he zig-zagged back and forth across America on Sol Hurok's meticulous itinerary, when he longed for home and Molly. "I miss you terribly and of course feel very homesick," he wrote from Princeton. From New York: "I shall miss you terribly darling and realise more and more how much you mean to me . . . I wish I could put into words my love for you – but I can't – will you try and take it for granted?"

Depression lifted when he appeared before an audience or picked up the latest witticisms circulating around New York. Under General Eisenhower's bland presidency, he reported, the White House had been christened "The Tomb of the Well-known Soldier." In November he went to the first night of Coward's *Nude With Violin*, done in London the previous year with Michael Wilding in the role which Coward himself took at the New York première. Emlyn drove down to the theatre "with Claudette Colbert and Cole Porter in his car, the full glamour: Noël in a crew-cut looking like the most intelligent old marmoset in a Chinese zoo – he got an exciting reception as you can imagine, but the play went steadily downhill, as you might expect – he gave it a sort of fake brilliance but it just isn't enough."

Within a few months he had a first night of his own. His new play *Beth* opened on March 20, 1958, at the Apollo. "Mr Williams," an elegant matron had recently said to him in New York on his Dylan Thomas tour, "do you ever act with actors?" On the occasion of *Beth* he did not, for he chose to direct, and, indeed, needed all his theatrical skill to make the play come alive. John Perry, Binkie Beaumont's partner at H. M. Tennent, had turned it down. "I think I ought to say straight out in my opinion it is impossible to write a play about a mental defective as the principal character," he told Emlyn. "I feel it would be too painful and embarrassing for the audience. I have a little experience of it in so much as my Mother was out of her mind for the last three years of her life."

Beth puts on stage a weird family whose head, a strong-minded, widowed mother, has just died. Her younger daughter Beth, a girl of sixteen with a mental age of eight, feels lost without her, as in fact the rest of the family does, and dresses her doll in black. Beth transfers her devotion to her sister Lydia who is about to marry a very rich man. Lydia, realising where her duty lies, nobly renounces her suitor and the prospect of a luxurious existence. At this point her uncle, an amputee in a wheelchair who has spent most of the time until now bitterly lamenting his fate, suddenly overcomes his innate selfishness and dedicates himself to looking after Beth. They are both, he says, "special persons", and "there are many others like us, all over the world. Beth, at the moment, you and I are alone. And nobody's any good alone." Critical response was flaccid, although, as *The Manchester Guardian* remarked, ". . . in the dramatic terms of tension and surprise his skill retains all its old compulsive *brio*; one may not entirely believe in his story when the curtain is down, but while the play is in progress it is impossible not to wonder with some eagerness exactly what is going to happen next." In *Beth* Emlyn's taste for the bizarre had misled him. Despite his skill the overall impression remains, as John Perry warned, uncomfortable and embarrassing. And there are inconsistencies. Would Beth's brother, a student pianist of virtuoso promise, endanger his hands through a holiday job working in a brickyard, even though he wears gloves? A more serious flaw is the amputee uncle's abrupt change of heart. In one sentence he is transformed from an egotistical moaner into a saintly pillar of strength. What saved *Beth* at the first night was the performance of Ann Beach in the title role, a psychological tour de force which brought special applause for her.

Since H. M. Tennent had rejected the play it was Stephen Mitchell, Emlyn's faithful ally ever since *The Corn Is Green*, who stepped in and presented *Beth*. After *Beth* Mitchell was often to remonstrate with him: why did he go on performing Dickens and Thomas instead of writing plays? Emlyn's answer was short and bleak. "I can't get any more ideas for plays".

(iii)
Pinterland

It was a refrain that echoed dismally throughout the rest of his life. A week or so after *Beth* started its short career he was touring New Zealand with the Dickens recital and writing to Molly: "I just haven't the deep waters to swim in, nor the inner urge to do the swimming. I have facility, ingenuity, stage sense, industry, the instinct for perfection – not enough . . . I *may* suddenly get the idea for an exciting play, but doubt it."

Miss Cooke did not help at all. She wrote to him enclosing the very bad notices for *Beth* and wandered off into a long farrago about whether children should go to state schools or not. Emlyn exploded: ". . . reckless-tactless-Miss Moffat . . ." Her letter ended: "Oh well, my boy, *Beth* isn't going to pay your overdraft, is it?" He complained to Molly: "I won't go into all this when I write, it would upset her, but I *must* ask her not to quote notices to me or to send them, the great thing at this distance is that I'm free of all that, or should be!"

If *Beth* failed to pay his overdraft, New Zealand on the contrary succeeded. In the first seven weeks he cleared £9,000 profit, and Australia, where he spent much of the summer, was even more rewarding with a twenty-one-week tour that netted £41,000. The price to be paid was boredom at official dinners and banquets. In Canberra there was a grand occasion honoured by the presence of his Excellency the Governor-General. "There will," noted the official programme, "be two intervals during the performance, during which the Vice-Regal party will remain seated." Emlyn scribbled across it: "As opposed to the Royal Family who invariably stand on their heads."

In Australia, too, he was challenged by a Mr Stanley Brookes – "The World's Greatest Dickens Platform Artist" – to give a three-hour performance without book or prompters. An additional titbit was promised: "Mr Brookes will play tape recordings of some of the conversations he has had with Dickens recently. As far back as thirty years ago he has spoken with the great Master." These tape recordings were but one example of his achievements. Mr Brookes also described himself as a "Stammering and Speech Defects and Voice Photography Researcher in American Universities; Specialist in English, Australian, Chinese Items, Pantomime Dames, Crazy Professors, Short Classics,

Screamingly Funny Characters, Spine-Chilling Tragedies, etc."
Gathering up all his energies for a final thrust, Mr Brookes added that
he was "the only Australian Red Indian Chief and was initiated into his
tribe, the OGALLALAS SIOUX, in the presence of three hundred
Redskins." Emlyn relished the baroque nature of one who might
himself have been a Dickensian character out of Crummles by Mr
Wopsle, but preferred to leave the challenge unanswered.

Brisbane was the scene of a reunion with Robert Helpmann, now
settled in his native Australia, an old friend from the days when Emlyn
and Molly lived out their idyll in the Thames-side bungalow. He was
agitated about Michael Redgrave's Hamlet. "He's too old!" he
snapped. "Oh, I don't know," said Emlyn, "he's much younger than
me." "He's not!" shrieked Bobby, "he's older than *me* – and I'm fifty
this year!" At that point, Emlyn remarked later, "we decided we were
splitting grey hairs." The gay community of Melbourne provided
charming diversion. Its denizens, Emlyn thought, made Bobby
Helpmann sound like J. B. Priestley. "But I'm very well-behaved",
said one blonde bombshell, christened David but known to intimates
as Diana Dors. "I *never* raise me voice above a scream!" He
accompanied "Uncle Emlyn", as he called him, to parties whose
tedium he dispersed with adroit campery. At one of them a drunken
hostess attempted to grope him. "My dear," he told her, "it's no good
looking for anything *there*. I always leave it at home in a drawer when I
go to parties." Afterwards Emlyn asked him: "What would happen if,
while you were at a party, your flat was burgled?" "Oh", came the
speedy answer, "it would depend on the burglar. I wouldn't mind if I
felt it was going to be in good hands."

In June Australian newspapers carried reports that the Birthday
Honours list had made Terence Rattigan a CBE. "What do *his* initials
stand for?" mused Emlyn. "Chorus Boys Everywhere?" But the
favourite traveller's tale he brought back to England was of a visit he
made to an elderly woman, a Mrs Potiki, who dwelt outside
Wellington in a little suburban villa. She resembled "a rather horse-like
spinster in some Bayswater boarding-house, knobbly knees, big feet –
Cockney." This seventy-six-year-old lady, brought up in Bethnal
Green, had lived in New Zealand for half a century. At tea they were
joined in the parlour by her husband, a gigantic, full-blooded Maori
who sat beside here as she dealt out fairy cakes. She was none other
than the sister of Lynn Fontanne, wife of Alfred Lunt in the world's
most glamorous theatrical partnership. Although Mrs Potiki remembered holding Lynn when she was born, she had not seen her for fifty

years, had never met her famous husband or seen her act. Lynn, she reminisced, "was *very* bad-tempered as a child, and strong-willed as a horse – Mum and Dad tried to get her to be a milliner, but she wasn't having any . . . I used to 'hear' her when she was practising, but never went to see her, I *hated* the stage." Emlyn was enchanted: "Lynn with a Maori brother-in-law – isn't it fantastic!" He wrote a long account of the meeting to his crony Gladys Henson. Why not, he suggested, take their friend Bobby Andrews, relict of the late Ivor Novello, to tea at Fuller's and read him the letter? Since Bobby watched his money rather closely when entertaining, Gladys was exhorted to "have at least a *try* at getting him to buy you a cake."

On the way back to England he played Dickens at the Munich Festival – "Mr Dickens – *fast persönlich*" read a newspaper headline – and on September 2 presented a new edition of "*Dylan Thomas: A Boy Growing Up*" at the Globe in London. His performance by now had reached a high state of perfection. "From the wings a stocky, white-haired sorcerer walks forward, papers under his arm, Wales in his voice, and the life of a dead poet in his head," wrote Richard Findlater. "He wears a navy blue suit, a red tie, and an air of deceptive neutrality; his trousers are, somewhat ostentatiously, supported by a belt; and he, no less conspicuously, is supported by nothing at all. Bowing sedately to the audience, he puts the papers on a chair, tests his aura, and begins to talk. It is Emlyn Williams at his wizard's work. For over two hours he is in command, alone on this bare stage, with the irresistible authority that marks the true star . . . unravelling a ladder of words, he climbs up with a knowing smile into a Welsh landscape of bawdy, lyrical fantasy and fun, and pulls the spectators up after him. It is a brilliant performance of the Cambrian Rope Trick . . ."

His audience at the Globe that night comprised what someone called "the stage in miniature": Edith Evans, Laurence Olivier, Richard Burton, Terence Rattigan, Sybil Thorndike, and Noël Coward wearing a dark red carnation in homage. "Your artistry is beyond words!" enthused Dame Sybil. In the foyer Epstein's bust of Emlyn frowned on Margaret Leighton, John Clements and Kay Hammond as they entered to take their seats. In the dressing-room stood a greasy milk bottle emptied to accommodate two pink roses offered by Diana Wynyard. On the table lay an illuminated scroll "presented by the men of this prison". Emlyn explained. "I was at Pentonville last night, entertaining the prisoners."

His two-week season at the Globe netted well over £7,000. Next month he appeared in a new play by Robert Ardrey, American author of the more famous *Thunder Rock*. Ardrey's latest piece, *Shadow of Heroes* at the Picadilly, dramatised events of the recent anti-Russian uprising in Hungary. Peggy Ashcroft played the wife of a Hungarian government minister, and Emlyn was "The Author", a character who introduces and comments on the action: "This is a drama with a cast of ten million characters." The play only enjoyed a short run, owing more to honest indignation at the plight of the Hungarians than to dramatic skill. It did, however, enable Emlyn, normally apolitical, to express, indirectly, his own feelings of outrage at the situation. He had, moreover, been personally involved. His elder son Alan had travelled to Hungary when Russian tanks were advancing on Budapest. Nothing was heard of him for several days. Emlyn flew to the country and at last discovered, after nearly a week of frantic searching, that he was safe in the British Embassy. Usually unaffected by world events, Emlyn found himself absorbed in the Hungarian affair. Later, he was deeply moved at the memorial service for thirty-one Hungarian youths hanged as freedom fighters by the Communist government. For once he shared Miss Cooke's anger at fellow-travellers in England who condoned the murders.

Vivien Leigh continued to give him concern. He went round to see her during a matinée interval and heard that she had just hit her dresser and accused her of stealing jewellery. That evening, at dinner Chez Nico, her balance and her sense of humour were restored. She told how she had first been attracted to Laurence Olivier when she saw him slide down the banisters in *Theatre Royal*. She said to her friend: "I'm going to marry that man." "But you're married already." "Don't be such an ass. What's that got to do with it?" After dinner with Emlyn she dashed off to meet another lover, Peter Finch: "He's always got a drink for me." An awkward weekend followed at Notley Abbey, the Olivier home. She took Emlyn down there in her car, talking all the way to an incessant accompaniment of moans from a dog and a Siamese kitten who shared the back seat with them. The household went to bed at four-thirty, but she was up walking in the garden next morning, fresh and pretty as a picture. At lunch she suddenly turned distraught because Olivier was nowhere to be found. "He always does this as soon as anybody arrives," she quavered. His technique of dealing with an impossible state of affairs was to be rude to her. "The trouble with you, my dear, is that you drink too much . . ." The remark was only half-disguised as comedy.

January came, and with it a five-month Dylan tour of fifty-nine cities in the USA. Welsh *hwyl* rang out in theatres, halls, colleges, universities, arts centres, women's clubs, gymnasia, academies, schools and once, even, a masonic temple. From San Francisco to Bethlehem (Pa), it seemed, there was not a theatre, not a fit-up that could escape the poetry of Dylan Thomas. One sombre day in Los Angeles Emlyn met Laurence Olivier who was filming there. Olivier spoke at length of his tormented life with Vivien Leigh. His long conversation with Emlyn provided, in some sort, a catharsis. He gave him a message for Vivien when he returned to London: Emlyn must tell her that he had decided to leave her. Life for another friend, Richard Burton, was brighter. Burton's twenty-two-month-old daughter lisped to her mother: "Daddy's shy . . ." Emlyn overheard and commented: "If she's being sarcastic, she's too young for that. And if she means it, it's a bad estimate of character." In the midst of all his travelling and entertaining he remembered, as always, to send a spectacular Valentine's Day card to Molly: "With all my love, darling."

Two films intervened, both taken from novels. *Beyond This Place* was an unmemorable English version of the book by A. J. Cronin. Hammond Innes furnished the basis for *The Wreck of the Mary Deare*, long on special effects, short on dramatic conviction. With these out of the way Emlyn celebrated his wedding anniversary on holiday in Spain. He returned to take part in the opening season of the new Rosehill Theatre, near Whitehaven, along with John Gielgud, Peggy Ashcroft, Yehudi Menuhin and others. Oliver Messel designed the interior – green silk in the foyer, dark red in the auditorium, white and gold brocade in the bar – to a commission from Nicholas (Miki) Sekers, the silk manufacturer who had business interests in the area. The enchanting little theatre seated two hundred people and created a neatly intimate setting for Emlyn as Charles Dickens. He was touched to receive a letter from Bransby Williams, the veteran actor now approaching his ninetieth birthday. For years uncounted the grand old performer had toured theatres and music-halls with his impersonations of characters from the novels, although he had never attempted Dickens himself. Not hale enough to attend in person, he relied on his wife's account of Emlyn's achievement. His generous praise opened with the jocular, affectionate salutation: "My Beloved Nevvy".

At lunch in December with Vivien Leigh at Notley Abbey Emlyn felt the stress of the encounter bringing on another kidney attack. He was rushed to an Oxford nursing home where yet another stone was extracted. "The newspapers tell us 'it isn't serious,' " wrote Miss Cooke in a flurry, "but hang it all your pain is serious. If only, if only, if only, they can hurry up and remove the cause of that pain . . . the doctor corroborates my first feeling – 'Oxford is a wonderful place to be ill in' – may it prove so." After a warm and sunny Christmas in Marrakesh with Molly and Alan, he chose Portugal for his convalescence. "My routine," he lamented, "seems to be to produce a stone every nine years. That's more than our projected National Theatre can boast!"

The early months of 1960 were spent touring the Midlands and the North. Just outside Barrow-in-Furness his car was held up in snowdrifts for two hours during the worst blizzards since 1947. As, at last, the vehicle crawled up and down the icy hills to Halifax: "This," said his chauffeur, "is called being in the sticks." Emlyn snuggled up at the back, face enveloped in a tartan cushion, and consoled himself with the thought that the BBC's most beloved soap opera was imminent on the car radio. "Soon we'll have Mrs Dale's Diary," he sighed.

Lausanne was to be vouchsafed a glimpse of *"le grand diseur Emlyn Williams"* – *"Grâce à Emlyn Williams l'on décèle le pouvoir dramatique de Dickens"* – and in between performances he went to the baptism at Celigny of Richard Burton's two little girls. Even grander events loomed: he and Molly were guests at the wedding of Princess Margaret and Tony Armstrong-Jones, the latter a nephew of Oliver Messel. "Thank you for that absolutely beautiful tea-set," wrote the polite bridegroom. The Moss Bros bill for Emlyn's wedding outfit was carefully preserved in the scrapbook under the solemn caption: "The Top Hat".

In 1961 he reached the fifty-sixth year of his age. It marked a sombre anniversary for one who, creatively at least, was struggling in the doldrums. Bereft of inspiration for plays, unable to develop satisfactorily even the fragile ideas that did succeed in breaking through, he realised that the irruption onto the scene of John Osborne and other young dramatists foreshadowed the end of the London theatre where he had grown up, learned his craft and triumphed. In the three years since *Look Back in Anger* the atmosphere had changed irrevocably.[2] At that very moment his friend Noël Coward was angrily attacking what he derided as the "dustbin drama" of contemporary theatre. Coward failed to see the irony of his position, since, forty years ago, he

---

[2] His seventeen-year-old son Brook, then a friend of Mary Ure and close to the Osborne circle, was present at the first night of *Look Back In Anger*. It was unpropitious and Osborne himself felt the play was doomed. Brook reported the evening to Emlyn whom he found reading a very unfavourable review in *The Times*. At Brook's urging Emlyn went to see it. At the time he was not impressed.

himself had been condemned by Gerald du Maurier. Emlyn was more subtle in his reaction. He envied young authors their freedom from tradition and the chance that had been given them of exploring new worlds. He decided that, if not as a playwright, then at least as an actor, he would come to terms with them.

Which is why, on January 18, the Arts Theatre opened with *Three*, a triple bill of one-act plays by John Mortimer, N. F. Simpson and Harold Pinter, featuring Emlyn, Richard Briers, Wendy Craig and Alison Leggatt. John Mortimer's *Lunch Hour* was a typically accomplished anecdote about a seedy businessman and a young businesswoman who hire a sordid room at lunch-time to indulge their furtive amour. They are shy, embarrassed, and as the precious minutes tick by they wallow in fatuous conversation. He passes her off as his wife from Scarborough, mother of three children, a subterfuge which the dotty girl takes seriously. By the time she has finished chattering about it, the hour has dwindled away and passion is unfulfilled. Emlyn was the businessman, nervous and ham-handed, Wendy Craig the gauche female, and Alison Leggatt a disbelieving manageress. At rehearsals John Mortimer found Emlyn "very funny, sharp and malicious." Believing Mortimer to be the oldest of the three young playwrights, (although in fact N. F. Simpson was his senior by four years), Emlyn joked to him: "*You* just got in to the New Wave as the tube doors were closing!"

The Form, a characteristically humorous fantasy by N. F. Simpson, presented a fat, foolish official (Emlyn again) who is agitated by a mysterious urge to tell a story about an elderly sheepdog. Forms and sheepdogs are, of course, merely an excuse for Simpson to embroider his own unique style of witty frivolity. The author felt that Emlyn gave "a bravura performance in it; but because my plays were essentially for ensemble acting, this had the effect of capsizing it. My fault, since I should have known my disposition towards understatement would not be best served by such casting. It is true, though ... that like Gielgud and others, he was open to approaches radically different from his own."

In Harold Pinter's *A Slight Ache*, the last of the three items, Emlyn played a tetchy writer of philosophical essays intent on working out his obsessions. His wife was Alison Leggatt, and the sinister tramp, who lurks with an air of menace, was a "massively inert" Richard Briers. Emlyn and Alison Leggatt, thought *The Times*, baffled by Pinterian obscurity, "act with great self-possession, but only at isolated moments do they throw any light on the characters they

represent." Ken Tynan, for once, was congratulatory and decided that
Emlyn gave "three patiently composed performances." Milton
Shulman remarked that, "seedy, senile and terrifying by turns, he has
an actor's field day with his three juicy parts."

As with Dylan Thomas, Emlyn enjoyed the richness of Pinter's
language without necessarily understanding it. "I couldn't possibly
have written plays like those of Pinter," he confessed. "If by chance I
had done so I should certainly want to ask myself several questions . . .
I'm sure I would be unable to answer them. Audiences *are* puzzled, I
suppose. But they are stimulated too . . . Imagination is needed when
you see these plays . . . From the purely selfish point of view of an
actor, though, I haven't enjoyed myself as I am doing now for a long
time." Yet still the shade of Dickens/Thomas loomed: Richard Briers
felt that, having been a star and done so many one-man shows, Emlyn
tended to be rather solitary and found it difficult to fit in with a team.

The triple bill was so successful that next month *Three* transferred to
the Criterion. At the end of the run everybody was invited to Pelham
Crescent and "a small party for the cast". This included some rather
nervous backstage staff who were reassured that there was no need to
dress up or do anything special for such a modest little get-together.
Wendy Craig was comforted by the thoughtfulness of Molly, a kindly
mother figure to them all. Richard Briers and his wife, at the beginning
of their West End careers, were flattered by the glamour of Emlyn.
N. F. Simpson, delighting in Emlyn's "wickedly accurate description" of
him looking like "a guilty monk", looked forward to the "small party"
with a writer's expectant eye for collector's items. He was not
disappointed. "When we all arrived we found – to my intense
amusement, and the consternation of some of the people to whom it
mattered – that we were there only to be ignored by such high-
powered nonentities as Jack Hawkins and Vivien Leigh . . . !'"

The *Three* party was one of the last receptions to be held at Pelham
Crescent. In July that year the Williamses decided they no longer
needed such a large home. Both their sons had grown up and embarked
on independent careers. Alan was now an established journalist soon
to hold important posts on the *Daily Express* and the *Guardian*. He
also inherited his father's gift for story-telling and was to write a
number of adventure stories which sold well at home and, in
translation, abroad. *The Purity League*, by "a master of adult
excitement", switched dizzily between Iceland and Poland, although
it set a moral problem: was it permissible to do evil in the name of a
good cause? Inspired by his professional experiences as a journalist in

troubled countries such as Hungary, Algeria and Vietnam, Alan went on to produce a series of thrillers, crisply written and tautly constructed, whose titles – *Barbouze*, for example, and *Snake Water*, *Dead Secret*, *The Widow's War*, *Long Run South* – held large promise. Brook, by a charming symmetry, inherited Emlyn's talent for acting. Following in father's footsteps he played Emlyn's old part as Lord Lebanon in *The Case of The Frightened Lady*. He was also to be Morgan in later productions of *The Corn Is Green*. Like every actor, he experienced the one obligatory, gigantic flop. In his case it was *Joie de Vivre*, a musical version of Rattigan's *French Without Tears*, which, opening with an enormous cast in a lavish production, closed after four performances. It must have been one of H. M. Tennent's most glamorous failures. Unabashed, he toured *Five-Finger Exercise* in South Africa, appeared opposite Margaret Rutherford, and did many radio broadcasts in between. Binkie Beaumont assured Emlyn that he had "enormous confidence in Brook's ability".

The birds had flown. So Molly was free to indulge one of her favourite pastimes: house-hunting. Throughout her married life she perfected the art of buying a house, renovating it, decorating it, turning into a home and haven, and then selling it at a profit. Park End, the country retreat bought in 1939, had since been replaced by Slade End at Brightwell in Berkshire. It was a rambling, heavily-thatched cottage, in appearance rather like a stylised toadstool with two immaculate black and white chimney pots. Roses and honeysuckle proliferated all around. In London she did not have far to look before she found a successor to Pelham Crescent. Dovehouse Street, off the Fulham Road and behind the Royal Marsden Hospital, contained a small, neat, post-war block of flats. She chose a two-bedroomed apartment on the first floor. The large drawing-room was warmed into life with antique chairs and tables, mirrored doors, swagged curtains, each element balancing the other to create perfect harmony. The double bedroom was large and bright. It looked out, as did the drawing-room, on a patio below filled with blossoming flowers and shrubs. Pelham Crescent was sold for £15,000 and the move to Dovehouse Street made in July. "So it is Dove House now – what a change," wrote Miss Cooke. "*Many, many happy days to you both*, May joins me in sending our loving thoughts for your peaceful happiness in Dove House."

For his study Emlyn chose the little bedroom at the front which gazed over the street. It was narrow and austere, much of the space being taken up by a small bed at the side and, at the end, a writing desk and capacious chair, the window on the left providing light from the correct position for a right-handed author. Here he kept his books, not necessarily the choicest or grandest which decorated the shelves in the drawing-room, but those which meant the most to him. They included the volumes he had owned as a boy and grown up with as a man. There were many in Welsh, and, of course, assorted volumes of the French "Collection Nelson", spick and span in their cream and gold bindings. A complete set of the Encyclopedia Britannica was accompanied by thirty-nine volumes of the Cambridge Shakespeare dating from the eighteen-nineties, a limited edition of five hundred. A curiosity was the *Cours d'anglais* (Nathan, 1958), an English primer for French students, which included an extract from *The Corn Is Green*: headed "Welsh and English", the text was printed on the left-hand page, with, on the right, vocabulary and grammar notes intended to aid Gallic schoolboys wrestling with the Welsh idiom. This, of a sort, was immortality. A long run of the Phoenix Library comprised forty-three items including the Scott-Moncrieff translation of Proust. Nearby stood a dozen novels by Aldous Huxley, very much a nineteen-thirties flavour. The Nonesuch anthology of John Donne was inscribed from Diana Wynyard, "*Watch on the Rhine*, 1942." The most heavily thumbed book was William Bolitho's *Murder for Profit* which comprehended the studies of mass-murderers such as Landru, Burke, and "Brides in the Bath" Smith. The chapter on Fritz Haarmann was closely annotated, especially the list of his victims which Emlyn had computed with meticulous pencilling. A photograph of Miss Cooke as a young woman was propped up between telephone directories and a recent edition of *Who's Who in the Theatre*. Copies of his own plays blushed unseen, for the most part, stored away in a drawer. The books he had used when a boy were originally inscribed "George Williams". In each case the name "George" had been carefully erased and replaced with that of "Emlyn". But no simple erasure could blot out the dual personality of George/Emlyn.

This duality, at the time of the move to Dovehouse Street, was very much in his mind. For the past fifteen months he had been writing his autobiography. If, for the time being, he could not find material for plays, there was more than enough for the story of his life. The formative period, from birth to the age of twenty-two, covered his poverty-stricken youth as a Welsh peasant to the end of his time at Oxford and his debut in *And So To Bed*. "My family tree is the shortest in the wood," he began the story of his days. "The Japanese variety, healthy but stunted. It would be the neatest feature of any landscape, for hardly a twig ventures outside Flintshire, the smallest county in Wales, the one in the top right corner next to Chester and Liverpool." He plundered the scrapbooks for photographs, certificates of birth, marriage and death, letters from long-dead relatives. A many-dimensional picture emerged of the introspective, book-loving child growing up in a narrow, alien environment of Welsh incomprehension. The portrait of the mother who neither understood nor sympathised with him is sharp but fair. In perspective, now, he could see and understand many of the reasons why she could not give him the love he so ardently desired and was obliged in his desperation to seek elsewhere. Even the constricting atmosphere of his early years – the bleak chapel, the pettifogging puritanism, the absence of art and literature – could not be passed over. It was a part of him, had made him what he was.

Until he started the autobiography his daily routine had been to get up at six in the morning if there was writing to be done, to have a snack lunch and an hour's nap, and then work until four in the afternoon. Friends might call for tea. Two hours later he would prepare for the theatre. After the play he would dine quietly at home or in a restaurant. In bed at midnight, he would read for an hour before going to sleep. The autobiography sent him into purdah, rising earlier still at five in the morning and working all day with passion. As he re-lived his childhood, in a mixture of pain and pleasure, his concentration was absolute. He was George Williams again, timid but proud, the awkward little boy often confused but always determined on . . . what?

The pages of his manuscript resembled a palimpsest. The first draft was rewritten again and again. Whole passages were crossed out and revisions pasted over them on slips of paper. Sentences were intercalated on scraps that fluttered awkwardly as pages turned. Handwriting mingled with typewritten thoughts. Each section was dutifully sent off to Miss Cooke for her scrutiny. Since she featured largely in his narrative he was anxious for her opinion. She gave her comments in detail. "Put it away for six months," she advised, "then read it through at one sitting, decide what effect you aimed at, decide what effect you made, and recast accordingly . . . The telling is beautiful and the telling is ordinary. May I suggest that close contact with Dylan Thomas has made you over-emphasise that side – the ordinary." The schoolmistress was dealing with her bright sixth-former. "Beginning Vol. III, page 493 and I am so hoping that I've got to the end of the sexual urges." On the other hand: "The episode with the French sailor struck me as beautiful. It is a very fitting climax, adolescence over, adult life begun."

He ended at the point when he loitered, heart thudding, about to make his first entry in *And So To Bed*. "A rustle and a sweep, like a strong calm wind. The curtain was up." So much rewriting, so much polishing and constant revision, produced a style that flowed with deceptive ease and spontaneity. As you read you think you can hear the tones of the author's voice. He called the book, simply, *George: an early autobiography*, and dedicated it to "my wife and our two sons, Molly, Alan and Brook". The frontispiece, reproduced on the dust jacket, showed a photograph of him at the age of sixteen, posed beside a table, right hand on an open book. The eyes are alert, the face is composed but wary.[3]

Brought up on the disciplines of concision demanded by the two hours' traffic of the stage, trained to express everything – plot, character, action – through dialogue alone, he found in writing the book an astonishing freedom and amplitude. It was, though, as he soon realised, a dangerous freedom, and discipline of another sort from that of the theatre was needed to curb loquacity. The fifteen months he took to complete *George*, compared with the shorter time needed for a play, had been, he admitted, ". . . a long period of gestation – longer than a baby. And it certainly has been a hard labour . . . But writing is absorbing. I enjoy it as much as acting."

The reader's report on *George* for the publisher Hamish Hamilton pronounced the book to be "fabulously good". After Hamilton had read it himself he wrote to Emlyn: "An utterly fascinating book, which combines the total recall of L. E. Jones's *Victorian Childhood* and Laurie Lee's *Cider With Rosie* (the two best childhood books I know) with flashes of Dylan Thomas, yet too individual to be influenced by any of them." The only drawback was that, at 200,000 words in length, it needed cutting to 160,000. Emlyn, the professional in everything he did, set about his cherished prose with a ruthless pencil.

George was published in October, had excellent reviews, and went into a second impression that same month. Noël Coward wrote in his diary: "It is perfectly enchanting. Beautifully written, honest, witty, compassionate and, at moments, profoundly moving. The Cinderella story of all time. His more than humble beginnings are never

[3] As Miss Cooke once said, ". . . it was certainly your solemnity that was your most striking characteristic. We always said you never smiled before you were 14!"

overstated and his early sex burgeonings in both directions described with exquisite taste. It is truly a marvellous exhibition of objective self-analysis as well as being a gripping story. I don't see how it can fail to have an enormous success." *George* was a milestone. In its pages Emlyn came to terms with his youth. After publication he gave up what had been the obsessive habit of keeping scrapbooks. Now that he had chronicled the vital formative years, did he feel there was no longer anything really worth recording? A ghost was exorcised.

He made a brief visit to America at the end of October for a part in a new play by Morris West, best-selling Australian novelist. A cast of twenty-five was assembled and two hundred thousand dollars were invested in *A Daughter of Silence*, a drama about a murder trial in an Italian village. The Mayor has been shot by a nineteen-year-old girl in revenge for her mother whom partisans killed during the war. A young lawyer takes her up as his first case and wins her acquittal on grounds of emotional immaturity, after which she goes screamingly insane at the fall of the curtain. This melodramatic framework was embellished with speculations on morality, justice, guilt and innocence. It was adapted from the author's novel and bore unmistakable traces of its wordy origin. Emlyn played the enigmatic role of a tyrannical father-in-law "with whitened hair and beard . . . a quiet, effortlessly authoritative performance that seemed to imply more than it said." He was, noted another critic, "urbane, judicious, exhaling his own little aura of perpetual mystery". At rehearsals for the pre-New York tour Morris West revealed himself to be jovial, skittish even, and bubbling with boyish enthusiasm. He told the cast that they would lay them in the aisles in Philadelphia. "Who's going to lay who?" grunted Rip Torn, the young actor who played the lawyer. Very few were laid in the aisles of New York's Music Box Theater, for the play closed after only thirty-six performances.

At home in England Miss Cooke, flattered by the portrait of her in *George*, found new windmills to tilt against on her seventy-eighth birthday. Flora Robson had just gone on a South African tour as Miss Cooke/Moffat in *The Corn is Green*, and was reported to have said of her: "I am steeped in Miss Cooke. She overrides people. She says cruel things!" The hermit of Roundhay came out fighting: "Yes, Miss Robson, it is true that you have met me. May I suggest it was under no circumstances that gave you any chance of probing my character. Really, the reviews of *George* have dubbed me Redoubtable, Formidable, Eccentric, but you are the first to dub me 'cruel' . . . Really, I cannot accept the charge cruel under any definition I know." Molly the peace-maker went round to see la Robson but retired, vanquished, describing her as "stupid and conceited." Miss Cooke decided that behind Robson's "armour," or "thick hide" as Emlyn termed it, ". . . is the most inhibited, frustrated of women, no matter *what* she achieves in this world, she never gets What Every Woman Wants – just plain love."

While these compliments flew and the two dragons breathed fire at each other, Emlyn escaped in January, 1962 with Molly to Barbados at Oliver Messel's home. Soon afterwards he appeared on the screen as one of the down-at-heel lodgers in *The L-Shaped Room* – others included Cicely Courtneidge, Pat Phoenix and Avis Bunnage – a version of the Lynne Reid Banks novel with Leslie Caron playing the girl who, intending to have an abortion, comes to live in a suburban London house. In June the Birthday Honours made Emlyn Commander of the British Empire. A flood of letters and telegrams cascaded into Dovehouse Street. "I don't know where the Empire is," wrote Felix Aylmer, "but I'm glad that you're in charge." Alec Guinness commented: "It seems to me nothing could be nicer than a CBE – and it's pretty to wear too." He remembered with gratitude how, in Algeria where he was on active service in 1943, Emlyn had written to his wife "whom you didn't really know at all, to say you had seen me and I was well. Many others, people whom I knew well, never bothered in spite of promises." To Sybil Burton, first wife of Richard who had already begun his liaison with Elizabeth Taylor, Emlyn quipped that CBE stood for "Can't Bear Elizabeth".

July found him in New York again taking over from Paul Scofield as Sir Thomas More in Robert Bolt's *A Man For All Seasons*. He had been reluctant at first. An actor who plays Hamlet is only one of the many to have essayed the rôle and will not be exposed to odious comparison. If, on the other hand, he is asked to follow an actor who has been the first to play a newly-written part, he will be hampered by memories of his predecessor. With this in mind Emlyn categorically refused Binkie Beaumont's offer of *A Man For All Seasons*, remembering that Scofield had been praised as "incomparable". He wavered only when the author "came to see me and wooed me and there we are". It had been a good decision. Reviews were favourable and no-one raised the ghost of Scofield. Emlyn gave ". . . a beautiful demonstration of flawless diction . . . Each line, each phrase, the very syllables are enunciated with a mastery . . ." Molly was due to join him in September, and he sent her a celebratory diamond bracelet from Bergdorf-Goodman. "Molly," he wrote. "My darling – My love always. Emlyn. Can be exchanged in September if you don't like it. The bracelet, not the love."

There was talk of his writing the book of a musical based on the play *Bell, Book and Candle* in which Rex Harrison had been very successful. (Harrison was then in the midst of his tempestuous marriage to Rachel Roberts – a situation, remarked Emlyn, described as "Rex v Rachel".) A suggestion had been made that he prepare a screenplay of *The Late Christopher Bean* for Ingrid Bergman. Neither idea reached fulfilment, but it was agreeable to toy with them. More tangible propositions earned him £500 for the commentary on a short film and £800 for playing television scenes from *A Man For All Seasons*. So well established had he become in the long-running play that his salary was raised to 1,000 guineas, or $3,000, a week.

A friend rang him one evening to invite him over at six o'clock for "something on a tray". He went, only to please her, because usually he never emerged before the performance except to eat ham and eggs at a drugstore opposite the theatre. "Five minutes after I got there, I realised why I had been bidden. In walked a slim, tallish woman in a brown dress, brown scarf high at the throat, long legs with low walking shoes, brown hair simply cut in a fringe – Garbo. Only three or four other people came over and she was completely relaxed, examining a book of paintings and borrowing somebody's glasses. The face is absolutely wonderful, especially when she smiles; and she turns Elizabeth Taylor into a vulgar trollop." Next evening he went as usual to the drugstore. Ray, the black barman, poured him a Coca-Cola and said: "I missed you last night – where'd yuh get to?" "Oh," replied Emlyn, "I went to dinner with Greta Garbo." "That's fine," answered Ray without even looking up. "I had lunch with President Kennedy, so we both had a good day, huh?"

New York was full of lonely people, especially widows and divorcées. He lunched with Vivien Leigh, her marriage to Olivier at an end, the latter, meanwhile, having found a new wife and mother of his future children in Joan Plowright. Vivien lived alone at a hotel, homesick but gallant in adversity, trying to forget the turmoil of her private life in singing and dancing lessons for the musical of *Tovarich*. There was no doubt, though, that Vivien could pall. At another meal, "in her goody-goody mood Vivien *is* in the end a bore – sweet and thoughtful and gracious to all, but a bore and a bit of a prig too until she laughs." Oliver Messel joined them one evening, and, *à propos* of someone having been sacked from the film of *Cleopatra*, said as a joke that he'd stuck pins into a manikin to wish him ill and the wish had come true. Vivien said, darkly: "Oh I wish you'd put pins into *somebody* for *me*, I'd be grateful." She did not specify whom. After lunching with her it became a ritual for Emlyn to escort her across Central Park to her dancing lesson. Her lavish hotel suite with secretary, maid, banks of flowers, seemed somehow lonely still. On a table, noted Emlyn, there was a box of Olivier cigarettes. After her opening night she entertained friends to dinner – Emlyn, Jean-Pierre Aumont, Charles Boyer. Also present was Vivien's mother, ". . . the stupidest most unhelpful piss-elegant Englishwoman you could imagine, not a trace of fun or humour, like the Queen of some Suburban Kingdom. I battled with her for ages. She wanted to know 'what plays one should see in NY.' I said (of course) *Who's Afraid of Virginia Woolf?* She stared at me and said, 'Who's afraid of the *Big Bad* Wolf?' and left it at that."

His stay in New York produced the usual crop of *bons-mots*. Someone had proposed a musical of *Lolita*, the notorious under-age romance, to be entitled "Take her, she's nine". The hit number would be "Stop the Girl, I Want To Get Off!" He met Terence Rattigan, in New York for the production of *Man and Boy*, and told him he had just seen John Gielgud, also on a visit to the city. "Is he behaving himself in New York?" asked Rattigan. A few days later Emlyn saw Gielgud again and mentioned he had spoken with Terry also. "Is he behaving himself in New York?" queried Gielgud.

He attended an inhospitable dinner with Hermione Gingold, "strong-faced, tight trousers, high heels, and a long Chinese coat that made her look *enceinte*. There were just two other guests and a pair of Gingold's thousands of indeterminate young men." He cheered himself up with a bit of scandal that had crossed the Atlantic from London: Binkie Beaumont's business partner and long-time lover had deserted him for an electrician in Putney. And a certain theatre director, very tall, had just married an actress, equally tall, because hers were the only women's clothes that would fit him.

By December 15 *A Man For All Seasons* reached its two hundredth performance and twenty-fifth week. There were twenty more weeks of Emlyn's contract to run. In March, 1963, the producer entered his dressing-room and said, "I've come to seduce you" – financially, that is. If Emlyn agreed to a year's tour of the play, he would be paid $5,000 a week plus a percentage, or a basic minimum of £1,800 a week rising to £2,500, an unheard of sum except for musical stars. No, said Emlyn, he needed at least a six-month break. Why not take the six-month holiday, argued his tempter, and come back for the big cities,

San Francisco, Chicago? Emlyn still said no. The producer delivered his clinching argument: Emlyn's tax adviser had said it would pay him to earn a lot in 1963–4 and as little as possible, according to the Alice-in-Wonderland logic of the Inland Revenue, in 1964–5. "*Will you come?*" Emlyn repeated his negative. "Without actually being Sir Thomas More, I am *not* Richard Burton either, and don't like the idea of my personal happiness being entirely governed by financial considerations – or in this case greed."

Once his contract ended the rest of the year was his own to be spent on vacation with Molly at Oliver Messel's home in Barbados and, afterwards, in Athens. Next year he accepted another New York engagement for a leading, and even more attractive, role as Pope Pius XII in *The Deputy*, Rolf Hochhuth's controversial play adapted by Jerome Rothenberg. Before going on what promised to be a long time away he called in at Roundhay to see Miss Cooke. It was January. Snow thickened on the ground and the bare black trees, crowned in white, had an eerie beauty. She was coasting, just, toward her eightieth birthday after a decade of ill health. During that time she had undergone two serious operations, a broken arm, two heart attacks, and now " – this. Hm!" "This" was a return of the cancer which had already haunted her. X-ray photographs showed results "not according to hopes but according to expectations," she told him stoically. He admired her fortitude and wondered if he would ever see her again. Having returned to London on route for New York, he left a note for Molly in Dovehouse Street: "My darling, Just to remind you of my undying love. Emlyn."

In New York he rehearsed *The Deputy* twelve hours a day at the Brooks Atkinson Theatre. He evolved an elaborate make-up for Pope Pius. His head was shaved and he had a wig specially made. (Passing a Beatles memorabilia shop in Times Square he "realised I'd got a Beatle wig on myself but I don't think anybody noticed".) The make-up was flour-white, complemented by rimless glasses, and he wore a robe of exquisite white silk trimmed in gold, presenting altogether an uncanny likeness to the late Pope. With him in the cast was Jeremy Brett as the young priest who unsuccessfully implores Pius XII to protest to Hitler about the slaughter of the Jews. *The Deputy* opened on the last day of February, 1964. Emlyn gave "a prim, studied, chalk-white performance". It was a commanding portrayal with "enormous authority and a sort of mystical detachment". He dominated the crucial second act with a cold, shrewd dignity. The play was a success, despite first-night pickets at the stage-door who protested loudly and flourished banners which read "God bless Pope Pius XII – down with *The Deputy*!"

Once the tension of the first night was over he could relax, although the spirit of the pickets lingered on. "Yesterday," he wrote to Molly, "a man came up to Jeremy in the street and said, 'Are you Jeremy Brett in *The Deputy*?' 'Yes,' said Jeremy, and the man pushed him off the sidewalk in the path of an oncoming car. Jeremy fell and just missed being run over. The man dived into a subway. So you see, there's never a dull moment." One evening, wearing the wig on his shaven pate, he went to a party with Jeremy. Beatrice Lillie was there, and he could not resist snatching off his own "rug" and exchanging it for hers. To it he added the hat she was wearing, and the party-goers were edified by a vision of Pope Pius crowned with one of Bea's flowerpot fantasies.

A letter arrived from Miss Cooke dated April 20. She had taken *Spring, 1600* to hospital with her and re-read it while enduring radiotherapy treatment that made her sick and weary. A hospital was like a gaol, she reflected wistfully, except that you could always leave a hospital. Once allowed back to the peace and quiet of home she began to feel better. The good days outnumbered the bad. She chatted on about the latest news and ended: "Oh! a sick room can be a very busy place. It really is beautiful out of bedroom window. Very affectionately, S. G. Cooke." The handwriting, always clumsy and big, had degenerated into a crabbed, shaky scrawl. On this letter, the last she ever wrote to him, Emlyn noted simply: "20 April – died May 1."

Molly and Brook went to the funeral, Emlyn being engaged with *The Deputy* in New York. He was glad that he had at least seen Miss Cooke in January, the champagne flowing as it always did on his visits to Roundhay. She left £8,521 gross. The manuscript of *The Corn Is Green* which he gave her went to the University of Wales. She bequeathed him "the chest with the initials EML carved thereon", and also £500 in Funding stock "as some slight remembrance of the endless kindnesses shown to me by him and which have done so much to make my life happy and full, and in reciprocation of the gift of £500 made by him to me".

The older of the two women who dominated his life had gone, and a relationship which had lasted nearly half a century was broken. Every week they had written to each other, often more than once. In the end, as old age emphasised her assertiveness, and her outspoken comments grated on him with their lack of tact, he sometimes dreaded the long rambling letters and put off opening them because he knew they would be difficult to answer without hurting her. Yet he preserved them carefully and even had many of them typed out and bound in duplicated files. Like *George*, she was a part of him that could not be shaken off. For her, he was the justification of her calling as a teacher. He stood as abundant, living proof of her vocation. True, his great success had brought her many incidental rewards, but the greatest of them was the fact that he had more than repaid her faith in him. When, however, people said that he owed everything to his teacher, she corrected them with typical bluntness. "Bunkum. I didn't give you your brain." They often had arguments. She was a doughty critic of his work if she thought something was wrong, and she always spoke her mind. Their debates were conducted with spirit but with respect. He would miss her very much. It was a long time before he grew out of the habit of looking through his daily post for the big, fat envelopes addressed to him in the familiar sprawling hand.

CHAPTER SIX

(i)
Waiting for Ideas That Don't Come

During the run of *The Deputy* Emlyn gave a party for his friends in New York. He drew up a guest list which included Bette Davis, Alec Guinness and the Burtons. Who were the Burtons now? They were no longer Richard and Sybil, his first wife. They were Richard and Elizabeth Taylor. Once Emlyn's protégé, a talented but unsophisticated Welsh boyo, Richard Burton had mutated into a star known throughout continents. Emlyn watched, in sadness, as Burton's private life dwindled into a sterile tangle and his gifts were shredded away on tawdry projects. What made the situation even more complex was the friendship between Burton and Emlyn's own son Brook, a popular member of the Burton caravan as it flashed expensively between Switzerland, New York, Hollywood and London. While Emlyn was away on his long tours Brook grew up to regard Burton as something of a father and, later, as a dear friend who taught him how to enjoy life. And now Elizabeth Taylor had taken over from Sybil, the girl whom Emlyn encouraged to marry his protégé and who was the mother of Burton's children. He did not warm to Elizabeth Taylor. As a pretty little moppet in *Lassie Come Home* and *National Velvet* she displayed a small talent as the co-star of a dog and a horse. In later years she showed a much more formidable gift as publicist. Even Burton, before he surrendered to her opulent charms, nicknamed her "Miss Tits". She walked, said Emlyn, "like a chorus girl". He went to see her and Burton in a sloppy production of Coward's *Private Lives*. "He's miscast and she's Miss Taylor," he commented.

From Phil Burton, Richard's guardian, he heard the whole story of the childhood and adoption. Richard, he was told, had always played people against each other since he was four years old and had ever been a consummate liar. He could not resist the urge to dramatise and to watch the havoc he created from outside. In New York Emlyn had painful discussions with Sybil Burton. She recounted how Burton would talk five hours into the night, would suggest they start together again, and persuade her to make a life with him once more. He would leave, having drunk in the meantime a full bottle of brandy. At eight next morning he would ring: "I was very drunk last night. You must forget all I said. I can't live without Elizabeth." On other occasions he would suddenly stop short and remark: "Well, I'd better get back to the Dorchester or there'll be a lot of breast-beating." With a flash of malice that Emlyn appreciated, Sybil added: "And indeed, there's quite a lot of breast to beat, isn't there?"

In the end she decided on a final break. The Burtons, that is Richard and Elizabeth, came roaring into Emlyn's party. They brought with them Cecilia, or "Sis", Burton's sister. She appeared quite beautiful, in black and haloed with perfect white hair. Someone told her how nice she looked. "Oh," she said, "Elizabeth has been dolling me up all day!" Emlyn politely asked Elizabeth Taylor how Sis was settling down in the Burton entourage. "I think," said Miss Taylor, "she's settling down very well, she's only called me 'Sybil' three times today."

When Miss Taylor subsequently appeared before a judge in 1991 to solemnise her eighth marriage, that official as a matter of form asked her to list her previous unions. "Is this a memory test?" she enquired irritably. Emlyn's own domestic life was, by contrast, positively Victorian. In July he celebrated his pearl wedding anniversary. He sent an elaborate card to Molly: "8 July 1934–8 July 1964. All my love always my darling. Emlyn." To it he added a list of the addresses they lived at during their married life, beginning with 71A Ebury Street and ending, currently, with 200 East 58th Street.

As soon as *The Deputy* finished its run in the autumn he set off on a Dickens tour of eighty American and Canadian tours which continued into 1965. "I'll settle down and enjoy the tour," he wrote to Molly, "it is after all my work and it's better than sitting in London waiting for an idea for a play or a book that doesn't come – and I must say that the show is as new to the audience as ever it was, and it's fresh to me too, I never feel stale and now I'm settling down will really enjoy it." Sometimes, though, conditions reminded him of the worst days with ENSA. In a small fit-up cinema ". . . I don't think they've ever had a live person backstage before, they've had to make a dressing-room with a bedsheet hanging on a rope, and I've just had to step out into the alley-way to have a pee before going on – not the most glamorous moment in a career, but it's all paying well."

Once the American tour ended the strolling player was away on an extended journey as Dickens throughout the Far East. The heat in

Dacca was so intense and unrelieved by any air conditioning that sweat poured down his beard on to the books each time he moved, soaked into his nose and eyes, and penetrated so deeply behind his moustache that it nearly dislodged the spirit-gum. A Pakistani boy at rehearsal saw him making up and said: "Old Master make magic?" From then on he was known to all as "Old Master".

In the brief interval between the USA and the Far East tours there had been disagreements at home. Molly was unhappy over his long absences and uneasy about those regions of his life which, as a woman, she could not approach. Once she had tried the experiment of accompanying him on one of his far-flung journeys taking Dickens to the uttermost extremities of the world. It had not been successful. In the middle of the night she packed her bags and took the next flight home. More important, she came to realise the truth of Heine's remark that a man's basic character remains, despite the passing of the years, as unchangeable as the rigid bones of his skeleton. Marriage could alter little. In Delhi he regretted the stormy fortnight they had spent together. "Every word you say is right about 'we must try not to quarrel', etc – absolutely right and sensible – but it left me so low that I haven't been able to write till now – it made me feel you think it's *all* my fault – made me feel guilty and unhappy. You say that 'nothing seemed to go right' – but surely *some* things during the two weeks did go right – was it so terrible *all* the time? . . . *Please* let us think of the good things, otherwise it seems such a poor outlook, doesn't it?"

He plunged doggedly on through India, Iran, Ceylon, Malaysia, Sabah, Vietnam, the Philippines, Singapore and Japan. Only in front of an audience, wooing them, cajoling them, did he achieve fulfilment, oblivious for the time being to all other things. This was, for him, the true reality, where each night he had to conquer a new group of people, as different in their reactions as the previous night's had been. The possible barriers of language only made the challenge more exciting. During the day he shopped and explored. A Chinese tailor in Hong Kong made him four suits. On the wall hung a signed photograph of Noël Coward – "he looks so much more Hong Kong than the tailor does that one wonders how they ever let him out!" At the Merlin Hotel in Kuala Lumpur after the show he sat next to a Malay gentleman. With typical Malay politeness the gentleman enquired: "How long have you been, Sir, in the theatre?" "Oh, since I was twenty-one." "And when, Sir, do you hope to retire?"

Retirement? At first the remark amused him, then it depressed. He could not exist without an audience, and the thought of vegetating within the four walls of his study was inconceivable. The record showed that to date he had given nine hundred and forty-five performances as Charles Dickens and three hundred and eight-six as Dylan Thomas. There would, he promised himself, be many more. In June, after his return from the Far East, he revived his 1943 adaptation of Turgenev's *A Month In The Country*. While playing Charles Dickens he had been visited in his dressing-room by a relative. Enquired the latter: "And what will you be doing after this, Emlyn?" "*A Month In The Country*." "Oh, you deserve it!" He played Ignaty Illyich, with Ingrid Bergman as Natalia, Jeremy Brett as Beliaev, and Michael Redgrave, who also directed, as Rakitin. It was the production chosen to open the Yvonne Arnaud Theatre in Guildford, and the play moved in September to the Cambridge Theatre. For the first time in his life he had trouble learning his lines and was haunted by the terrible fear of drying, even though he himself adapted the text. Again, too, it was difficult playing as one of a team after long periods as a solo performer.

At least, however, Molly was happily occupied with a fresh project. Having bought and sold several country homes which, in the meantime, she had transformed into comfortable family retreats, she was now looking more ambitiously abroad. The flat in Dovehouse Street was completed to her satisfaction, the current home in Berkshire had reached her idea of perfection, and she hungered for new worlds to conquer. Their holiday visits to Oliver Messel in Barbados gave her an inspiration. They had often stayed with their friend the designer Roger Furse, brother of the actress and director Judith, at Benitsa on Corfu. In that sunny island, she decided, they would build a house, and Emlyn, as usual, acquiesced. The land was bought in 1966 and the foundations were dug in October that year. By November the walls were rising steadily. In February, 1967, the structure was complete and the roof in place soon afterwards. The local priest, venerable in white beard and pillbox hat, conducted a ceremony of blessing on the "Villa Ilios", as they christened it. Emlyn gave a speech in Greek and wine was drunk. The company sat on the terrace beneath white walls in sparkling sunshine and looked out over the tops of trees which descended to a sandy shore below, a wine-dark sea and a coast romantically vague in the distance. The house had two double bedrooms and one single. Emlyn's library contained *Greek Made Easy*, heavily annotated, and textbooks which gave instruction on how to hold the pen correctly and how to write characters of the alphabet. As a trained linguist he tackled the new language with informed enjoyment. Grammars were covered with marginal notes on prepositions and adjectives. Exercise books rapidly filled up with model sentences. On the back of old play manuscripts he practised the formation of characters and accents. A little scrapbook was inaugurated to record life at the villa. It was embellished with a specially designed bookplate which read "Molly and Emlyn Williams, Villa Ilios, Benitsa, Corfu".

Among their callers on the island was Vivien Leigh. She was in one of her high-strung brittle moods, despite the break with Laurence Olivier, and accompanied the Williamses to a party given at a palazzo by a Greek dowager, "a cross between Lady Bracknell and a Proustian blue-blooded lady," as Emlyn put it when describing the scene to Alexander Walker, Leigh's biographer. The night was hot and stuffy, the function solemn. "It's going to be a long, long haul and I know I'm going to fall asleep in the middle of it. Come with me," Vivien said to Emlyn. They went behind a pillar. She opened her bag, impish, and took out an eyebrow pencil. "If I do fall asleep, it'll seem so *rude*. Darling, make me up." Emlyn stared, bewildered. She closed her eyes and brandished the pencil. "Draw me some eyes, on my eyelids, so that if I close my eyes it'll look as if I'm wide-awake and taking everything in." Fascinated but aghast, Emlyn temporised. After two more glasses of ouzo he agreed. "So I gave her new eyes, considerably less beguiling than her own and the effect was macabre. And yet when she opened her own eyes, *alles in ordnung*." He was grateful that, for the rest of the evening, he was dining at another table with his back to her.

Like all the other homes Molly created, the Villa Ilios was a place of much ease and happiness. Jeremy Brett came to stay and she greeted him with the news that Emlyn had been bitten on the tongue by a wasp. It was heaven, she said half-humorously, because it stopped him talking all the time. Another actor friend, Peter Bull, who also had a house on the island, albeit considerably more modest, put it differently. In a reference to Emlyn's waspish wit, he observed: "Poetic justice."

For all the tranquillity the Villa Ilios conferred on their marriage, soon there were new arguments between Molly and Emlyn. He had not lost his taste for murder trials, and the recent Moors Murders, as they became known, gripped his imagination more strongly than any other had done. The personalities of Ian Brady and Myra Hindley obsessed him. Their trial at Chester Assizes in 1966 was the beginning of a quest that led him to examine once again the nature of evil. With his son Brook as chauffeur he drove around the Yorkshire Moors inspecting the scene of the crimes and interviewing, where possible, the policemen and others who had been involved in the affair. Once all the material was assembled, he proposed to write a book about it. Molly was horrified and disgusted, as were many in his circle. She had had enough of his lust for the macabre. If, she threatened, at the end of her tether, he published the book, she would leave him. But he did.

He called the book *Beyond Belief: A Chronicle of Murder and its Detection*, and it was brought out in 1967 by Hamish Hamilton who had earlier published *George*. In the Foreword he wrote, defensively: "For me, just as no physical aberration can ever be too extraordinary to interest the medical scientist, so no psychological phenomena can be forbidden to the serious and dispassionate writer, however 'unsavoury' the details. Who expects savour from a story of noisome evil? When a shocking scandal blows up, with all the attendant sensationalism, there is in some people an instinct to avert the head and shovel the whole thing under the carpet, 'I don't want to know.' But some of us *do* want to know, and it is salutary to inquire: the proper study of mankind is Man. And Man cannot be ignored because he has become vile. Woman neither." Three hundred and fifty-nine pages later he ends, referring to the murderous pair, still alive though separated in prison: "But their souls are together, buried in one grave on moors of their own making. And when on Judgment Day those souls will be dug up, they will stink to heaven."

In between these two comments are many passages of brilliant writing, impressionistic, horribly convincing in the re-creation of the evil atmosphere. But "serious and dispassionate", as he claimed in the Foreword? More vivid, admittedly, than a *News of the World* report, but hardly adequate as a serious attempt to explore the nature of wickedness. There is a difference between making the flesh of a theatre audience creep with unnamed menace – they are, after all, like children who enjoy the horror of a nightmare fairy tale, comfortable in the assurance that all will end happily when they are tucked up for the night – and retelling in ghastly detail one of the most hideous child murders of the century. Ever since writing *Night Must Fall*, he said, he had wondered if a murder case would one day come along and challenge him to write a book which aimed at "the accuracy of history and the accuracy of imaginative understanding" which Hector Bolitho, author of *Murder For Profit* so admired by Emlyn, was said to have achieved. The reader must decide for himself, provided he can bear to study the repellent contents of *Beyond Belief*.

Emlyn was very proud of *Beyond Belief*. Molly, in the event, did not leave him. Yet disharmony persisted. From Princeton, New Jersey, where he toured after publication of the book, he wrote: "We must forget the meaningless quarrels and just think of the wonderful times we've had together, and will have, the rows are like sudden terrible unexpected illnesses but they're over so quickly and no need even for a minute's convalescence. We must just think of our love for each other as being the reality nothing can destroy, and hold on to that." Despite the quarrels, despite the high words, there were times when he longed to be back with Molly. In Denver, Colorado, he had ". . . the most terrible reaction, waves of homesickness for you and Corfu, I looked at my Greek dictionary and burst into tears and thought, I must go back, I must go back . . . It was reaction and maybe I was sickening for the cold . . . Anyway I felt much better after the show . . ." He usually did. There were few illnesses, few indispositions, that the magic of applause did not cure. Off the stage he was easily bored, especially when he could find no entertainment at the local theatre other than Pinter's *The Homecoming* which he had seen twice and considered, each time, to be "awful." And most of all: "If only I were writing, but I can't think of anything."

The current American tour ended in Spring, 1968. The Dickens frock-coat and prop books were put away in a cupboard for the next two years. Odd jobs came to the rescue. The Investiture of the Prince of Wales at Caernarvon found him giving a commentary on television, very proud, very Welsh. For television also he played the part of the dotty Mr Dick in *David Copperfield*, obsessed by King Charles's head and for ever memorialising the Lord Chancellor without being able to keep the monarch out of his address. Laurence Olivier was the schoolmaster Mr Creakle, fiery-faced, thick-veined, bald except for a strand of wet-looking hair, who vastly enjoyed beating small boys. As is often the case, Emlyn never met Olivier on the set as their scenes were filmed separately. He thought of the whirligig of time and, wryly, of the occasion thirty-four years ago when Olivier, over a midnight meal at Lyons, exclaimed in his wretchedness: "I'm all washed up – I'll never make it!"

An opportunity to appear on the West End stage materialised in September, 1969. After a very successful run of nine months John Gielgud had decided to withdraw from the cast of Alan Bennett's play *Forty Years On* at the Apollo. "I suggested he should be invited to follow me as the Headmaster," says Sir John, "since I felt he was feeling neglected as an actor after his long years of the Dickens and Dylan Thomas one-man shows which were both so brilliant." The speeches were learnt, the part was rehearsed, and Emlyn duly joined the production. "I am *delighted* to think you will take over the Headmaster ..." Sir John wrote to him. Things went badly, however. Emlyn did not get on with the other people involved. Perhaps the spectres of Dickens and Dylan Thomas were too potent. "He never blamed me for the disaster," Sir John continues, "but I know how deeply he was hurt. Some months later, when he was about to resume his one-man show, he told Binkie Beaumont that he would only take it on if he was allowed to give a special matinée at the Apollo, using his old dressing-room with the photographs replaced just as they were, before an invited audience, to lay the ghost of his failure, and this was accordingly arranged."

Forty Years On closed abruptly. Emlyn, steeling himself for discomfort and expense, entered the Harley Street Nursing Home to undergo an operation. Barely out of the anaesthetic, he wrote to a friend: "I have long felt that Senior Citizens with a place in the sun, such as Corfu, should take pride in looking their best on the beach *in shorts*, as I shall certainly do next summer; trim from knee to ankle, none of those unseemly bulges. Not to mince matters, I've had my varicose veins done." The anaesthetic had not blunted the edge of his tongue. He was, he added, looking forward to the birthday party of an old friend – "... the Noël celebrations – Coward, not Christmas, you'd think nobody had ever reached the age of seventy before since Shakespeare passed away in his early fifties."

The hundredth anniversary of Dickens's death fell in 1970 and Emlyn free of, but still smarting from, his varicose veins, decided to lead a quiet life until the centenary events. "I started my stage career by walking *on*," he said. "I don't want to have it ended by walking *off*." A ceremony at which he took part was held in Westminster Abbey on June 9. "Reading from Dickens?" enquired a friend. "No," he retorted with some asperity, for his leg was still hurting. "From Dorothy Parker."

That year saw the release of an undistinguished film in which he played called *The Walking Stick*. The plot featured a girl polio victim enamoured of a painter who entangles her in his crooked schemes. Exquisitely photographed in Metrocolor and Panavision, it was a slow and indecisive affair which gave little scope either to Emlyn or to his co-star Phyllis Calvert. He left England soon afterwards for a mammoth Dickens tour sponsored by the British Council which took him to Australia, Czechoslovakia, all over Scandinavia, Russia, Yugoslavia, Bulgaria, Greece, and, for the rest of the year, the USA.

His repertoire included the Veneerings from *Our Mutual Friend*, the short ghost story *The Signalman*, "Mr Chops" from *Christmas Stories*, "Paul" from *Dombey & Son*, "Once Upon a Time" from *The Battle for Life*, high society scenes from *Little Dorrit*, "The Fancy Ball" from *A Tale of Two Cities*, and "The Nurse's Story" from *The Uncommercial Traveller*. This time Molly insisted very strongly on going with him. She did not want to be left alone in London. After a great deal of argument he persuaded her to drop this idea. As he put it: "I know it's tough that I should have to be away so much at the moment, but it *is* in the course of my work and we know too well how miserable and uncomfortable you would be on these trips . . ." He was later to regret the decision, very bitterly, very deeply.

Molly was tired and dispirited. For nearly forty years she had been his loyal companion. During that time she played many parts: mother, hostess, housekeeper, adviser, wife, lover. As Miss Cooke once told her: "I realise that you must have got quite a kick – shall I say out of the financial benefits of Emlyn's success but goodness only knows what Emlyn has absorbed from you – how shall I put it – imponderables such as few women have it in them to give. 'Imponderables' is a good 'get out' for me – all the things that cannot be weighed and counted." He had been lucky in his choice of wife, and he knew it. But over the past decade she had become increasingly weary. The strain of raising a family during his prolonged absences and the responsibility of making important decisions had worn her down. Elusive, too, was the character of the man she loved so deeply: although he had brought her great happiness, although she would never have wished to live with anyone else, she knew that despite his own love for her and the years of intimacy they shared, certain areas of his personality were denied to her. Her disquiet surfaced in the arguments that boiled up so frequently these days between them. All this was concealed behind "the astonishing glass shade" that protected them from the gaze of the outside world. They never confided their troubles in anyone else. Old friends like John Gielgud and Stephen Mitchell could only stand aside and speculate on the intimations, faint and occasional, of unease.

Emlyn embarked for America at the end of October, 1970. Before he left he gave some friendly advice to Jessie Matthews who was to play the hypochondriac Mrs Bramson in *Night Must Fall*. He had known her as the pretty fresh-faced ingénue for whom he wrote the script of *Evergreen* many years ago. "I don't know why they always have to have these college boys writing my scripts," Jessie had said in lofty tones: she was then twenty-six years old and Emlyn twenty-eight.

Remembering the young star of *Evergreen* he found it hard to imagine her in the part of Mrs Bramson, even though she had made another name for herself as the plump, maternal heroine of the BBC radio soap opera *Mrs Dale's Diary*. "Way-out casting!" he wrote to her. "But it will be fascinating. You will have to play right against yourself for she has to be an out-and-out bitch, mean, selfish, and cruel, also very silly and vain when flattered by the boy. The more horrid she is, the better for the comedy. I should wear an old-fashioned grey wig – nothing modern about *her*! – and steel-rimmed glasses which you might take off once or twice when feeling a little girlish with Dan, then put them on again. Keep her strong and horrid (strong that is until her hysteria when alone)." He was touring when she gave her first-night performance confined to Mrs Bramson's wheel-chair. In a reference to the hit song associated with her, "Over My Shoulder Goes One Care," he sent her a good-luck cable which read: "Just think of over my shoulder goes one wheel-chair."

The American phase of the Dickens Centenary Tour began in New York. Emlyn was accompanied by his manager Bob Crawley, a very tall, big American, an efficient organiser and invaluable on the road. Molly, for some reason, had taken a dislike to him. "My darling," Emlyn reassured her, "I miss you very much . . . but I know you are happier at Fieldings [their current home in the country]. We are just not meant to travel continuously together while I'm working and we should know it by now . . . I do hope you feel differently about Bob – I know what we two say to each other in anger we neither of us mean but I'd hate to think you've turned against him. He is indispensable to me on this tour . . . I couldn't have done it without him possibly . . ."

New York was followed by Susquehanna University in Philadelphia, and a series of one-night stands took him by mid-December to Chicago. Here unexpected news arrived, shattering, overwhelming. Molly was dead.

(ii)

Alone

In the evening of December 14 Molly had suddenly been taken ill. She collapsed and was driven urgently to hospital. There, soon after, she died. She was sixty-four, one year younger than Emlyn. The widower, stricken, hurried back to London. "There is no doubt that we love each other very much," he had told her in one of the very last letters she was to read from him. Never again would he be able to say so to her in person.

She had asked for "no outward signs of mourning" and stipulated that no flowers be sent and no memorial service be held. Instead, donations were requested to the Actors' Orphanage or the Actors' Benevolent Fund. The income from her estate, proved at £33,466, went to Emlyn, and, after his death, to children and other descendants under the usual provisos. Such, declared Mary Marjorie Williams, was her last will and testament made on January 5, 1961, nine years before her death.

At first he was numb. The thing was inconceivable. He could not comprehend what had happened. The only remedy he knew was work. Surrounded by his family and friends at Dovehouse Street, where everything spoke of Molly, everything reminded him of their years together, he grimly concentrated on arrangements for the continuation of his Dickens tour. On January, 13, 1971, he started again in Ontario on a journey that did not end until March. "I'm glad of course that you are working again so soon," wrote John Gielgud, "but the eternal packing, and making polite nothings to strange people, and never knowing quite what city one is in, must be infinitely trying to your nerves and patience. Still, the old cliché, of 'work the great healer' has, I imagine, something to be said for it . . . How long ago it is since *Spring, 1600* – and Molly fresh from *Battling Butler . . .* – and then the success of your marriage and your own enormous success . . . And now it's like a dream – very strange isn't it, getting old – somehow one never thought it quite possible – for oneself, I mean."

Sometimes, for a moment or two, he could submerge himself in the Veneerings, forget himself in Paul Dombey, blot out everything in the applause of an audience. Then, all too soon, the fog of misery would descend again. He would remember Molly's voice, her turn of phrase, the way she walked. Thirty-six years of his life had vanished with her. He sat alone in blank hotel rooms. There would be no more letters to her. So many things he wished he had said were unspoken. If only . . .

Remained Alan and Brook, the two sons who had, between them, inherited his dual talent. Eventually there would be grandchildren. Such was Molly's true bequest, more precious than any trust fund. Too, there was Ann Plugge, Molly's oldest friend, and, apart from Miss Cooke, his own also. She had known Molly even before Emlyn met her, and worked in the theatre with her, later becoming a model. Her beauty and her poise, indeed, had attracted the unwelcome notice of Molly's first husband whose advances she skilfully parried, as she was often obliged to do with many admirers of her elegant charm. She had eventually married Captain Leonard Plugge, an Englishman of Norwegian descent, scientist, inventor, former pilot and alert entrepreneur. He was an early pioneer of broadcasting and set up programmes sponsored by Gordon Selfridge direct from the Eiffel Tower. His car, he claimed, was the first in the world to be equipped with a radio. In the nineteen-thirties, having built an intricate network of contracts and agreements throughout Europe, he established, among other things, one of the earliest commercial broadcasting stations and called it Radio Normandy. Then, having stood for Parliament in Chatham and vanquished an opponent whose name was Hugh Gaitskell, he became an MP.

Ann shared the life of the Williams family from the very beginning. She went with Molly to America, saw the boys grow up, helped nurse them through childish illnesses, and was involved in every important matter that concerned Emlyn and his wife. She was now a widow. On Emlyn's return from the USA in 1971 it was entirely logical that she should come to Dovehouse Street and run his household for him. He moved into his study and slept at night in the little bed. She was to organise receptions for him, help with his manuscripts, hear him rehearse his lines, and accompany him on tour at home and abroad. He proved an easy man to cater for. So long as he had a modest dish of scrambled eggs, he was content. Whenever she hosted a party for him and his guests at Dovehouse Street, next morning she would find, tucked under her bedroom door, a little note expressing thanks in graceful, often witty words.

In April, 1972, another friend came into his life. His personal manager, John Roberts, had recently died in the Royal Marsden Hospital just across the way from Dovehouse Street. Dead, too, was Bob Crawley. When Roberts died his last words had been: "Ask John to look after Emlyn." He meant John de Lannoy, a theatre administrator of wide experience. De Lannoy arrived in Dovehouse Street at the cocktail hour for the first of what was to become a series of regular visits. After a hospitable welcome from Ann he would go with Emlyn into the little study. There the contents of what became known as "John's Drawer" were discussed: business letters, cheques, bills, contracts. Problems were talked through and ideas for future plans argued over. While Sol Hurok was responsible for American tours, anywhere else in the world, including the United Kingdom, became the fief of de Lannoy. His arrangements bristled with efficiency and immaculate attention to detail. Naturally, the agreements he drew up were scrupulous in separating the cost of "holiday periods" from the expense to be borne by impresarios. Understandably, managements were held responsible for airport clearance formalities. Reasonably, individual insurance policies covering each eventuality were drawn up for Emlyn, Ann, and his stage-manager Martin Beckwith. Punctiliously, time of arrival and departure, mileage and passport numbers were noted. What compels admiration is the all-embracing foresight that could envisage the provision of a cushioned day-bed in the dressing-room together with an iron and board to ensure that Charles Dickens and Dylan Thomas appeared on stage in garments that were well pressed and neatly creased.

Before he started the first tour organised by de Lannoy, a trip round South America under the aegis of the British Council, Emlyn holidayed with Ann in the Villa Ilios on Corfu. Their guests were Laurence Olivier, accompanied by Joan Plowright to whom he was now married, and three of their children. He was in lazy, happy mood after the years of strain with Vivien Leigh, and resembled more a sedate retired bank manager than a person of the theatre. They talked, inevitably, about the stage, and Emlyn, to check a point, looked up a *Play Pictorial* of 1930. "I was one year old then," remarked Joan Plowright, a glint of mischief in her eye. Olivier said nothing but smiled benignly at her over his spectacles.

While Emlyn revealed the humour of Dickens to the inhabitants of Trinidad and São Paulo and Bogota and Panama and Mexico City, he was at the same time working hard on a new project. Years ago someone had proposed to turn *Night Must Fall* into a musical, though the improbable suggestion never fructified. Now he was engaged on a similar venture with *The Corn Is Green*. Since his attempts to find inspiration for a new play were unsuccessful, why should he not profit from the modern craze for musicals? The idea came from his old friend Joshua Logan, the theatre director he and Molly had known ever since 1944 when Logan was in London to produce Irving Berlin's *This Is The Army*. He met Emlyn while the latter was rehearsing *The Druid's Rest*, and Gladys Henson introduced him to those whom he later called ". . . two of the closest friends I would ever have, Emlyn Williams and his wife Molly." Often on visits to New York Emlyn put up in the apartment where Logan and his wife Nedda lived. He stayed there during the run of *Montserrat* in 1949 when Logan was grappling with the production of *Mister Roberts*. Although later a success, *Mister Roberts* wallowed in rehearsal problems, the most intractable being its length. It overran by fifteen minutes, and Logan, who had, he thought, cut it to the bone, could do no more. He appealed to Emlyn, who said: "Give me the script and a pencil and I'll have it cut for you by morning." Next day, punctually, he appeared with the edited script. "I was only able to do a minor super brilliant job," he said. "I cut sixteen minutes and haven't eliminated one scene." This had been done by excising nearly every adjective, adverb and needless dependent clause. Repetitions of the same idea were elided and the briefest verb forms used. Logan was overjoyed. He and his collaborators presented Emlyn with a pair of gold scissors.

Like Tyrone Guthrie, Josh Logan was a man of enthusiasms. He was also a manic-depressive subject to repeated nervous breakdowns. One of these, not surprisingly, was brought on by the experience of directing Marilyn Monroe in the film *Bus Stop* and he was only rescued from it by a drastic session of electro-convulsive therapy. He visualised *The Corn Is Green* as a vehicle for Mary Martin and engaged the composer Albert Hague, whom he flew to London at his own expense to work with Emlyn on the libretto. Musician and writer collaborated well. At Logan's suggestion the setting was changed from Wales to a sugar cane plantation in the deep South of the USA. The young hero Morgan Evans became a black boy of academic promise who is groomed by his teacher Miss Moffat. Emlyn entered the game with wholehearted commitment. He had studied the medium, a new one to him, with care, and wrote lyrics of the requisite streamlined inanity. Miss Moffat inculcates the joy of reading with a bouncy number called "A Book":

> "It's true a book's a box
> A treasure chest for ever;
> You'd think it would have locks
> To guard the treasure. Never!
> The treasure's there for you
> You've only got to grab it –
> But one thing you must do
> And make it a regular habit
> It's why I'm here today
> To supply just what you're needing
> To show you how to play
> A wonderful game called . . . READING!"

Later Miss Moffat becomes briefly enamoured of a senator and chirrups:

> "If you weren't you,
> And I weren't me –
> What a different world it would be!
> Bright sun without rain,
> True love without pain –
> Nobody tearful
> The news always cheerful . . .
> All colours would blend –
> All fractures would mend –
> The inflexible boughs all would bend . . ."

Et patati et patata. The resulting farrago, in which all the cast except for teacher and senator are black, was christened *Miss Moffat*.

Much of this was written in the Hotel Continental, Buenos Aires, during Emlyn's South American tour. When score and book and lyrics were complete, Josh began his search for a leading lady. His first choice, Mary Martin, disliked the songs. Katharine Hepburn also refused. Irritated, Josh demanded to know why, if Miss Hepburn did trash like *Coco*, she turned down a fine piece like *Miss Moffat*? "Because" came the answer, "*Coco* gave me a chance to rant and rave all over the stage and have some fun – and in this I'd have to hold myself in." Rosalind Russell wanted something lighter for her comeback, and anyway the poor thing had arthritis which would hamper her in the dance numbers. Other notables were approached, among them Deborah Kerr, Julie Harris, Anne Bancroft and Shirley Maclaine. None of them responded. "The only name not to have come up so far has been that of Liberace," observed Emlyn.

In the end a really big name was snared, that of Bette Davis. For many years she had wanted to repeat the role she played in the film of *The Corn Is Green*, and *Miss Moffat* in its new guise seemed to give her just that opportunity. "It's marvellous!' she breathed. Exultant telegrams flew: "Bette Davis loves script hears score 27th." She did not love Josh Logan, whose reputation for slave-driving actors gave her pause. Even this obstacle was overcome, however, when, intent on coaxing her, he wrote her a letter in which he promised to behave himself. She made a dozen copies of it and prudently kept one in all her pockets and handbags so that she could confront him with his own words should a reminder be needed. The ploy did not work. It never could have with such an untameable creature as Josh.

In 1974 *Miss Moffat* began a provincial tour and sold out completely, on the strength of Bette Davis, six months in advance. Josh, keen for a Broadway hit, kept tampering with the play from the very first week. More used to the cosier habits of the film studio, Bette Davis had difficulty in learning her lines, especially when she was given ten pages of new dialogue to absorb each day and as many pages were withdrawn. She did not get on with the talented black boy who played Morgan Evans and she disconcerted the rest of the cast with unexpected pauses. A sore throat intervened, and neuralgia and hysterics. Severe back pains, the legacy of a fall some years ago, racked her frame, and a pinched nerve forced her to wear each night on stage a viciously tight corset. In Philadelphia she retired to bed. Accompanied by a train of doctors and insurance representatives, Logan charged in and angrily accused her of swinging the lead. She called her own doctors. They told the fulminating Josh that the lady was elderly and might well die on his hands. He, with a history of breakdowns, confessed to wife Nedda that Davis could well bring on "the grand extravaganza nervous breakdown of my life." Charges of cowardice and unprofessionalism shattered the tranquil air of Philadelphia. Miss Davis, "the Wicked Witch of the West", as Josh called her, withdrew from the show and hundreds of thousands of dollars were lost. He never forgave her, nor she him.

There is a postscript to this. Josh did not lose faith in *Miss Moffat*, and, some years later, in 1983, he persuaded Ginger Rogers, statuesque survivor of feathery dance films with Fred Astaire, to play the lead relinquished by Bette Davis. The cast was a mixture of professional and amateur players, and they opened in the town of Indianapolis. Ginger was, said Josh, "excellent", sang well and was a good actress. He fell ill during rehearsals and had to go back to New York and a long rest in bed. Unlike Miss Davis, Ginger was eager for the attention of a play doctor. He was not there. Neither was the playwright nor the composer. *Miss Moffat* lasted two weeks. One reason for the collapse of Josh may have been the unappetising news that Elizabeth Taylor, now dabbling in management with a partner, had bought the rights of *The Corn Is Green* and planned a version to be set in West Virginia. This latest turn in the hilarious saga delighted Emlyn. As he put it to Josh, the novelty value of two different productions would be great, since one was a musical with a white female star and a black male lead, while the other was the original play with a black female star and a white male lead. By now, though, an exhausted Josh had lost his sense of humour. Emlyn, as author, could not lose either way, which is more than might be said of the embattled director.

Emlyn had tasted blood. He enjoyed it so much that, even while Josh Logan was scouring Hollywood on behalf of *Miss Moffat*, he had already started turning *Spring, 1600* into a musical. Obedient to the convention that titles must be short and end with an exclamation point, he called his version *Spring!* The goodies he envisaged included a pavane which moved through the centuries, beginning with a couple in Elizabethan dress and ending with a couple in denims and leather. On the way there were coy jokes such as a sign that read: "WETTE PAINT." The big production number, "Spring!", opened:

> "Ev'rything's happening – here in London Town,
> It's the Spring!
> Dump all your cares in the Thames, an' watch 'em drown –
> Have a fling!
> Dreary December's forgotten – long live *May* –
> It's the Spring!
> Trees are in blossom down Covent Garden way –
> Have a fling!"

Lady Coperario revealed her secret to Burbage in a sprightly duet:

> "Out of pride
> I have tried
> To hide my love for you –
> To swear it wasn't true . . .
> I swore in vain . . .
> When *you* were bold
> I turned cold;
> And at your ev'ry smile
> I had to run a mile
> It caused me pain . . .
> But now the cloud is off my mind,
> Both pride and pain are well behind."

Once the deed was done, Emlyn looked around for a composer to set his lyrics. He never found one, and *Spring!*, doomed to nestle unsprung in a drawer, marked the end of his flirtation with the musical.

He had, in any case, found for the moment an answer to the question "If *only* I could fix on something to write!" which recurred throughout his later years. In September, 1973, he published the second volume of his autobiography. *George* had covered his life from 1905 to 1927. The next instalment recounted an even shorter period, from 1927 to 1935, the year in which he attained his thirtieth birthday and, as playwright and actor, startled the town with *Night Must Fall*. The book was called *Emlyn: An early autobiography*. While telling the story of his initial career on the stage, of his excursions into films, of the first plays like *A Murder Has Been Arranged* and *Spring, 1600*, of his friendships with Laughton, Coward and Gielgud, he spoke frankly of his personal life. These were the years of his search for the elder brother, the perfect companion, which led him on a stumbling quest to Bill, to Fess, and, in the end, to Molly. With *George* he had decided not to go beyond his first two decades. A second volume, he felt, risked becoming a catalogue of professional ventures interspersed with "cautious anecdotes". Could he equal the challenge of being as honest about his life as he had been in *George*? The challenge was successfully met. He wrote with a candour that shocked some but would not do so today.

Now that Molly had gone he could tell the whole story as he saw it. The professional career was smoothly woven into the fabric of his private existence. All that could be said, with deference to people still living, was duly uttered. With *George* and *Emlyn* he sketched to his own satisfaction the Janus-faced character of George Emlyn Williams. The book had glowing reviews and was widely noticed, both here and in America. It became a best-seller along with Graham Greene's *The Honorary Consul*, and rivalled Harold Macmillan's memoirs in the lists. Later he read it as a serial on BBC Radio 4. *Gay News*, in particular, lauded him for, in a phrase newly imported, "coming out". He clipped the review and filed it punctiliously, without comment.

That year he holidayed at the Villa Ilios. His study of modern Greek had advanced so far that he was able to play the part of narrator in a local performance of *Peter and The Wolf*, that piece of jocularity by the overrated Prokoviev – in any case Emlyn was not particularly interested in music. His delivery was notable for a mastery of the language which got all the accents and quantities right. With such diversions did he strive to lay the ghost of the companion who accompanied his thoughts everywhere on Corfu, in Dovehouse Street, in their country home. A close friend who happened to be with him on the island received tragic news about the death of her young son. She had already lost her daughter, murdered some years previously. He tried to comfort her. "Oh, I do miss Molly!" she cried. At which point he could bear it no longer. The old wound reopened and he broke down.

On his return to London he found another subject which might help to keep at bay memories which persisted in haunting him. His old friend Margaretta Scott, who had acted in *A Murder Has Been Arranged*, invited him to dinner one evening. The other guest was Frank Hauser, director of the Oxford Playhouse, who looked forward to talk about Oxford and mutual friends. He was to be disappointed. Came a ring at the door and Emlyn presented himself, bright and trim after walking briskly from Dovehouse Street in Chelsea across the Park to Margaretta's Scott's home in Molyneux Street, Marylebone. In his hand he carried a large bag. Scarcely was he in the house than he produced from the bag a straw boater, a blazer, a bow tie, and various Edwardian props. Throughout dinner and long into the evening he chattered excitedly about his new idea, another solo entertainment to feature the short story writer "Saki". Then he went ahead and gave his audience of two a privileged recital. Frank Hauser never reached the point of exchanging the Oxfordian reminiscences for which he had hoped.

"Saki" was H. H. Munro (1870–1916). His pen name he borrowed from the woman cup-bearer in a wry, disillusioned but stoic verse of the *Rubáiyát of Omar Khayyám*. As a journalist he had all the resource and despatch of the ready writer who, strictly on time, never fails to supply the precise number of words to fill the precise amount of space. These limitations helped him achieve the balance and economy which characterise his best stories. He had been a foreign correspondent in the Balkans where he much enjoyed the company of gypsy boys whose grace reminded him of "black panthers". In Poland he found the young men adequate but lethargic. St Petersburg was the nicest place of all, for there he discovered he could enjoy a private life unhampered by the social conventions of Edwardian London, although Russian youth often seemed oddly jaded by the age of seventeen. Neither did Paris disappoint, for here, in his last posting, he set up his usual unorthodox household run by a male cook whom his sister innocently described as an "original". Finally he came back to London, resolved to make his living as a free-lance writer of stories and articles. Although the liberty he had enjoyed in foreign capitals was denied him, he made up for it by discreet attendance at the Turkish Baths in Jermyn Street.

Saki was a handsome man with pale features, cool eyes and slim lips. His place in English literature, which he shares with Ronald Firbank, is that of a consummate dandy. The heroes of his stories are languid young men called Reginald, Clovis and Bertie who wander through fashionable drawing-rooms murmuring epigrams and upsetting dowager duchesses. The wit is sometimes Wildean: "To have reached thirty is to have failed in life." "No really provident woman lunches regularly with her husband if she wishes to burst upon him as a revelation at dinner. He must have time to forget; an afternoon is not enough." But there was plenty of Saki's own. "She was a good cook as cooks go, and as cooks go she went," is the most famous. His stories, often no more than anecdotes, are exquisitely constructed and beautifully proportioned. In the course of his short life he produced over a hundred and twenty of them, all written at speed to meet a deadline. Not a word is superfluous, not a phrase too long. He is on the side of children against adults, of life-enhancers against bores, of frankness against pomposity. Beneath the glittering surface is a moralist who satirises greed, cupidity, hypocrisy and snobbery. He could also be very feline. "You're looking nicer than usual, but that's so easy for you", was a typical greeting to a woman friend. The death of this fastidious writer was brutally ironic. As a sergeant at the Front (he had refused a commission) sheltering his men from enemy fire, he rebuked someone for giving away their position by lighting up. "Put that bloody cigarette out!" were his last unstylish words before a sniper shot him dead.

Emlyn had when young read and enjoyed Saki. In 1972 his son Alan gave him the Bodley Head collected edition of the stories with Noël Coward's introduction. It reawakened his interest. "I knew him in my early twenties," he said, "and, like most people of that age, I fell in love with him ... I read the stories again. I suddenly realised that the dialogue and the prose absolutely leapt to the stage. It was the same way I had felt about Dickens and Dylan Thomas and I don't feel about any other authors."

The problem was which, among Saki's many small masterpieces, to choose? He selected fifteen items. Although he had been wholly faithful to the texts of Dickens and Thomas, rearranging but always respecting the original, with Saki he had no such scruples. He concocted an introduction putting Saki in context and using some of the famous witticisms – "To be clever in the afternoon is to argue that one is dining *nowhere* in the evening" – which gave a foretaste of what was to come. His selection portrayed the range of Saki's gift. "The Secret Sin of Septimus Brope" illustrated the purely mischievous aspect in a tale about the respectable and learned editor of *Cathedral Monthly* who secretly makes a large revenue by composing pop songs to be performed "in Blackpool and places where they sing". The unscrupulous Clovis discovers his dreadful secret, and, in return for a handsome royalty, supplies him with the lyric of his next hit. "The Disappearance of Crispina Umberleigh" concerns a husband whose wife is seized by kidnappers. So relieved is he to be shot of her that he gladly pays them a yearly ransom to keep her.

The more sinister regions were charted in "Laura". "You are not really dying, are you," asks Amanda. "I have the doctor's permission to live till Tuesday," says Laura. "But today is Saturday; this is serious!" gasps Amanda. Laura dies on Monday but is reincarnated as an otter which ruins Amanda's garden and raids her larder. Her husband kills the beast out hunting. Unfortunately Laura comes back again, this time as "a naked brown Nubian boy" who lays waste to her husband's dressing-room. "And now Amanda is seriously ill." Even more macabre, erotic, even, was "Gabriel Ernest". A fussy bachelor who lives with his aunt finds that in a coppice on his property a boy of about sixteen lies "asprawl, drying his wet brown limbs luxuriously in the sun." His light-brown eyes have a tigerish gleam in them. The boy, it seems, is a werewolf who enjoys the flesh of rabbits, hares, poultry and the occasional child. The spinster aunt, feeling maternal, adopts him as she would a stray kitten. After a Sunday-school party she gives for local children she dotingly allows him to take home one of Mrs Toop's infants. "A shrill wail of fear" is heard and neither is seen again. "Mrs Toop, who had eleven other children, was decently resigned to her bereavement."

Sometimes the underlying cruelty of Saki is playful. "Waldo is one of those people who would be enormously improved by death," says Clovis. Most of us have a Waldo in our life and have, on various occasions, felt that way about him. At other times the cruelty can be implacable and chilling. *Sredni Vashtar* is very characteristic of him, both in his fellow-feeling for children and in his detestation of unsympathetic adults. When Saki was a boy his much cherished pet had been a Houdan cockerel. It fell ill, and although a veterinary surgeon could have saved it, the aunt under whose domination Saki lived ruled that it should be put down. His misery was intense. Thirty years later he used the incident as the basis of *Sredni Vashtar*. The protagonist, ten-year-old Conradin, belongs reluctantly to the household of an elder female cousin. She delights in thwarting his every pleasure, "for his good", as she explains. (One is reminded of another Saki story where a woman is annoyed by a page-boy who delivers an unwelcome message. "Eleanor hated boys, and would have liked to have whipped this one long and often. It was perhaps the yearning of a woman who had no children of her own.") One of the few delights Conradin has left to him is a dilapidated shed in a forgotten corner of the large garden. Here lives a ragged Houdan hen on which he lavishes his affection. Here, also, is a hutch containing a large polecat-ferret sold him by the friendly butcher-boy. Conradin baptises the animal Sredni Vashtar and invents elaborate pagan rituals in his honour. One of them celebrates the occasion when his cousin suffers for three days from acute toothache, and the boy almost convinces himself that Sredni Vashtar is responsible. She finds out about the hen and arranges for it to be sold. That night Conradin prays earnestly to Sredni Vashtar. Still suspicious about the contents of the shed, the cousin sneaks the key from its hiding place in his bedroom and goes to inspect the shed in person. Conradin, from a distance, watches her enter. The minutes pass. He chants a defiant hymn:

> "Sredni Vashtar went forth,
> His thoughts were red thoughts and his teeth were white.
> His enemies called for peace, but he brought them death.
> Sredni Vashtar the Beautiful."

Soon he is rewarded. Out through the doorway comes ". . . a long, low, yellow-and-brown beast, with eyes a-blink at the waning daylight, and dark wet strains around the fur of jaws and throat." The animal drinks from a brook and disappears into the bushes. Tea is served. The mistress is absent. Amid screams and sobs a heavy burden is carried into the house. "Whoever will break it to the poor child?" exclaims a shrill voice. Conradin makes himself another piece of toast and joyfully smothers it in butter.

With "The Lumber Room", a story in which a small boy traps a detested aunt in a malodorous rainwater tank, Emlyn completed his selection of items showing Saki's darker nature. They were alternated with others of a more comic flavour to provide changes of mood in a varied evening's entertainment. Sometimes, however, he broke down a story to its barest elements, preserving only the outline and suppressing the ironic flavour which is among the greatest pleasures of reading Saki. One must needs broaden effects for the stage, but even so it was a pity that he sacrificed so many of the delicate touches in the prose of an expert miniaturist. Even titles were not sacrosanct: for no apparent reason he changed "The Secret Sin of Septimus Brope" into "The Secret Sin of Septimus Grope". And one story at least, "The Open Window", was so maltreated that the sly, gossamer humour evaporated.

He found the title of his entertainment in an article by Christopher

Morley on Saki: "The Playboy of the Weekend World". It was some time before he was ready to present it, for adaptation and rehearsals took many months of work in between tours. The years 1975 and 1976 were taken up with more travels as Dickens and Dylan Thomas around the USA, Israel and Asia, by which time the records showed that he had given one thousand nine hundred and twenty-one performances and six hundred and sixty-two of Thomas. "I'm more relaxed doing this than when doing a play," he explained. "With other actors you feel terribly responsible if you go wrong and spoil it for someone else. Playing Iago in *Othello* was much more exhausting for me than this." Critics, though, were beginning to tire of these performances. He had been giving them for twenty-five years, and there were those who detected a mechanical note in his delivery. The novelty had long since vanished. It was time to introduce something new, and Saki gave him the opportunity.

He chose 1977 as the year of Saki. It was also his Jubilee, the fiftieth anniversary of his first professional appearance in *And So To Bed*. He was seventy-two, the hair entirely snow-white but the features still smooth. He had become, he said, more "narrow-eyed" about his performance, and would not commit himself to Saki beyond a five-week tour of the provinces. "If you're sure of the ice, you can skate. I'm hoping I can skate again."

The Playboy of The Weekend World opened at the Yvonne Arnaud Theatre in Guildford on August 15. Emlyn came forward on an empty stage. He wore a blue blazer, perky bow tie and white flannels. The atmosphere of Edwardian country houses entered with him. "Of course," wrote a reviewer, "it is no mere reading of Saki's stories – rather, it is a highly dramatic, exhilarating acting performance in the same mould of Charles Dickens." He ended with "Birds On The Western Front", a poignant coda in which Saki depicted skylarks building nests in ruined trenches, crows locked in combat with sparrow-hawks while fighter planes above them attacked enemy aircraft, and rooks poking through bombed-out streets beneath a thunderous rain of shells. At the exact moment when Emlyn uttered the word "thunder" in his script, a noisy storm crashed out over Guildford.

He gave fifty performances on a tour of the provinces and in a short season at the Apollo. Next year he took Saki to Canada and America. Before he left he gave a party at Dovehouse Street. The windows stood open to admit rays of pallid sunshine as he bustled around fetching ginger beer and proffering ice cubes. He wore a short-sleeved shirt outside his trousers. Royal blue spectacle frames dangled on a cord over his chest. His manner, said a guest, was "elegant yet insouciant, with the bow of a boy, a scholarly boy's shy precision of speech." A friend asked him about the poetry of Dylan Thomas. "Some of it I find wilfully obscure," he avowed. "Sometimes you can't even find the verb."

The Playboy of the Weekend World opened at Harvard in February, 1978. This American tour was organised by Arthur Cantor, the Boston-born impresario who had promoted many successful plays in New York and London, where he was joint managing director of H. M. Tennent Ltd. One of his associates was Greer Garson, the film actress doomed for eternity to be known as Mrs Miniver, although she fought bravely against the notoriety of her most celebrated rôle by founding the Greer Garson Theater in Santa Fé, New Mexico. The most orchidaceous of Cantor's solo entertainers was Barry Humphreys, whose *Housewife! Superstar!!* toured under his auspices. As a counter-balance to the secular nature of Moonie Ponds, Cantor also represented *The Gospel According to St Mark* told by Alec McCowen.

Boston followed, then Washington, and so to New York, where Clive Barnes in the *New York Post* wrote of Emlyn as Saki: "He looks like a languid dandy – a soft shoe shuffle of a man crammed with tea and crumpets . . . Williams is such an extraordinarily gifted actor – he holds the stage with the naturalness of an unspoken reality. He lounges, he moves with calculated exaggeration, he mugs, he underlines with an elegantly grotesque style of gesticulation, yet he never wavers from character . . . But it is all, yes, urbane. Williams, looking like a transcendental choirboy with white mice in his pockets, is superb . . . enchantingly funny . . . It all gives the evening the genial poignancy of crushed violets – of elegance expended at the expense of truth . . . of all three of Williams' personifications this one is the most personal and sensitive. I suspect it is an actor's testament to his art." Perhaps the essential Englishness of Saki had a strange, exotic appeal for Americans, whereas in his native England *The Playboy of The Weekend World* never really achieved the success of Emlyn's other two shows.

Besides the pleasure of winning fresh acclaim in the USA Emlyn enjoyed a privilege extended to few except Mark Twain and C. B. Cochran.[1] He found that his obituary had been published in an

---

[1] To which famous names may be added that of the Victorian actor, Charles Brookfield. He was a noted clubman and raconteur, and, according to Ellen Terry, delighted in retailing the final sentences of his premature obituary: "Never a great actor, he was invaluable in small parts. But after all, it is at his club that he will be most missed."

American newspaper and the date of his death given as 1974. "I have racked my brain," he remarked helpfully, "and cannot recall anything untoward happening that year."

(iii)
Floating Cues

From the Cupola and the Tower of Winds, perched on the airy heights above Hastings whence might be glimpsed the misty reaches of Romney Marsh, came a brisk letter. "You have an individualistic attitude to life," it told Emlyn. The writer of the letter went on to express his fear that individuality was endangered, that the collectivist state loomed. It was therefore needful to make a record of Individuals for posterity. Would Emlyn pose for John Bratby, a leading member of what was known as the Kitchen Sink School of Painting?

In December, 1979, Emlyn went down to Hastings and duly posed. "It was a most enjoyable afternoon," Bratby told him. Emlyn's was not the easiest face to paint, he discovered to his surprise, because his appearance was most definite. "But it was elusive, and the afternoon like trying to catch butterflies, groping and grasping for changes of form, trying to grab the swell of the cheeks, the character of the strong nose, and the distinctive upper lip." He was easier to catch in profile, "for there your identity is writ most clearly . . ." First refusal of the portrait was offered at £400.

The imputation of individuality was flattering for a writer who still wanted urgently to write something original but who had not yet found a subject. A reminder of what he could once achieve came when *The Corn Is Green* was made into a television film with Katharine Hepburn in the role played earlier by Sybil Thorndike and Bette Davis. "Oh indeed a wonderful part," said Miss Hepburn. "My, I laughed and I cried and cried. Lovely for me. A woman alive. Not half dead." These were words to cheer an author's heart.

He thought, in fact, that he had at last written a play that would work. Profiting from the end of censorship and the air of freedom that blew through the theatre, he finished what he described as "a new comedy by Emlyn Williams". After considerable rewriting and extensive revision, he noted the date on the manuscript, a tangle of holograph and typed amendments: "7 am, July 18, 1980." The new comedy had a sex-change as its subject.

"I want . . . to feel silk next to my skin," says the husband who longs to become a woman. "To slide my hand between the silk and the skin, and to feel the one as smooth as the other. I want . . . to bind my hair in a knot on the top of my head, and to walk barefoot in the sand." He has already shaved off the disgusting "mat of hair" from his chest. "It isn't a mat," rejoins his poor bewildered wife indignantly, "it's smooth and glossy – like babies' hair." He borrows, unknown to her, items from her wardrobe and preens himself in them. "What's he doing?" she asks. "Sitting in front of the mirror with one of your lipsticks, in a slip and black stockings," she is told. "If anybody asks me out to dinner tonight," she laments, "I'd have to say: 'Sorry, I haven't a thing to wear'."

Since his name is Gerald, he wishes to be known henceforth as "Geraldine." An operation is planned in Switzerland. His biologist father-in-law explains that he wants to have "it" removed. "But it's *his*", remarks his son. "What do you mean, his," cries his wife. "It's *ours*! . . . It's *vandalism*!" The would-be woman starts a course of pills which will hasten the much-desired change. His father-in-law and son connive to push him into the swimming pool, for they know that salt water will negate the effect of the pills. So it does, and "Geraldine", restored to normality, brings down the curtain by kissing his wife lovingly and passionately. To make quite sure the audience realised how up-to-date his play was, Emlyn also included a Lesbian in the cast.

Neatly constructed, with curtain-lines in all the right places and the seeds of later developments cunningly planted, the piece fails utterly to work. The plot is ludicrous and the dialogue inept. *Transformation Scene*, as Emlyn entitled his new play, is a bizarre excursion. Casting around for a leading man, he bethought himself of Richard Briers, now an established name, with whom he had appeared in *Three*. The actor was summoned to Dovehouse Street. Emlyn, full of charm, pressed drinks into his hand, autographed books for him, took a flattering interest in his career. The atmosphere was delightful. Then, gently, Emlyn introduced the subject of *Transformation Scene*. The play, he was convinced, would be a tremendous hit for the actor who played the leading rôle. His enthusiasm grew in proportion as that of his guest dwindled. Dismayed and embarrassed, Briers sought to disengage himself as tactfully as possible. Gerald/Geraldine was, he agreed, "a splendid part," but . . . The air grew chill. Emlyn's eyes narrowed.

The charm dissolved to show the steel beneath. He loathed being thwarted. Still he did not get his way, and none of the other people he approached about *Transformation Scene* would have anything to do with it. The manuscript returned to his bottom-most drawer.

More successful was another piece of writing which he completed at this time. In September that year he published a novel called *Headlong*. He and Molly belonged to a generation that had been fascinated by the abdication of Edward VIII. He was intrigued by the royal family, and the scrapbooks are full of press cuttings and photographs concerning them. In 1940 a bomb had landed on Buckingham Palace. What, he thought to himself, if it had wiped out the entire family? In *Headlong* the whole tribe of them, even unto Prince Paul of Kenilworth, twenty-seventh in line of succession, are incinerated at the launch of the gigantic new airship which explodes and collapses on them. The year is 1935. Frantic courtiers search the genealogical trees and find that the heir presumptive is an obscure actor, illegitimate grandson to the Duke of Clarence, eldest son of Edward VII, who died in 1892. He is spirited off to the Palace, bathed, coiffed, tailored, and proclaimed King. At first he plays the part with conviction. Then, like the Prince of Wales, later Edward VIII, he becomes distressed about the plight of the poor and the unemployed. The inability of government to solve the problem appals him, and he decides to stand down. His place is taken by his private secretary, who, as great-grandson to George III on the right side of the blanket, has an even better claim to the throne. The ex-king is given a tax-free pension of £50,000 a year, which he accepts only on condition that the greater part of it be paid into a fund for relieving the unemployed. Back to the theatre goes Jack Sandring(ham), whose name was a joke invented by his father the Duke of Clarence when the latter eventually married a respectable woman.

Although Jack comes from a remote part of Cornwall, his youthful background and career are strangely reminiscent of Emlyn's. The theatre world of the nineteen-thirties is, of course, extremely well done with its echoes of Jack Buchanan, Ivor Novello, late-night snacks at the Strand Corner House, and libidinous impresarios. So, too, is the detail of procedure at investitures and meetings of the Privy Council. Emlyn, the scholar, prided himself on his research and took expert advice from an unnamed lady who had in her time graced the royal court. His copious notes included a full ground-plan of Buckingham Palace. He also introduces, and draws with striking realism, such characters from the period as Lloyd George, Stanley Baldwin, Ramsay

MacDonald and John Reith. Emlyn enjoyed himself very much and was satisfied with the result. "When writing a play you are in a strait-jacket governed by the fact that it should not take more than two hours to perform," he said. "The danger in writing a novel is to allow yourself to spread too much. I don't think I've done that."

Though not in complete agreement, the *Daily Express* liked *Headlong*. "This loquacious Welshman writes very much as he talks," it decided. "The words tumble out in a non-stop untidy flow. But what energy!" *The Times Literary Supplement* called the book "a good, old-fashioned read." The late John Braine, novelist and grumpy old man, wrote: "It would pass the time on a long railway journey and is always agreeably high-spirited." *The Times* found it ". . . a real chatterbox of a book, bursting with good humour and keen observation and written with vigour, skill and a wicked sense of malice." The autumn of 1980 was spent in promoting the book at literary luncheons up and down the country organised by Emlyn's publishers. At the age of seventy-five he was still able to withstand long journeys and the ordeal of appearing in public with persons such as Jilly Cooper and Val Doonican. On entering Heinemann's offices and overhearing publishers' jargon about "tele-ordering", he remarked: "I feel as though I have been brought to a house of ill-fame and am learning how it all works."

In 1991 *Headlong*, a frothy *jeu d'esprit*, was brutally assaulted and wrenched into a Hollywood film called *King Ralph*. The protagonist was the fat husband of an even fatter American television comedienne, and he played the role of a Las Vegas pianist who is catapulted into the kingship. Local colour included references to "spotted dick" as a favourite British dessert, and "fox hunting" was construed as the pursuit of women. At a state banquet the newly-proclaimed monarch hammers out "Good Golly, Miss Molly" on the harpsichord, and later drops his crown into a royal foam bath. Emlyn was in his grave by then, and the only good thing about the movie was the sale of film rights. He might, though, have been comforted to learn that in the end the throne of Great Britain was inherited by Peter O'Toole.

The destiny of the royal family having been settled, Emlyn embarked in the dying days of 1980 on a twelve-week tour of the USA. He was Charles Dickens again, for although his Saki had enjoyed a *succès d'estime*, it was as Dickens that audiences most wanted him. In New York he stayed with Josh and Nedda Logan, walking each day through stinging cold and snow to the Century Theater where he was appearing. A reporter asked him if he liked walking. "Yes," he replied, "when it's over. I feel better because I think I've done a good deed." There followed a well-timed pause. Then: "Oh, I don't enjoy it as much as all that, you know. I think that the things you really enjoy are the things you feel guilty about afterwards." Did the "enjoyable" things include acting? "Oh, no-o-o-o-o, because one is not guilty afterwards. One is pleased it's over. It's work and it's nervous. One is always nervous. It's a sort of enjoyment but it's more of a challenge. You're never sure that it's all right until it's over. Then you can relax and have a drink." On one of his solitary promenades he arrived at the Century Theater to find two hundred or so actors and actresses gathered round the stage-door. When he asked one of the hopeful actresses what was going on, she explained that they were auditioning for *Jitters*, a back-stage comedy. Glancing at his hair, white as the snow that lay all about, she added kindly: "I wouldn't bother hanging around if I were you, there aren't any parts for old men."

He was seventy-six in 1981, and although the vigour and the faultless memory he displayed continued to impress, what remained most astonishing of all was the freshness he brought to every performance. It seemed as if the phrases were being uttered for the first time. This is one of the greatest triumphs an actor can achieve. By that date Emlyn had given over two thousand performances as Dickens. Yet, as one reviewer noted: "Mr Williams reminded us of what it was like to read Dickens for the first time: the words had a bloom on them, the phrases glinted like new coins. It was like a magician taking you into the secret of his act, one responded with uncomplicated pleasure and an excitement that was not far from childish." And another, in Philadelphia: "I first heard him read Dickens fifteen years ago, and in the intervening time, as if to prove that life is unfair, I've gotten older and crankier, while he and Dickens have kept their vitality, passion and wit."

After playing Kenya, Zimbabwe and South Africa, he returned to the USA in autumn and remained there until the spring of 1982. On the thirtieth anniversary of his Dickens recital he wrote a letter to the shade of the novelist. "Dear C.D.," he began, "I should have penned this thirty years ago, but I was too much in awe of you. Now I realise, from my stage presentation of you, that you are not only a genius but an amusing and approachable fellow – a comic if there ever was one! I know you'll understand. For this is a letter of apology.

"As I was first preparing my pieces, I was excited to hear your words spring to vivid life when spoken on the stage – but I realised too that not *all* the words do that. Because – forgive me – there are a great many of them. Millions. And in between the words that soar like birds (or like jets, as we say now) there are areas of overweight stuff that refuses to stir. So I've had to cut."

As an example he went on to excuse himself for cutting "the brilliant opening of *A Tale of Two Cities*", and explained why. He ended: "I'm sorry. But I know with your sense of theatre, you will understand.

"With homage, and thanks for adding a dimension to my life, E.W." A postscript read: "Since I am told that owing to inflation, like everything else the postage rate to the Other World has risen out of all proportion, I'm afraid this missive must stay where it is. Sorry, Master."

When he came back to London he found a real letter awaiting him with real news about a real friend. John Gielgud had just been filming *Wagner* with Richard Burton. "Richard seemed dreadfully sad and ravaged," Gielgud wrote, "lonely and unhappy, but acting well, though under physical troubles with his back and I fear too much drink after work in the evenings . . . They have two or three months to go yet before the picture is finished. I only hope for everyone's sake he will stay the course. I believe the insurance is enormous and no wonder. The Press hounded him for copy all the time. He was sweet to me and gave me a wonderful present when I left . . . I suppose he is so lavish as a kind of guilt complex. All very sad . . ." The handsome Welsh boy of *The Last Days of Dolwyn* had become an international star, raddled, shaky, alcoholic, and even now approaching his own last days.

Emlyn also returned, briefly, to the television screen next year. He was Harold Brittling in episode one, "Rumpole and the Genuine Article", of the third Rumpole series. His role was that of an old painter. John Mortimer remembers: "He tried to change all his lines and then found they didn't work so went back to what I had written." Later he was to play another elderly character, a judge, in Mortimer's radio play *Edwin*. He was, says the author, "very good."

His own *The Corn Is Green* turned up again in the summer of 1983. This was the production mounted by Elizabeth Taylor through her company the Elizabeth Theatre Group. It went on a pre-Broadway tour and opened at the Lynn Fontanne Theater in New York. Miss Moffat had been rewritten for a black actress and endowed with Caribbean ancestry. "When Miss Moffat confronts a group of young coal miners, their faces blacker than hers," wrote an English correspondent, "the play seems strangely topical and its meaning still fresh. Some young black actors could easily have been cast as the miners and it would have made little difference." Cicely Tyson, who played Miss Moffat, was a handsome woman "with a fine-featured severity." But her voice, said a reviewer, was monotonous. "A black Miss Moffat is not the issue. Tyson's Miss Moffat is." With her was Elizabeth Seal as her fellow teacher Miss Ronberry. The box-office languished and the cast agreed a cut in salaries to help the play along while Emlyn took a smaller royalty for the same reason. The sacrifice availed little. There were disagreements with Miss Tyson and she withdrew. The interesting experiment closed after a month or so. Emlyn consoled himself with three weeks' comparative idleness in Crete and Turkey. Guilty at not working, he remarked defensively that it was ". . . my first real (tourist) holiday since my last one with Molly in 1964!"

He need not have felt culpable. Royalties on previous work still came in, and although they may not have been so abundant as in earlier years, other sources began to flow. In January, 1984, he received his first cheque of £424.94 from the new Public Lending Right, a modest attempt to compensate authors whose books were borrowed free from libraries by people ready to spend money on anything but literature. Later that year, in July, he opened at Bromley in a new production of *The Doctor's Dilemma*. Why should a famous West End star submit himself to a humble provincial tour? He did not need the money. He did need, like all actors, an audience, and he enjoyed the challenge of speaking Shaw's dialogue. Besides, listening to the other actors was ". . . very good for me because . . . it's not easy to listen in a one-man show; also waiting for floating cues is very good for the concentration and for the realisation there are other actors in the profession. And of course I'm occasionally puzzled by the sheer presence of the crowd (of five) surrounding me . . . As I wait in the wings for thirty seconds, a chair is produced. In the end I had to say, 'Respect is welcome, but one draws the line at veneration.' "

As the oldest and wisest of the doctors in the cast, Emlyn gave a well-tuned and wholly professional performance. At the age of seventy-nine, though, he occasionally found it difficult to remember his lines, and sometimes he forgot vital business. *The Doctor's Dilemma* travelled no further than Guildford since casting difficulties prevented a West End booking. Back home in Chelsea he started looking at his earlier plays in the hope of revival. He rewrote *Beth* and called the result *Cuckoo*, for that was the name of the central character, originally a young girl but now a grown woman in her late thirties. Joan Plowright, approached to take the lead, turned it down with the frank, or polite, admission that she was too old for the part. *Cuckoo* reached the stage at Guildford but was heard of no more. He took up *Someone Waiting* again, and, because the subsequent abolition of the death penalty had nullified its dramatic point, revised it to take this into account. The list of actors who were offered the part of the young man but who refused it is sadly impressive: Alan Bates, Tom Courtenay, Tom Conti, Anthony Hopkins, Ian McKellen, Alec McCowen.

On August 30 he delivered his tribute at a memorial service for Richard Burton who had died at the age of fifty-eight. Though the features had become haggard and the body weary, some spark still remained of the dazzling boy in whom Emlyn had seen so much of himself. He was glad that, after the rift between them caused by the marriage with Elizabeth Taylor, they had come together again. While playing *The Deputy* in New York he had had a telephone call one night from Elizabeth. She, daring to take the initiative, invited Emlyn and Molly to their hotel suite for a drink. Burton kissed them both. All was well, and at last Emlyn became reconciled to a situation which had distressed him. He said, wonderingly: "I never thought, when I gave that boy his first part in a film, that when he died he would be front page and *headlines*." His memorial address at St Martin-in-the Fields was a difficult task, given the number of wives who remained. He tackled it boldly, ignoring all but Sally, the last wife, whom he mentioned briefly, and speaking of Elizabeth as if she had been the sole Mrs Burton. Sir John Gielgud, due to give a reading from *Hamlet* committed a typical "Gielgoodie": he arrived very late, having driven in the wrong direction along Shaftesbury Avenue under the impression that the service was being held in an altogether different church.

In 1985 Emlyn reached his eightieth birthday. Even he, the energetic, the lively, the irrepressible, thought it was time to prepare for the moment when he would follow Molly. On June 13 he made his will. Trust funds were set up for his sons Alan and Brook, and should these funds determine they were to benefit his nephews, the children of his late brothers Thomas and Job. He also remembered Ann Plugge, the family friend whose care for him had helped lighten, if anything could, the blow of Molly's death. Like Molly, he asked only for a simple and private service with no outward signs of mourning and no flowers. "I also have an earnest wish," he continued, "which I hope will not be interpreted as a gesture against organised religion. It is not. I earnestly request that there should be no Memorial Service held for me. As members of the 'Entertainment' Professions get older they find that more and more of these tributes have to be arranged and attended, in the course of extremely busy lives more and more mornings have to be set aside for deliberately solemn faces and deliberately hushed voices. I am sure my friends will see the commonsense of this. If anybody feels strongly that they wish to enter a church at any time to think of me I am touched and welcome it. Otherwise I know my family and friends will remember me with love, and if they spontaneously foregather to think of me and drink to me and to one another, I welcome that. But no Memorial Service please."

He went on writing plays, among them *The Sound of Horses* and *Fess*. The former never emerged from his files. Actors who turned down the latter when approached included Peter Barkworth and Tom Conti. On November 26, his eightieth birthday, he was interviewed for television by Terry Wogan. Trim, alert, he bounced up to the dais wearing a neat blue suit and red tie, white hair glinting in the studio lights. He was, he told Wogan, employing the formula he usually adopted in the hundreds of interviews to which he had been subjected, "a Welsh peasant". The smooth chit-chat proceeded, Wogan feeding his guest with cues that were instantly taken up and expertly dispatched. Then, suddenly, a small boy and girl appeared bearing champagne and a birthday cake. They were Emlyn's grandchildren, the son and daughter of Alan. He got down, loping somewhat stiffly, from the dais and joined them to cut the cake and open the champagne. And so the interview ended in a flush of Woganised sentimentality.

After the Wogan interview he resumed the new international tour he was making as Charles Dickens. It had begun in Poland where he did a good turn to John Gielgud who, of Polish ancestry, still had relatives in that country. "Ah," said Sir John when he heard of the impending trip, "I wonder if he could take a few small gifts to some of my cousins there?" Emlyn, he was told, would be delighted. The small gifts which arrived at Dovehouse Street, beautifully and individually gift wrapped, amounted to a considerable bulk. Somehow they were squeezed in with all the props and baggage that went on the tour. "Dear John," said Emlyn gently, "never does things by halves."

In December he was at the Bayview Playhouse in Toronto, and from there went to Florida, Los Angeles and a series of American towns which ended in North Carolina by March, 1986. Although he was in his eighty-first year the compulsive urge to make up, to go out on a stage, to dominate an audience remained as compulsive as ever. To satisfy this he gladly put up with the discomfort of ceaseless travelling, of lonely nights in dull hotels, of inane conversations with boring people. What else was there to do but work? Besides, it was the only activity that helped, ever so little, to keep his regret for Molly in check. When he returned to Dovehouse Street the tally of Dickens performances amounted to two thousand three hundred and sixty shows. Saki, caviar to the general, could only muster a hundred and thirty-one.

He found awaiting him the pleasant news that he was entitled to a monthly pension of some $450 a month from American Equity. Ever since his first appearance in New York he had scrupulously paid his dues and contributed to the pension fund. Another $10,000 or so were owed him in arrears. His mother would have applauded such thrift.

Less pleasing was a bodily condition that persisted. The symptom was bowel disturbance which upset routine and began to restrict his life. He underwent the usual examinations. The appetite remained good, the heart proved in excellent condition for a man of his age, the blood-pressure was wholly satisfactory. Might the cause be an inflammatory bowel disease complicated by ulcerative colitis, an unusual form of Crohn's Disease? (As Sacha Guitry once observed, when doctors don't know what is wrong with us they give it a name.) A colonoscopy showed no obvious colitis. After a simple sigmoidoscopy consultants spoke of lesions and villous adenomas. Cancer of the bowel was suspected, and Emlyn went into the Princess Grace Hospital for an operation.

At first it appeared to have been successful. He left wintry London in January, 1987, and flew to the Canary Islands for a warm convalescence. Such were his good spirits that he started to write a book he had long contemplated: a third volume of autobiography as the successor to *George* and *Emlyn*. It would, he decided, be called *From Stage to Stage: An Adventure*. "Chapter I," he wrote boldly. Another chapter was to be entitled "Brief Encounters" and in it he drafted his memories of Laurence Olivier, Vivien Leigh and Lillian Hellman. The book was to include his reminiscences of the Duchess Theatre, scene of his first great triumph with *Night Must Fall*. "Then there was the night," he wrote, "Sweetie Sugarbowl came round after the play to see us because she had heard that Robert Montgomery was coming round too; I shan't tell you her real name, she used to grace the boards in an ineffectual way before she retired into the comparative obscurity of a small title and a mink coat.

"I was talking to Robert Montgomery in my room when I heard her languish into Angela's [Baddeley] room with the helpful comment: 'My dear, *what* tiny dressing-rooms they are here!'

"It turned out to be her only comment of the whole evening. A moment later I opened Angela's door to tell her Montgomery was anxious to meet her, and opened the door wider to let him pass me into the room. Sweetie had disappeared.

"Angela looked rather worried for a minute. We talked, and then went out again. It turned out that in opening the door I had pinned Sweetie behind it and she had been five minutes in a room with a film star without even seeing him. Angela, who bears no malice, was rather sorry for her. I was delighted."

Neither cancer nor old age had succeeded in dulling Emlyn's acid wit.

Another literary work that had recently absorbed him was published later in the year. The case of Dr Crippen had long been one of his favourite murder trials, and in *Dr Crippen's Diary: An Invention* he combined the methods of scholarly research with imaginative recreation. There is, as one might guess, a plethora of macabre detail. The diarist recounts how, with the aid of Cunningham's *Manual of Practical Anatomy* ("bought in Charing Cross Road all those yrs ago!"), he dissects the corpse of Belle Elmore, cuts off the head and drops it in the sea on a trip to Dieppe. ("The fishes are welcome. As the French put it, *bon appétit*.") If one accepts the morbid fascination with death and dissection, *Dr Crippen's Diary* is a more successful piece of writing than *Beyond Belief*. It reads as a convincing psychological portrayal of a human paradox, a strange mixture of the mild-mannered and the cold-blooded. A further merit is that, even though one knows the end of the story in advance, the telling of it conveys real excitement. When Crippen nearly bungles the murder one is on tenterhooks about the result. At his first interrogation by detectives one feels the suspense he goes through as he recalls the mistakes he might have made before, as he thinks, he manages to deflect their suspicions. Even Ethel le Neve's infatuation with the unattractive little man is made believable. The style of the diary is perfectly in character for one who is not a professional writer: the spelling mistakes, the vocative "Well" at the beginning of sentences, and the erratic punctuation. Prim locutions such as "Intimacy took place" complete the impression.

Emlyn never completed *From Stage to Stage: An Adventure* and did not go beyond the few tentative sketches he left among his papers. The title, however, is a good choice for an autobiographer whose life was dominated by, and dedicated to, the theatre. An "Adventure" it most certainly was. Where did he get his talent from, this son of a stoker and a housemaid? There was nothing in his ancestry to suggest either scholarship or acting. His gifts flowered spontaneously. Children of semi-literate parents often surprise their families with intellectual brilliance, as did Emlyn, whose first language was Welsh, his second English, and his third, fourth and fifth French, Italian and German, with, in later years, a good enough command of modern Greek to speak it in performance on the stage. What is really puzzling is his genius for the drama. He grew up in a remote part of Wales and did not see a play until he was sixteen. The world of fantasy in which he lived was nourished by the cinema rather than by the stage. Then, while performing his Dickens recitation at a school concert, he began involuntarily to flesh out the text with gestures and grimaces, so discovering for himself the craft of acting. Like his compatriot Ivor Novello he did not go to a drama school and never had any sort of training. His mastery of technique was the result of close observation supported by lightning intuition.

It was Miss Cooke who channelled his intellectual ability and turned him into a scholarship boy, although, as she was often later to say, she claimed no credit for the brains without which he would have achieved nothing. The strength of his imaginative power survived what might have been the cramping influence of an academic education, and for the rest of his life he remained both a scholar and creator. While on the one hand he could carry out research with precise attention to detail, on the other he could create from his native wit alone plays of dazzling theatrical effect. One remembers Macaulay's epigram on Sir Richard Steele: a rake among scholars and a scholar among rakes.

This duality influenced his life from the very beginning. His parents were a study in contrasts, the father an improvident toper, the mother a spartan pessimist. While he reacted violently against the depressing confines of a Welsh Nonconformist childhood to become a sophisticated metropolitan man, he could not shake off the legacy it gave him of two disparate characteristics: thrift over money and the *hwyl* that infused his writing with passion. His attachment to his native land was always clear-eyed. "Welsh," he once said, "is a *bona fide* literary language – not just a quirk of some fanatics. But not worth dying for." The "George" of youth grew into the "Emlyn" of maturity. Yet there remained always a George and an Emlyn within his character.

In his time he loved both women and men. Women, indeed, played a very important part in his existence. For Miss Cooke, who shaped his scholastic career, he had a lifelong affection. For Molly, his wife, he had a deep and passionate love which endured in spite of the disagreements that characterise any lengthy relationship and, in their case, the arguments that shadowed the later years. He was frank on the subject of his bisexuality. She was no less frank in her acceptance of it, for she realised, as the heroine of *Accolade* puts it, that: "It's no use pretending I don't wish he were – otherwise . . . But if he were, how do we know he'd still have talent? And he might not even be human . . ."

"The history of this little Welshman is a romance," wrote his headmaster when the boy was eighteen years old. "He is a splendid reciter, fond of dramatics, and unusually successful in portraying life on the platform." Is he to be pigeonholed as actor or playwright? Again duality intervenes. On his passport he described himself as "Actor" alone. In the thirty years that followed the production of his last successful play, he concentrated on acting: Shakespeare, the one-man shows and rôles in films and plays by others. This, however, was only because he could no longer find the inspiration to write plays himself. George/Emlyn was also actor/dramatist.

George was the boy who dreamed creatively. Emlyn was the doer, the man of action whose immense determination and energy propelled him from the Welsh backwoods to the glamorous life of the West End stage. George had charm and kindness. Emlyn could, when thwarted, be cold and ruthless. Gentle George was, despite himself, fascinated by evil and murder. Emlyn boldly expressed this fascination in *Night Must Fall*, *Beyond Belief* and *Dr Crippen's Diary*. As an actor George/Emlyn, in private life the most generous and sympathetic of men, excelled at rôles which were sinister and villainous.

His film appearances were slickly professional. The finest of them were the decadent Lord Lebanon in Edgar Wallace's *The Frightened Lady*, the rôle he originally played in the stage melodrama; the slimy blackmailer in *Friday the Thirteenth*; the hunted man in *They Drive by Night*; and the cuckolded husband in *The Deep Blue Sea*. Standing quite apart is his portrayal of Caligula in the aborted *I, Claudius*, a superbly tantalising fragment. *The Last Days of Dolwyn*, the only cinema production wholly his own as writer, director and star, is a pointer to the even greater things he might have achieved if the British film industry had been better organised and in a position to encourage his talent. On the stage, which he liked best of all, he will be remembered as the murderous Danny in *Night Must Fall*, the young hero of *The Corn Is Green*, the showman Ambrose Ellis in *The Wind of Heaven*, and the medium Saviello in *Trespass*. Memorable contributions to other writers' plays include the chilly advocate in Rattigan's *The Winslow Boy* and the austere Pope Pius in Hochhuth's *The*

Deputy. To these must be added a truly wicked Iago, a not unsympathetic Shylock, and a complex Angelo. His inspired re-creations of Charles Dickens, Dylan Thomas and Saki began a fashion for one-man shows and are a part of stage history.

What remains of George/Emlyn the playwright? He made no grand claims for his work and insisted that his purpose was to entertain. If, by entertaining, is meant the ability to engage an audience, to amuse, to thrill, to make it continually wonder what is going to happen next, his plays stand up well. "I always felt," says John Gielgud, "his narrative talent had something of the Welsh streak about it which brought Ivor Novello such success. A kind of story in the dorm schoolboy gift which he could employ with great invention and freedom, but which could not bear too close investigation." While the action of *Night Must Fall* proceeds the author's stagecraft bewitches his audience into suspending disbelief. The same gift is at work in *Trespass* and *Someone Waiting*. *The Corn Is Green*, revived in 1985 at the Old Vic to celebrate the dramatist's eightieth birthday, proved that, despite miscasting, the play could still move and delight. This piece, together with *The Druid's Rest*, *The Wind of Heaven* and the film *The Last Days of Dolwyn*, shows best his Dickensian gift for creating character and for bringing to the stage a true breath of his native country. The fresh and buoyant lyricism of *Spring, 1600* certainly deserves revival. *The Light of Heart*, with its bravura leading role and gallery of picturesque minor characters, is a lively evocation of the theatre by one who loved it profoundly. All these plays belong to a period of the London stage which has since passed away, and they might even be described by that disdainful phrase "well-made." Do critics, one wonders, prefer plays that are "badly" made? Just as his contemporary Noël Coward was sentenced to neglect and then gradually emerged to be hailed as something of a modern classic, so Emlyn Williams, at the moment, is undergoing the purgatory which follows soon after the death of an author. What will survive cannot be foretold. It is probable, however, that the plays mentioned above are likely to figure among it.

Whatever the fate of his work for the stage, his two-volume autobiography has established itself as one of the most readable and lasting of theatrical memoirs. When, in 1987, he returned from his convalescence in the Canaries, he started toying again with *From Stage to Stage*. He did not live to write more than a few scattered drafts. Illness depleted him and took away even his appetite for work. It was clear that his first operation had been unsuccessful and that another would have to be carried out. Resignedly he went back into the Princess Grace Hospital and submitted himself to the surgeon. He came home depressed and humiliated by the daily routine a colostomy imposes. No one dared tell him the thousands of pounds his medical treatment had cost. Throughout the last months he was nursed devotedly by Ann Plugge who had run his household ever since Molly's death. In mid-September he had a visit from Stephen Mitchell, his old friend and producer of so many of his plays from *The Corn is Green* to the ill-fated *Beth*. Other friends stood around in the drawing-room at Dovehouse Street. Emlyn sat in characteristic pose, his typewriter placed before him, though his fingers did not move. He seemed very distant, withdrawn, as if he were about to go on a long journey. On September 21 his daughter-in-law Maggie Noach was at his bedside. A sudden happy smile passed over his features. "Oh darling," he murmured as she held his hand, "how lovely to see you!" He thought she was his wife Molly. Five days later he died in the little study which also served as his bedroom.

His death occurred only a short while before the "Black Monday" of 1987 on the Stock Exchange when share values were drastically reduced. This meant that his holdings were valued at a much higher price than that which obtained while the estate was being wound up, and many shares had to be sold. Even so, the final figure was put at £552,916.

The funeral on Friday, October 2, was, as he requested, a simple one. In St Paul's, Covent Garden, the "actors' church", gathered the family and Ann Plugge. Sally Burton, Richard's widow, was there, with old friends like Sir John Gielgud, Robert Hardy, Robert Fleming, Ronald Fraser, Susan Hampshire and John Casson, the son of Sybil Thorndike. Two of Emlyn's favourite hymns were sung: "He Who Would Valiant Be" and "Guide Me, O Thou Great Redeemer." In place of an address Brook Williams read the Dylan Thomas poem, "And Death Shall Have No Dominion". After the service the coffin, bearing a single bouquet of red roses, was carried out past the numerous memorials to other people of the theatre commemorated there. Cremation at Golders Green followed. It was all plain and straightforward according to his wish. There was no memorial service. As he had joked some time before, he did not want to risk drawing a poor house.

THE WORKS OF EMLYN WILLIAMS

Original Plays

1926 March   *Vigil*
Playhouse, Cambridge. OUDS

Issaiah	Emlyn Williams
Atherton	Robert Speaight
Richman	Leslie Nye

Director: John Fernald
(Published: *The Second Book of One Act Plays*, Heinemann, 1954)

1928 December 10   *Glamour*
Embassy, London

Eve Lone	Mary Dibley
Rupert Onslow	Harold Anstruther
Louise	Monica Stracey
The Hon Mrs George Pettifer	Haidée Gunn
Jack	Emlyn Williams
Jill	Betty Hardy
Rhys Price Morris	Frank Royde

Director: Charles B. Williams

1929 January 30   *Full Moon*
Arts Theatre, London

Terry Sanding	Felix Irwin
Mrs Brentwood	Margaret Watson
Charles Terra Ferma	Alfred Clark
Ross	Robert Haslam
Gordon Brentwood	Cecil Parker
Anna	Margaret Delamere

Director: John Fernald
(Originally produced at the Playhouse; Oxford, OUDS)

1930 November 9   *A Murder Has Been Arranged*
Strand Theatre, London

Miss Groze	Ann Codrington
Cavendish	Guy Pelham Boulton
Mrs Wragg	Amy Veness
Jimmy North	Whitmore Humphreys
Beatrice Jasper	Margaretta Scott

Emlyn Williams

Mrs Arthur	Violet Farebrother
Sir Charles Jasper	Wilfrid Caithness
Maurice Mullins	Henry Kendall
A Woman	Veronica Turleigh

Director: Emlyn Williams

Later presented at the St James's Theatre from November 26, 1930, with the following cast changes:

Cavendish	John Cheatle
Mrs Arthur	Viola Compton
Sir Charles Jasper	J. M. Roberts

(Published: Samuel French, 1931)

1931 November 1   *Port Said*
Wyndham's Theatre, London

Suleiman Ali	Rodney Millington
Jo Barmouth	Finlay Currie
Ibrahim Abdou Ali	Percy Parsons
Suzy	May Agate
Edith	Dorothy Minto
Mr Vint	Brember Wills
Youssef el Tabah	Emlyn Williams
Ruth Blair	Jessica Tandy
Mrs Frankiss	Ann Codrington
Narouli Karth, the Dove	Maria Burke
David Frankiss	Jack Hawkins

Director: Emlyn Williams

1933 July 3   *Vessels Departing* (Revision of *Port Said*)
Embassy Theatre, London

Suleiman Ali	Rodney Millington
Ibrahim Abdou Ali	Frank Royde
Suzy	May Agate
Edith	Dorothy Minto
Roger Blair	David Hawthorne
Ruth Blair	Stephanie Rivers
Youssef el Tabah	W. Cronin Wilson
Narouli Karth	Flora Robson
Mrs Frankiss	Edith Sharpe
David Frankiss	Eric Berry

Director: John Fernald

1934 January 31   *Spring, 1600*
Shaftesbury Theatre, London

Mistress Ellen Byrd	Renée de Vaux
Mary Morley	Gwendolen Evans
John Amery	Valentine Rooke

Kit Cooper	Ellis Irving
Ann Byrd	Joyce Bland
Will Kempe	Lawrence Baskcomb
Salathiel Pavy	Harold Reese
Henry Condell	Scott Russell
Augustin Phillips	H. O. Nicholson
Ned Pope	Frank Pettingell
Tom Day	Anthony Bruce
Richard Burbage	Ian Hunter
Winifred	Margaret Webster
Rachel Frost	Casha Pringle
George Pearce	Anthony Pelissier
Peter Cook	John Dennis
A Blackamoor	James Rich
Lady Coperario	Isabel Jeans

Director: John Gielgud
(Published: Heinemann, 1953)

1935 May 31   *Night Must Fall*
Duchess Theatre, London

The Lord Chief Justice	Eric Stanley
Mrs Bramson	May Whitty
Olivia Grayne	Angela Baddeley
Hubert Laurie	Basil Radford
Nurse Libby	Kathleen Harrison
Mrs Terence	Dorothy Langley
Dora Parkoe	Betty Jardine
Inspector Belsize	Matthew Boulton
Dan	Emlyn Williams

Director: Miles Malleson
(Published: Heinemann, 1961)

1937 May 26   *He Was Born Gay*
Queen's Theatre, London

Prissy Dell	Betty Jardine
Francis	Harry Andrews
Mrs Georgina Dell	Elliot Mason
Miss Mason	Gwen Ffrangcon-Davies
Lewis Dell	Glen Byam Shaw
Lady Atkyns	Sydney Fairbrother
Sophy Raffety	Carol Goodner
Mr Leroy	Frank Pettingell
Mason	John Gielgud
Lambert	Emlyn Williams

Director: John Gielgud with the Author
(Published: Heinemann, 1937)

1938 September 20   *The Corn Is Green*
Duchess Theatre, London

Mr John Goronwy Jones	John Glyn Jones
Miss Ronberry	Christine Silver
Idwal Morris	William John Davies
Sarah Pugh	Dorothy Langley
A Groom	Albert Biddiscombe
The Squire	Frederick Lloyd
Bessie Watty	Betty Jardine
Mrs Watty	Kathleen Harrison
Miss Moffat	Sybil Thorndike
Robbert Robbatch	Kenneth Evans
Glyn Thomas	Wynford Morse
Will Hughes	Jack Glyn
John Owen	Glan Williams
Morgan Evans	Emlyn Williams
Old Tom	Frank Dunlop

Director: The Author
(Published: Heinemann, 1938)

1940 February 21   *The Light of Heart*
Apollo Theatre, London

Mrs Banner	Gladys Henson
Barty	Arthur Powell
Fan	Megs Jenkins
Bevan	Edward Rees
Maddoc Thomas	Godfrey Tearle
Cattrin	Angela Baddeley
Robert	Anthony Ireland
Mrs Lothian	Elliot Mason

Director: The Author
(Published: Heinemann, 1940)

1941 December 10   *The Morning Star*
Globe Theatre, London

Mrs Lane	Gladys Henson
Mrs Parrilow	Elliot Mason
Alison	Angela Baddeley
"SD"	Frederick Lloyd
Brimbo	Roddy Hughes
Cliff	Emlyn Williams
Wanda	Ambrosine Philpotts
Sir Leo	Walter Piers

Director: The Author
(Published: Heinemann, 1942)

1943 December 22   *Pen Don*
Grand Theatre, Blackpool

With Marie Ault, Morgan Johns and Emlyn Williams as "Bran".

Ran for ten nights.

1944 January 26   *The Druid's Rest*
St Martin's Theatre, London

Kate Edwards	Gladys Henson
Glan	Richard Burton
Tommos	Brynmor Thomas
Sarah Jane Jehova	Nuna Davey
Job Edwards	Roddy Hughes
Issmal Hughes	Neil Porter
Zachariah	Lyn Evans
A Mysterious Wayfarer	Michael Shepley

Director: The Author
(Published: Heinemann, 1944)

1945 April 12   *The Wind of Heaven*
St James's Theatre, London

Dilys Parry	Diana Wynyard
Bet	Megs Jenkins
Manna	Dorothy Edwards
Gwyn	Clifford Huxley
Pitter	Arthur Hambling
Ambrose Ellis	Emlyn Williams
Evan Howell	Herbert Lomas
Mrs Lake	Barbara Couper

Director: The Author
(Published: Heinemann, 1945)

1947 July 14   *Pepper and Sand*
Radio Play. One Act. BBC Light Programme

George Pepper	Emlyn Williams
Georges Sand	Françoise Rosay

(Published: H. F. W. Deane & Sons Ltd, 1948)

1947 July 16   *Trespass*
Globe Theatre, London

Bill	Raymond Westwell
Gwan	Daphne Arthur
A Maid	Frances Bates
Mr Grice	Roddy Hughes
Mrs Henting	Gladys Henson

Christine	Françoise Rosay
Dewar	Leon Quartermaine
Mrs Amos	Marjorie Rhodes
Saviello	Emlyn Williams

Director: The Author
(Published: Heinemann, 1947)

1950 September 7 *Accolade*
Aldwych Theatre, London

Will Trenting	Emlyn Williams
Albert	Anthony Oliver
Rona	Diana Churchill
A Parlour Maid	Meg Maxwell
Thane Lampeter	Anthony Nicholls
Marian Tillyard	Ruth Dunning
Ian	John Cavanah
Harold	John Stratton
Phyllis	Dora Bryan
Daker	Noel Williams

Director: Glen Byam Shaw
(Published: Heinemann, 1951)

1953 November 25 *Someone Waiting*
Globe Theatre, London

John Nedlow	Campbell Cotts
Martin	John Stratton
Miss Lennie	Dorothy Baird
Hilda	Gabrielle Brune
Vera	Adrianne Allen
Fenn	Emlyn Williams
Mrs Danecourt	Gladys Henson
Neighbours }	Edward Rees Eileen Dale

Director: Noel Willman
(Published: Heinemann 1954)

1958 March 20 *Beth*
Apollo Theatre, London

Beth	Ann Beach
Lydia	Pauline Yates
Owen	Derrick Sherwin
Powell	Robert Flemyng
Madame	Irene Brown
Jerome	Michael Scott
Benjy	Edward Cast
Mrs Dix	Nan Munro

Director: The Author
(Published: Heinemann, 1959)

Adaptations by Emlyn Williams

1933 May 16   St James's Theatre, London
The Late Christopher Bean: from Sydney Howard's version of *Prenz garde à la peinture* by René Fauchois. (Published: Gollancz, 1933.)

1934 September 25   His Majesty's Theatre, London
Josephine: from the original by Hermann Bahr.

1943 February 11   St James's Theatre, London
A Month In The Country: from Turgenev (Published: French, 1943.)

1946 May 21   Embassy Theatre, London
Guest In The House: from the play of the same name by Hagar Wilde and Dale Eunson.

1964 June 9   Old Vic, London
The Master Builder: from Ibsen. (Published: French, 1943.)

Solo Performances by Emlyn Williams

1951 November 19   Criterion Theatre, London, after provincial tours.
Charles Dickens
Many subsequent London seasons and tours throughout the world until 1986. Total of performances: 2,261.

1955 May 31   Globe Theatre, London, after provincial tours.
Dylan Thomas – A Boy Growing Up
Many subsequent London seasons and tours throughout the world until 1986. Total of performances: 842.

1977 September 22   Apollo Theatre, London, after provincial tours.
The Playboy Of The Weekend World (Saki)
Subsequent performances in Great Britain and North America until 1978. Total of performances: 131.

Major Appearances on Stage

1923 December   First appearance on the amateur stage as the Maître d'hôtel in *La Poudre aux yeux* (Labiche and Martin), for the Oxford University French Club. Thereafter he made many appearances in OUDS productions of classical and modern plays. He also played Issaiah in the OUDS production of his own *Vigil* (see list of plays).

1927 April 4   Savoy Theatre, London.
First professional appearance as Pelling's Prentice in *And So To Bed* (Fagan).
Thereafter many small professional rôles.

1928 December 10   Embassy Theatre, London.
Jack in own play *Glamour*.

1930 April 2   Wyndham's Theatre, London.
Angelo in *On The Spot* (Wallace)

November 20   Wyndham's Theatre, London.
Commissar Neufeld in *The Mouthpiece* (Wallace).

1931 February 17   St James's Theatre, London.
Etienne in *Etienne* (Deval/Wakefield).

August 18   Wyndham's Theatre, London.
Lord Lebanon in *The Case Of The Frightened Lady* (Wallace)

November 1   Wyndham's Theatre, London.
Youssef el Tabah in own play *Port Said*.

1932 May 6   Garrick Theatre, London.
Jack in *Man Overboard* (Vane).

1933 May 26   Apollo Theatre, London.
Patrick Branwell Brontë in *Wild Decembers* (Dane).

1934 September 8   Westminster Theatre, London.
Piers Gaveston in *Rose and Glove* (Ross Williamson).

September 25   His Majesty's Theatre, London.
Eugène Beauharnais in *Josephine* (see adaptations).

1935 May 31   Duchess Theatre, London.
Dan in own play *Night Must Fall*.

1937 May 26   Queen's Theatre, London.
Lambert in own play *He Was Born Gay*.

August   Buxton Opera House (Old Vic).
Oswald in *Ghosts* (Ibsen).

October 12   Old Vic, London.
Angelo in *Measure for Measure* (Shakespeare).

November 2   Old Vic, London.
Duke of Gloucester in *Richard III* (Shakespeare).

1938 September 20   Duchess Theatre, London.
Morgan Evans in own play *The Corn Is Green*.

1941 June 4   Globe Theatre, London.
Takes over from Godfrey Tearle as Maddoc Thomas in own play *The Light of Heart*.

December 10   Globe Theatre, London.
Cliff Parrilow in own play *The Morning Star*.

1943 December 22   Grand Theatre, Blackpool.
Lan in own play *Pen Don*.

1944 Feb–Dec   ENSA tour abroad as Peter Kyle in *Flare Path* (Rattigan), Dan in *Night Must Fall* and Charles Condamine in *Blithe Spirit* (Coward).

Emlyn Williams

1945 April 12	St James's Theatre, London. Ambrose Ellis in own play *The Wind of Heaven*.
1946 May 23	Lyric Theatre, London. Sir Robert Morton in *The Winslow Boy* (Rattigan).
1947 July 16	Globe Theatre, London. Saviello in own play *Trespass*.
1949 October 13	Fulton Theatre, New York. Izquierdo in *Montserrat* (Robles/Hellman).
1950 September 7	Aldwych Theatre, London. Sir Will Trenting in own play *Accolade*.
1953 November 25	Globe Theatre, London. Fenn in own play *Someone Waiting*.
1955 December 21	Saville Theatre, London. Hjalmar Ekdal in *The Wild Duck* (Ibsen).
1956 April–August	Stratford Memorial Theatre, Stratford-on-Avon. Shylock in *The Merchant of Venice*; Iago in *Othello*; Angelo in *Measure for Measure*. (Shakespeare).
1958 October 7	Piccadilly Theatre, London. The Author in *Shadow of Heroes* (Ardrey).
1961 January 18	Arts Theatre, London. The Man in *Lunch Hour* (Mortimer); Mr Chacterson in *The Form* (Simpson); Edward in *A Slight Ache* (Pinter).
November	Music Box Theatre, New York. Ascolini in *Daughter of Silence* (West).
1962 June	ANTA, New York. Sir Thomas More in *A Man For All Seasons* (Bolt).
1964 February	Brooks Atkinson Theatre, New York. Pope Pius XII in *The Deputy* (Hochhuth).
1965 September 23	Cambridge Theatre, London. Ignaty in *A Month In The Country* (Turgenev:Williams).
1969 September	Apollo Theatre, London. Took over from John Gielgud as the Headmaster in *Forty Years On* (Bennett).

Major Film Appearances

1932	*The Frightened Lady* *Sally Bishop* *Men of Tomorrow*
1934	*Friday The Thirteenth* (also wrote screenplay) *My Song For You* *Evensong* *The Iron Duke*

1935 *The Love Affair Of A Dictator*
Roadhouse
The City of Beautiful Nonsense

1936 *Broken Blossoms* (remake – also wrote screenplay)
I Claudius (unfinished)

1938 *Night Alone*

1939 *Dead Men Tell No Tales*
The Citadel
They Drive By Night
Jamaica Inn

1940 *The Stars Look Down*

1941 *You Will Remember*
The Girl In The News
Major Barbara
This England (also wrote screenplay)

1942 *Hatter's Castle*

1949 *The Last Days Of Dolwyn* (also directed and wrote screenplay)

1951 *Three Husbands*
Another Man's Poison
The Scarf

1952 *The Magic Box*
Ivanhoe

1955 *The Deep Blue Sea*

1957 *I Accuse*

1959 *Beyond This Place*
The Wreck Of The Mary Deare

1962 *The L-Shaped Room*

1966 *The Eye Of The Devil*

1969 *David Copperfield* (TV film)

1970 *The Walking Stick*

Gramophone Records

1958 *Emlyn Williams Talks*: London, Qualiton Records. QLP 1004. 33⅓.

1960 *Emlyn Williams Reading Charles Dickens*: London, Decca/Argo. TA 507/8.
2 records. 33⅓.
Vol 1: *Our Mutual Friend*; *Dombey and Son*; *Pickwick Papers*.
Vol 2: *Christmas Stories*; *A Tale Of Two Cities*.

1969 *Dylan Thomas, Poems – A Boy Growing Up*: London, Decca/Argo.
TA 509/10. 2 records. 33⅓.

Includes "Memories of Childhood", "Who Do You Wish Was With Us", "A Visit to Grandpa's".

1971 (?) *The World of Dylan Thomas*. London, Decca/Argo.
PA/A/166. 33⅓.
Selected readings by Emlyn Williams, Richard Burton and others.

Books and Miscellaneous Writings

Readings From Dickens: With an introduction by Bernard Darwin. Heinemann, 1954
George: An early autobiography. Hamish Hamilton, 1961
The Collected Plays of Emlyn Williams. Volume 1. (No more published.) Includes *Night Must Fall, He Was Born Gay, The Corn Is Green, The Light Of Heart*. Heinemann 1961
Beyond Belief: A Chronicle of murder and its detection. Hamish Hamilton, 1967
"Dickens and the theatre" – chapter in: *Charles Dickens 1812–1870. A Centenary Volume*. Editor, E. W. F. Tomlin. Weidenfeld and Nicolson, 1969
Emlyn: An early autobiography, 1927–1935. Bodley Head, 1973
Dr Crippen's Diary. In: *Great Cases of Scotland Yard*, Reader's Digest. 1978
Headlong: A Novel. Heinemann, 1980
Dr Crippen's Diary: An Invention. Robson Books, 1987

Unpublished Works

Hearts of Youth. Novel. (Written at age 13.) 1918
The Blue Band. Drama. (Written at age 14). 1919
The Tombs of Terror. Unfinished novel, April, 1919.
The Mists of Babylon. Unfinished novel. (Written age 15). 1920–1921
Sinner in the Sun. Draft of play. 1924
Cinderella. Play. c 1925
Poems. 1926
The Long Vacation. Short story. c 1928
Glamour. Play in three acts. 1928
Full Moon. Play in three acts. 1929
Patrick's Mother. Comedy in 1 act. 1929
Tom. Comedy in 3 acts. c 1929
Up at Cardinal's. Play in 3 acts. 1933
Shocking Fatality. Play in 2 acts. 1933
Celebrity. Comedy in 3 acts. 1934
Pen Don. Legend in 4 scenes. 1943
Gala Night. Film scenario. (Based on *The Terror* by Arthur Machen.) c 1960
Memory Lane. Short story. 1963
Fess. A play. c 1970
The Sound of Horses. Play in 3 acts. c 1970
Miss Moffatt. Musical based on *The Corn is Green*. 1973
Spring! Musical based on *Spring, 1600*. 1976–77.
Transformation Scene. Comedy in 3 Acts. 1980
From Stage to Stage: An Adventure. Unfinished autobiography. 1980–87
Someone Waiting. Revision of play of same name. 1984
Cuckoo. Revision of play called *Beth*. 1986

Bibliography – Manuscript Sources

Correspondence dating from 1917 onwards and comprising some seven hundred letters exchanged between Emlyn Williams, Richard Williams (father), Mary Williams (mother), Molly Williams (wife), Alan Williams (son), and Miss Sarah Grace Cooke.

Approximately eighty letters from colleagues and friends such as Sir John Gielgud, Sir Noël Coward, Sir Alec Guinness, Sir Hugh Walpole, Sir Charles B. Cochran, Sir Terence Rattigan, Dame Sybil Thorndike, Dame Marie Tempest, etc.

"Emlyn Williams and Family" scrapbooks in seven large bound volumes covering the period from 1869 to 1961.

Bibliography – Printed Sources

Agate, James. *First Nights*. Ivor Nicholson and Watson, 1934
—— *Ego 2*. Gollancz, 1936
—— *Ego 3*. Harrap, 1938
—— *The Amazing Theatre*. Harrap, 1939
—— *Ego 4*. Harrap, 1940
—— *Ego 5*. Harrap, 1942
—— *Brief Chronicles*. Jonathan Cape, 1943
—— *Red Letter Nights*. Jonathan Cape, 1944
—— *Ego 7*. Harrap, 1945
—— *The Contemporary Theatre*, 1944 and 1945. Harrap, 1946
—— *Ego 8*. Harrap, 1947
Anon. *Who's Who In The Theatre*, 15th edition. Pitman, 1972
Batters, Jean. *Edith Evans*: A Personal Memoir. Hart-Davis, MacGibbon, 1977
Black, Kitty. *Upper Circle*: A Theatrical Memoir. Methuen, 1984
Braden, Bernard. *The Kindness of Strangers*. Hodder and Stoughton, 1990
Bragg, Melvyn. *Rich*: The Life of Richard Burton. Hodder and Stoughton, 1988
Callow, Simon. *Charles Laughton*: A Difficult Actor. Methuen, 1987
Castle, Charles. *Oliver Messel*. Thames and Hudson, 1986
Cotes, Peter. *J.P.*: The Man Called Mitch. Paul Elek, 1977
Coward, Noël. (Ed. Graham Payn and Sheridan Morley). *The Noël Coward Diaries*. Weidenfeld and Nicolson, 1982
Curtis, Anthony. (Editor). *The Rise and Fall of The Matinée Idol*. Weidenfeld and Nicolson, 1974
Darlington, WA. *Six Thousand and One Nights*. Harrap, 1960
Darlow, Michael, and Hodson, Gillian. *Terence Rattigan*: The Man and His Work. Quartet Books, 1979
Dent, Alan. *Preludes and Studies*. Macmillan, 1942
—— *Nocturnes and Rhapsodies*. Hamish Hamilton, 1950
Findlater, Richard. *Emlyn Williams*. Rockliff, 1956
Forbes, Bryan. *Ned's Girl*. Elm Tree Books/Hamish Hamilton, 1977
Forsyth, James. *Tyrone Guthrie*. Hamish Hamilton, 1976
Gänzl, Kurt. *The British Musical Theatre*, Volume 2. Macmillan, 1986
Gaye, Freda (Editor). *Who's Who In The Theatre*, 13th and 14 editions. Pitman, 1961
Gielgud, John. *Early Stages*. Hodder and Stoughton, 1987
—— *An Actor In His Time*. Sidgwick and Jackson, 1979
—— *Backward Glances*. (*Time For Reflection. Distinguished Company*.) Hodder and Stoughton, 1989

Guinness, Alec. *Blessings In Disguise*. Hamish Hamilton, 1985

Herbert, Ian. (Editor) *Who's Who In The Theatre*. 16th edition. Pitman, 1977

Huggett, Richard. *Binkie Beaumont*. Hodder and Stoughton, 1989

Jenkins, Graham, with Turner, Barry. *Richard Burton, My Brother*. Michael Joseph, 1988

Junor, Penny. *Burton: The Man Behind The Myth*. Sidgwick and Jackson, 1985

Lane, Margaret. *Edgar Wallace*. The Book Club, 1939

Lindley, Sandra. *A Bibliography of Emlyn Williams*. College of Librarianship, Wales. Aberystwyth, 1979

Logan, Josh. *Josh: My Up and Down, In and Out Life*. W. H. Allen, 1977

Mander, Raymond, and Mitchenson, Joe. *The Theatres of London*. N.E.L., 1975

Morley, Sheridan. *The Great Stage Stars*. Angus and Robertson, 1986

—— *Our Theatres In The Nineties*. Hodder and Stoughton, 1990

Moseley, Roy. *Bette Davis:* An Intimate Memoir. Sidgwick and Jackson, 1989

O'Casey, Sean. *The Flying Wasp*. Macmillan, 1937

Parker, John. (Editor). *Who's Who In The Theatre*. 7th, 8th, 9th 10th, 11th and 12th editions, 1933, 1936, 1939, 1947, 1952, 1957. Pitman

Plomley, Roy. *Days Seemed Longer*. Eyre-Methuen, 1980

Quirk, Lawrence, J. *The Passionate Life of Bette Davis*. Robson Books, 1990

Roberts, Edward W. *The Emlyn Williams Country*. (Foreword by Emlyn Williams.) Penarth. Penarth Times, 1965

Rogers, Ginger. *Ginger: My Story*. Headline, 1991

Sherrin, Ned. *Ned Sherrin's Theatrical Anecdotes*. Virgin, 1991

Thornton, Michael. *Jessie Matthews*. Hart-Davis, MacGibbon, 1974

Trewin J. C. *Dramatists Of Today*. Staples Press, 1953

—— *The Turbulent Thirties*. (Foreword by Emlyn Williams.) Macdonald, 1960

Walker, Alexander. *Vivien*: The Life of Vivien Leigh. Weidenfeld and Nicolson, 1987

INDEX